ic Quarter Library leeds metrop

the l

SOCIAL POLICY REVIEW 20

Analysis and debate in social policy, 2008

Edited by Tony Maltby, Patricia Kennett and Kirstein Rummery

First published in Great Britain in 2008 by

The Policy Press
University of Bristol
Fourth Floor
Beacon House
Queen's Road
Bristol BS8 1QU
UK

Tel +44 (0)117 331 4054
Fax +44 (0)117 331 4093
e-mail tpp-info@bristol.ac.uk
www.policypress.org.uk

British Library Cataloguing in Publication Data
A catalogue record for this book is available from the British Library.

Library of Congress Cataloging-in-Publication Data
A catalog record for this book has been requested.

ISBN 978 1 84742 077 0 paperback

Cover design by Qube Design Associates, Bristol.
Front cover: photograph kindly supplied by www.alamy.com
Printed and bound in Great Britain by MPG Books, Bodmin.

Contents

List of tables and boxes

Tables

Boxes

List of abbreviations

BERR	Department for Business, Enterprise and Regulatory Reform
CO_2	carbon dioxide
CRE	Commission for Racial Equality
DCLG	Department for Communities and Local Government
DCSF	Department for Children, Schools and Families
DIUS	Department for Innovation, Universities and Skills
DTI	Department of Trade and Industry
DWP	Department for Work and Pensions
EES	European Employment Strategy
EGGSIE	Expert Group on Gender, Social Inclusion and Employment
ELSA	English Longitudinal Study of Ageing
ESB	Employment and Skills Board
EU	European Union
EUA	European Union allowance
EU ETS	European Union Emissions Trading Scheme
GDP	Gross Domestic Product
GHG	greenhouse gas
GP	general practitioner
ILO	International Labour Organisation
IPCC	Intergovernmental Panel on Climate Change
IT	information technology
JER	Joint Employment Report
JSA	Jobseeker's Allowance
LSC	Learning and Skills Council
MP	Member of Parliament
NDC	New Deal for Communities
NGO	non-governmental organisation
NHS	National Health Service
NIACE	National Institute of Adult Continuing Education
NRF	Neighbourhood Renewal Fund
NRP	National Reform Programme
ODPM	Office of the Deputy Prime Minister
PAT	Policy Action Team
PCDL	Personal and Community Development Learning
PPG	planning policy guidance
PPS	Planning Policy Statements
PSA	Public Service Agreement

RSC	Royal Society of Chemists
SERPS	State Earnings Related Pension Scheme
SEU	Social Exclusion Unit
SSC	Sector Skills Council
SURF	Centre for Sustainable Urban and Regional Futures
UN	United Nations
UNFCCE	United Nations Framework Convention on Climate Change

Notes on contributors

Nahid Ahmad previously worked for the Policy Research Institute, University of Wolverhampton, and is now a Senior Researcher at the Applied Research Centre of Health and Lifestyle Interventions at Coventry University. She is a chartered health psychologist and has conducted research in areas of health psychology, health policy, and within the wider policy context. Nahid has also lectured in various areas including social psychology, health psychology and qualitative research methods.

Roberta Blackman-Woods MP is Member of Parliament for the City of Durham. Before entering Parliament in 2005 she was a social policy academic and was Dean of Social and Labour Studies at Ruskin College, Oxford, and Head of Social Sciences at Northumbria University. In Parliament she is a member of the new Select Committee on Innovation, Universities and Skills and is Parliamentary Private Secretary to the Secretary of State for Defence.

Ingo Bode was until November 2007 Lecturer in the School of Social and Political Studies at the University of Edinburgh. He is currently Visiting Professor for Sociology at the University of Wuppertal, Germany. His research interests include the organisational foundations of welfare and health care provision, the role of the non-profit sector in contemporary welfare regimes, and the development of welfare markets on which he has recently completed a research project based on investigation conducted during academic stays in Canada, Germany, France and the UK.

Beth Breeze is a member of the School of Social Policy and Social Research at the University of Kent. She is completing her doctoral thesis on 'The meaning and purpose of contemporary philanthropy in the UK' and will take up a post as a researcher in the new ESRC-funded Centre for Charitable Giving and Philanthropy in January 2009.

Hartley Dean is Reader in Social Policy at the London School of Economics and Political Science, University of London. His research interests include poverty and exclusion, welfare rights and citizenship, discourses of welfare, and the survival strategies of marginalised social groups. He has recently completed two studies funded by the Economic and Social Research Council (ESRC), one on the labour market experiences of people with multiple problems and needs, the other on popular and welfare provider discourses concerning dependency, responsibility and rights.

Patricia Kennett is currently a Visiting Research Fellow at The Hong Kong Polytechnic University, Hong Kong, and Senior Lecturer in Comparative Policy Studies at the University of Bristol. Her research includes work on issues relating to governance and public policy; the welfare state and citizenship in comparative perspective; housing, homelessness and social exclusion. Recently completed projects include 'Women and material assets in Britain and Japan' funded by the Institute for Household Economy, Japan, and 'Cohesive neighbourhoods and connected citizens in European societies' funded by the European Science Foundation.

JaneMaree Maher is the Director of the Centre for Women's Studies and Gender Research at Monash University, Melbourne. Her current research is focused on birthing, pregnancy, women, family life and work and new models of motherhood. She has recently published in these areas in *Australian Feminist Studies* and *Journal of Sociology*.

Tony Maltby is CROW Research Fellow and Deputy Director at the Centre for Research into the Older Workforce at the National Institute for Adult Continuing Education (England and Wales) based in Leicester. His research interests embrace the range of work, income and the social policy of later life. His many publications include *Ageing Europe* (Open University Press, 1997), with Alan Walker. He was founding editor of *Social Policy and Society*.

Catherine Palmer is Reader in Sport and Social Policy at the School of Applied Social Studies, University of Durham. She joined the staff at Durham in September 2006 after teaching appointments at the University of Adelaide and Flinders University, South Australia. Her teaching and research interests include the anthropology of sport, social research methods and social theory, particularly as these relate to applied or 'real-life' settings.

Gillian Pascall is Professor of Social Policy at the University of Nottingham. Relationships between welfare states and gender have been at the centre of her research and publication since *Social Policy: A Feminist Analysis* was published in 1986 (Tavistock). More recently, work with Professor Anna Kwak at the University of Warsaw on *Gender Regimes in Transition in Central and Eastern Europe* (The Policy Press, 2005) studies gender and parenting in the changing social policy environment after Communism. 'Innovative Policies for Gender Equality at Work' (2006) was supported by the European Social Fund and drew comparative social policy into a national context to explore the relevance of a range of European policies to lower-paid workers in England. Currently, with Sirin Sing of Queen's University Belfast, she is developing an edited collection on *Gender and East Asian Welfare Studies*.

Alison Porter is a Research Officer and Deputy Director of AWARD's Mid and West Wales office at Swansea University. She is primarily a qualitative researcher, with a research background and interests including health inequalities, disability, older people, and the interface between health and social care. She was the AWARD lead investigator for the Strategy Interim Review undertaken for the Welsh Assembly Government during 2006/07.

Debora Price is Lecturer in Social Gerontology at the Institute of Gerontology, King's College London, having previously practised as a barrister in the Middle Temple. Her research focuses on pensions and the poverty of older people, with particular interest in gender inequalities across the lifecourse. Current ESRC projects include a review of poverty measures for older people in the UK, and research into how older couples negotiate and manage household money.

Jill Rubery is Professor of Comparative Employment Systems and Director of the European Work and Employment Research Centre (EWERC) at Manchester Business School, University of Manchester. From 1991 to 2007 she coordinated the EU's research group on gender, social inclusion and employment. Her research work and publications include work on labour market regulation policies and the role of minimum wages; new forms of work and flexibility; women's employment and pay; employers' working-time policies; and international comparative labour market analyses.

Kirstein Rummery is Professor of Social Policy at the University of Stirling. Her research interests include gender, particularly the way in which welfare policies affect older and disabled women; welfare partnerships and governance; and issues concerning citizenship, social participation and access to services, particularly for disabled and older people.

Alison Smith is Lecturer in Social Policy at the University of Edinburgh. Her research interests include the labour market and family life, European social policy, adult education, longitudinal secondary data analysis and quantitative and comparative research methods. She is a member of the RECWOWE (Reconciling Work and Welfare in Europe) group.

Carolyn Snell is a Lecturer in Social Policy at the Department of Social Policy and Social Work, University of York, and is also a Research Fellow at The Stockholm Environment Institute at the University of York. Carolyn specialises in environmental policy and the links between poverty, the environment and sustainable development.

Alastair Thomson is Senior Policy Officer at the National Institute for Adult Continuing Education (England and Wales) based in Leicester. He works to the Director on matters relating to government, advocacy and membership with a particular focus on political and policy matters.

Gill Windle is a Research Fellow based at the Dementia Services Development Centre at Bangor University. Her research interests extend across quality of life and social policy in older age, in particular health promotion, mental health and well-being. She was seconded to the Older People's Strategy Unit at the Welsh Assembly Government during the 2006/07 interim review period, and was a member of the Strategy Advisory Group at this time.

Introduction

Tony Maltby, Patricia Kennett and Kirstein Rummery

Overview

This year's *Social Policy Review* (SPR) follows the tried and tested structure of previous years. It is divided into three distinct parts, each edited by one of the three co-editors who provide below an introduction to their section. Part One, commissioned and edited by Tony Maltby, provides a review of some of the significant developments in social policy during 2007; Part Two, edited by Patricia Kennett, is a selection of papers from those delivered to the annual international Social Policy Association (SPA) conference held at the University of Birmingham in July 2007; and the final part, edited by Kirstein Rummery, focuses upon the important issue of gender inequality within the policy process and provides a selection of papers from a SPA-sponsored workshop.

Part One: Current developments – *Tony Maltby*

The first part differs slightly from previous years. The aim, as in previous editions of the *Review*, is to provide the reader with a review and analysis of the key developments in UK social policy during the previous year. However, my aim as lead editor was to broaden the perspective away from what I regard as a rather dated and somewhat narrow 'five giants' framework.

Hence, the chapters comprising this section also reflect the areas of policy that are now pertinent to the key challenges and debates within social policy in the 21st century. My view is that the 'five giants' framework is now more relevant to the 1940s and 1950s than to 2008. To suggest that we continue to operate within Beveridge's 'five giants' framework, at least for this review, seems to suggest that the discipline has failed to reflect the rapidly changing agenda of social policy as a 21st-century discipline. We no longer have central government Departments for (of) Education or Social Security or, for that matter, Housing. Would anyone argue that we should ignore the debate on the impact of sexuality, sexism or racism (for example) upon policy, as Beveridge did? Let us celebrate the vibrancy of our discipline, and allow the exploration of new avenues by building upon Beveridge's legacy.

The current debate about global environmental change and its impact upon the 'social', and indeed social policy issues (for example, work, lifestyle, leisure, housing, transport, poverty), and the participation of adults in learning and training are two such examples of debates that should be included. These do not readily fit within the 'five giants' policy framework. Yet both are central elements of the policy agenda of the present government.[1] Slaying the giant of Ignorance was largely focused upon those aged 5 to 21 and not beyond. Responding to the giant of Squalor was more about public housing than about maintaining the 'green belt' and planning issues. The environmental impact of industrialisation and global capitalism were not of key importance in the 1940s and hence did not figure anywhere on the policy agenda until more recently.

Consequently this part considers two very important central government reviews (those by Leitch and Stern) and the exciting policy developments in the field of health and social care in Wales. Part One has also sought to look beyond the university sector for its authors in order to offer a different perspective, from those directly involved in the policy process. Hence, one of the chapters is written by a sitting MP (Roberta Blackman-Woods) and the other by a NIACE colleague (Alastair Thomson). My hope is that this slightly different twist to this part of *SPR* this year will enrich the academic discourse in social policy and engage its audience in a wider debate.

The first chapter in Part One, by Alastair Thomson, reflects upon a necessarily selective account of developments in the field of post-compulsory education and training. Similarly, it has a focus on England, reflecting the devolved nature of policy in this area within the UK. His central theme is to assess the impact of 'the Year of Leitch' and *the* major review into the long-term skills needs of the UK. Thomson outlines the main elements of this key report and offers a critique and analysis of its impact. He suggests that it rapidly became part of a 'new orthodoxy' among the policy community. He then describes how, with Leitch's patron now Prime Minister, the main elements of his strategy for world-class skills was implemented. This has more recently been through a White Paper offering the hope for a 'more integrated employment and skills policy', and the chapter offers a detailed description and analysis of the main provisions. There are many difficulties with a single focus upon the acquisition of qualifications (per se) rather than skills. The chapter concludes by suggesting that despite the hope for a workforce with world-class skills, over the past year 700,000 learners have been lost to publicly funded adult education.

The next chapter, by Roberta Blackman-Woods MP, offers her own unique and personal insights into the area of planning, housing and regeneration now more usually termed the built environment. Her chapter stresses the importance of this field for social policy because she suggests that, in any discussion, the 'aspirations of individuals and communities are played out on a daily basis' locally and nationally unlike most other areas of policy. She reviews the Labour governments' record since 1997, placing the considerable body of legislation since then into some sort of meaningful context, before a thoroughgoing description and analysis of the range of policy measures introduced during the past year. These include the 2007 Planning Bill, built largely out of the influential Barker and Eddington reports of 2006. In conclusion it is suggested that how the legislation is implemented is key, since there is still a need for local and national policy making in this area to become better aligned.

The following chapter, by Debora Price, discusses the implementation of the reforms to the state pension following the major Turner Commission on Pensions. In her detailed and engaging analysis she documents the decline of defined benefit schemes in favour of defined contribution schemes, together with the new development of Personal Accounts and an assessment of their likely impact. In conclusion, she suggests that the new pensions structure is a return to the Beveridge flat-rate system. Furthermore, she suggests that low earners and those with intermittent employment records may make 'bad' decisions about their pensions due to a lack of clear guidance and advice available to this group. This may result in increasing inequalities between public and private pension provision. Clearly a need, perhaps, for better adult education in this area?

Chapter Four, by Carolyn Snell, addresses a distinctly new focus of policy development, that of environmental policy. It is an area that has an impact upon the everyday lives of every individual and affects the impact of a range of social policy concerns, for example poverty, economic and social globalisation, transport and housing, to name a few. As Carolyn indicates, it was considered important enough to be discussed at the G8 summit in 2005 and for a government report to be commissioned and authored by Stern. After providing a substantiation of 'climate change as a policy problem', she discusses the Stern report and its main recommendations in some detail, together with the notable policy developments arising out of this, including the Climate Change Bill, which should receive Royal Assent early in 2008.

The final chapter in this part is by Gill Windle and Alison Porter. It reviews the progress to date on the implementation of the Older People's Strategy in Wales. Gill was seconded to the Older People's Strategy Unit at the Welsh Assembly Government during the review period, and was a member of the Strategy Advisory Group. Alison was the AWARD Lead Investigator for Strategy Interim Review undertaken for the Welsh Assembly Government. Their chapter outlines and reviews the implementation of this significant new approach in addressing population ageing. Its objective was the adoption of a holistic approach to policy towards older people's health and well-being. This was to be achieved through the engagement of older people within the planning and implementation phases using a thoroughgoing participative framework. The chapter comments upon similar schemes introduced in the two other devolved governments in Northern Ireland and Scotland.

Part Two: Current debates – *Patricia Kennett*

The second part opens with a chapter by Hartley Dean, who draws on a small-scale, qualitative study to explore the experience of work–life balance amongst households in a low-income neighbourhood. Work–life balance is defined as 'flexibility' in relation to employment and family commitments. Bargaining power is identified as an essential component in establishing this flexibility. He begins the chapter by identifying three different perspectives on the relationship between the worlds of paid employment and family life; the social welfare perspective, the liberal/ business perspective, and the 'Third Way' public policy perspective. He then focuses on bargaining power in relation to employer practices, income maintenance and childcare arrangements. The chapter concludes by integrating the analysis of the various perspectives on work–life balance with the experiences of households, most of whom were identified as having very limited bargaining power.

Nahid Ahmad's recent research, on which her chapter is based, explores the levels of non-political civic participation, and the motivations and barriers to participation among different ethnic groups. While it has been recognised that civic participation has the potential to promote self-confidence, this chapter discusses the importance of self-confidence in enabling and motivating people from ethnic minorities to take advantage of civic participation opportunities. Ahmad recommends that policies to encourage inclusion and participation should progress beyond information access. They should instead include active consultation with communities and community leaders, and a recognition of the importance and potential of political identity and confidence in enhancing civic participation amongst minority groups.

Beth Breeze focuses on the under-researched theme of philanthropy. Drawing on original research of 150 of the most significant UK donors in 2006 she highlights the distinct characteristics and ideal types of UK philanthropy. The chapter then goes on to consider the potential for significant charitable gifts to overcome the 'problem of riches'.

Catherine Palmer focuses on the processes and politics associated with undertaking action research with refugee women soccer players in Adelaide, South Australia. The focus of the research is a group of young Muslim women, recently resettled in a public housing estate, playing for the New Arrivals soccer team. The chapter draws out the contradictions and challenges of conducting publicly funded, qualitative research in the context of shifting government policy priorities. The research raises important issues in relation to the nature of evidence in social policy, research transfer and the governance of knowledge.

In the final chapter of this part, Ingo Bode explores the nature and substance of social citizenship in Britain and Germany, focusing particularly on unemployment protection, retirement provision and health care entitlements. The chapter begins by arguing that the concept of social citizenship established by T.H. Marshall in the 1950s and, to varying degrees, fostered through the welfare states of Western Europe has been undermined, curtailed and replaced by strategies of activation, consumer choice and self-government. However, Bode suggests that this is not a unilinear process and argues in the remainder of the chapter that while there is clear evidence for the emergence of a fragmented configuration of citizenship with the marketisation of citizenship in some policy areas, one can also identify a re-emphasis on universalism.

Part Three: Engendering policy and politics –
Kirstein Rummery

The chapters in the final part are drawn from a selection of papers presented at the Engendering Policy and Politics conference held at the University of Manchester in June 2007 and supported by the SPA. Collectively, the authors aimed to examine the issue of how governments address gender inequality through the political process and the formation and implementation of policy, bringing an international and comparative dimension to a project started by the Gender Research Network at the

University of Manchester focusing on New Labour's record in this area (reported in Annesley et al, 2007).

In Chapter Eleven Gillian Pascall looks at the way in which New Labour in the UK has moved away from a male breadwinner model of welfare policy, and at the impact that recent developments have had on policies on employment, care, the division of labour and time, income and the political process. She usefully shows how, in comparison with the more gender-friendly social democratic 'Nordic' model of gender policy, New Labour's continued commitment to the neo-liberal model has compromised its achievements on gender equality.

In Chapter Twelve Jill Rubery draws on a project looking at the development of gender-sensitive employment policies in the EU to report how policy tensions have evolved between national and supranational agencies. She focuses particularly on the implementation of the European Employment Strategy, and the role that active labour market policies (or 'activation' policies), targets and childcare strategies have played in addressing gender inequalities in the workplace. Like Pascall, her chapter shows how a return to a narrow 'economic' perspective in policy and away from more 'social' perspectives has slowed down progress in gender mainstreaming, and she argues that the economic, social and political challenges being faced by the EU mean that it will have to address gender issues in a more systematic way.

The final two chapters in this section take us from policy to practice and show how economic and social policy impact on gender relations in society and within families. JaneMaree Maher's chapter shows how the normative underpinnings of policy reflect gendered assumptions about work and care in Australian families. Drawing on the *Families, Fertility and the Future* study she shows how policy concerns about fertility rates were reflected in decisions about family configuration, and shows specifically how such considerations are differentiated along gender lines. The burden of work *and* care seems to be falling on women within this policy context, and this is demonstrated through the views expressed that policies about combining work and care are about women's concerns. Correspondingly, she shows that less attention has been paid to the role that fathers play or are expected to play: a gendered preoccupation echoed in policy across several national and international contexts.

Alison Smith's chapter is a welcome counterbalance to the assumption that combining working and family life are women's concerns. She draws on an ESRC-funded study on how working fathers are reconceptualising fatherhood as being about combining economic provision *and* caring, usefully taking the theoretical debate on fatherhood beyond issues of breadwinner versus carer. Her analysis of working time and paternal time show that there is a distinct class basis to both the quantity and quality of time that fathers spend with their children: that, perhaps counter-intuitively, it is the fathers who work the hardest in the economic arena (both in terms of hours and income) who also work the hardest in the caring arena (in both quantity and quality). Put simply, fathers who earn more care more for their children. Her findings have important implications for the way in which we might think about developing theory and policy around fathering, caring and working, as well as the impact that has on mothering, caring and working and gender relations within families and societies.

Note
[1] I am writing this in December 2007.

References
Annesley, C., Gains, F. and Rummery, K. (eds) (2007) *Women and New Labour: Engendering politics and policy?* Bristol: The Policy Press.

Part One
Current developments

ONE

A year of transition in post-compulsory education and training

Alastair Thomson

This chapter reviews some of the main developments that occurred during the year in the UK and highlights some of the connections and themes. It is, of course, a selective account. First, it focuses on the written and spoken words of legislators and their officials rather than the voices of learners and their teachers. Second, it focuses on the majority of the UK's population, who are adults rather than children. Third, it concentrates not on the education and training of elites (whether in the academy or in the workplace) but on the changes that impact most on the lives of people who gained least from their initial education. Fourth, in a State where the education and training systems of the four component parts are divergent, it does not presume to describe dynamics of relevant policy development within Scotland, Wales and Northern Ireland – nor indeed the impact of European Union policies.

The central theme – Leitch

There can be few who would deny that 2007 might best be described as 'the Year of Leitch'. When, in 2004, former insurance company chief executive, Lord Alexander Leitch, accepted an invitation from then-Chancellor, Gordon Brown, to undertake an independent review of the UK's long-term skills needs, he may not have realised just how central his report would prove to be to the start of his patron's premiership.

The report, *Prosperity for All in the Global Economy: World Class Skills* (Leitch, 2006), appeared in December 2006 and immediately framed subsequent debate. In some ways this was odd since the document itself was seen as a disappointment in several quarters. This was due in part to a sense of déjà vu. The overall analysis seemed often only to rework and update that of earlier initiatives such as the National Training Task

Force of 1988 and the National Skills Task Force that had reported six years before (National Skills Task Force, 2000). Some of the most interesting areas opened up in the review's interim report were not carried through to the final one, an example being the analysis of the potential impact of an ageing population on training and labour market supply. In other areas, such as inward and outward migration and how to bring people some distance from the labour market closer to it so that the government could achieve an employment rate of 80%, the report was largely silent.

Box 1.1: What the Leitch review recommended

- The state, employers and individuals will all have to pay more if the UK is to succeed in increasing adult skills at all levels by 2020.
- Employers should be given control over training by funnelling all public funding for adult vocational skills in England through the Train to Gain initiative.
- Community learning plus funding for adults with learning difficulties and disabilities should remain with the Learning and Skills Council (LSC).
- Individual learners to be given greater control through Learner Accounts – virtual funding to be used at accredited providers and aimed at giving individuals greater purchasing power.
- Vocational skills courses should only receive public money if they have been given the all-clear by business-led Sector Skills Councils (SSCs). A question mark was placed over the future role of the Qualifications and Curriculum Authority.
- The creation of a new Commission for Employment and Skills with local Boards to further strengthen the voice of business. The Skills Alliance, national employers' panels and the Sector Skills Development Agency will be folded into this. Individual SSCs to be re-licensed.
- Business to 'pledge' voluntarily to train more employees at work or, if insufficient progress is made by 2010, workers to get a statutory right to access workplace training.
- A new universal adult career service to be established in England, integrated with Jobcentre Plus.

New targets for 2020:

- 95% of adults to achieve basic skills of functional literacy and numeracy (currently 85% and 79%).
- Level 3 intermediate skills to take priority over Level 2.
- 40%-plus of adults to be qualified to Level 4 or above (currently 29%).

In 148 pages, the review set out changes at national and subnational level, in funding flows, funding responsibilities and financial support, with different roles and responsibilities for the LSC, SSCs and employers.

Two of the sharper critiques of the review came from Keep (2007) and Unwin (2007). The former observed that skills are a necessary but insufficient precondition for economic success – 'Scotland already has a more highly qualified workforce than England but its productivity still lags behind' (p 15) – and went on to highlight the importance of research and development, employee relations and work organisation in a successful economy. Keep's overall verdict was that 'Leitch overloads expectations onto skills' (p 15). Unwin, the UK's only Professor of Vocational Education, claimed that the review failed 'to ask tough questions about how skills are developed and used in the contemporary economy. Leitch refers to employers as one homogeneous community that has the capacity to tell education and training providers exactly what it wants' (Unwin, 2007).

She went on to point out the heterogeneity of employers before concluding:

If we agree some competitor countries have more skilled people, is it because their apprenticeship programmes are more demanding? Or because, unlike the UK, most jobs require a 'licence to practice'? Or is there a greater sense of shared enterprise, with trust and respect between government, employers, education and training providers, trade unions, and citizens?

While academics were among the more public critics of the review, many others involved in teaching and training had misgivings about how the aspirations expressed in the review were to be translated into practice and concentrated on the 'how' rather than the 'what'. Among parliamentarians and the social partners, however, there was little by way of a sustained critique and the Leitch analysis rapidly became part of the new orthodoxy.

First days of the Brown premiership – new structures and holistic solutions

The appointment of Gordon Brown as Prime Minister on 27 June led to a rush of documents in the month before Parliament rose for the summer. These were intended to signal a new style and a change of emphasis. Three of these documents are covered below but the very first act of the new Prime Minister was to reorganise the machinery of government – especially those parts concerned with education.

The first piece of the jigsaw was to establish a new Department for Children, Schools and Families (DCSF), bringing together key aspects of policy affecting children, young people and families. These included pre-19 education (with funding for 16- to 19-year-olds to be routed to schools via local authority education budgets from 2011 rather than through the LSC, a non-departmental public body). As well as responsibility for the funding and standards of pre-19 education, the new Department's role included the promotion of the well-being, safety, protection and care of all young people – including, through policy, responsibility for children's social services and (with the Department for Work and Pensions [DWP] and HM Treasury) for ending child poverty. With the Department of Health, the new DCSF was to promote children's health and, with other departments of state, youth sport and the reduction of youth homelessness. The first significant result of this bringing together of different policy strands was revealed on 11 December with the publication of *The Children's Plan – Building Brighter Futures* (DCSF, 2007).

The response was underwhelming. The left-leaning *Guardian* newspaper's verdict was: 'impressive in its interventionist ambition but leaving doubts about whether that ambition can ever be met', adding 'The public may ask why, after a decade of public spending and a succession of plans, problems are as great as they are' (*Guardian*, 2007). In the more right-wing *Daily Telegraph*, the Conservative shadow to the Secretary of State observed that:

> Ten years of government micro-management have resulted in our schools plummeting down the international league table for numeracy, literacy and science. But the Government's response, the Children's Plan that was unveiled this week, takes micro-

management to a whole new level of intrusiveness, with more than 500 targets for the education of toddlers and rules on how babies should play with rusks. (Gove, 2007)

The approach of seeking to tackle policy in a more holistic way and to overcome Whitehall's perceived 'silo culture' carried through into other elements of the machinery of government changes. The second piece of the jigsaw was the establishment of a new Department for Business, Enterprise and Regulatory Reform (BERR) that was to be responsible for leading government engagement with business, for competitiveness, consumer choice and regulation. This replaced the former Department of Trade and Industry (DTI) and included the joint appointment of a junior minister, Lord Jones of Birmingham, with the Foreign Office. Other parts of the DTI were to become the responsibility of the third new creation – the Department for Innovation, Universities and Skills (DIUS). Mr Brown announced it thus:

> In the years ahead, countries will increasingly derive their competitive edge from the speed with which they are able to innovate, building on a world-class research base, creating new products and markets and driving enterprise and efficiency. Seizing these new opportunities will also require a world-class skills base – both through the expansion of high-end graduate skills, but also by raising the skills of the wider adult workforce, including those currently unskilled. (Brown, 2007)

Brown went on to say that the Department would, in addition to leading on the public funding of science:

> be responsible for the development, funding and performance management of higher education (both teaching and research) and further education, working closely with the Department for Children, Schools and Families. The Department will also be responsible for taking forward the Government's wider skills agenda – including the implementation of Lord Leitch's review of skills, published last year. (Brown, 2007)

It is worth noting that, as a consequence of the restructuring, the UK government, for the first time in more than 100 years, no longer had a Ministry, Board or Department of *Education*. Despite the absence of such a word in the titles of Secretaries of State, the move did double the number of voices at the Cabinet table with a concern for education and a practical imperative to cooperate. The split of the former Department for Education and Skills into the DCFS and DIUS was, however, complicated (for example around the lead department for apprenticeships, access to higher education and family learning) and undoubtedly created a more complex working environment for colleges of further education, many of which had student bodies ranging from 14-year-old school pupils to adults retired from the labour market.

The first major publication from the new DIUS was the government's response to the Leitch review – *World Class Skills: Implementing the Leitch Review of Skills in England* (DIUS, 2007a). Most of this was drafted prior to the restructuring but publication was held back to 18 July so that the incoming Secretary of State, John Denham MP, could inject something of his preferred approach into the document.

Mr Denham entered the post with a high reputation. Having resigned as a Home Office minister on a matter of principle (the Iraq war), he had gone on to become an effective Select Committee chairman, leading parliamentary scrutiny of ministers and their officials. During this backbench period he had also made a well-received speech to a party think-tank on the theme of 'Making work work' (Denham, 2004). In it he argued for the establishment of 'Advancement Agencies' that would:

> explore with each individual their personal options to improve their position. [The new service] would look at access to in-work support (tax credits, disability assistance, and childcare). It would discuss whether employers were complying with employment law on parental leave, holiday provision or the minimum wage. It would examine the training provided and whether this was meeting the needs of both employee and employer. It would help the individual to improve their current employment or to prepare to look for other work, perhaps in jobs that they had previously thought beyond their reach. If the latter, the routes through training could be mapped. (Denham, 2007, p 4)

The lecture went on to set out Mr Denham's broader thinking:

> Creating and simplifying the opportunities to improve skills and productivity is, clearly, very important. But we are still tending to separate different elements of the problem – aspirations, employment rights (including work–life balance), skills and

training and employer attitudes. We cannot tell in advance whether each person's problem will be the lack of skills, their own self-confidence, or their employer's attitude.... We need an approach that can offer support to the individual around all these issues. I believe that can come best from an organisation that has the simple and unambiguous commitment to helping them progress. An organisation that can offer support on each of the problems that they face. (Denham, 2004, p 5)

The subtle, person-centred and holistic approach illustrated by these words was seen as a refreshing change from the Skills Strategies promoted by the former Department for Education and Skills, which were perceived as unhelpfully, even dogmatically, favouring employers over employees and reducing skills acquisition to a process of qualification collection. When the new Secretary of State appointed as a special adviser one of the leading members of Lord Leitch's review team, expectations were high.

A new tone was apparent from the start. This was commented on in the media and not denied by the Permanent Secretary of the new DIUS and its Director General for Lifelong Learning.[1] More junior officials commented informally at other events about a ministerial team with few inhibitions about challenging and questioning their officials' submissions and less patient than their predecessors. In this respect, it would appear that while civil servants may have seen the Blair–Brown transition as being about the move to Year 11 of a Labour government, for Mr Brown's ministers this was Year Zero – and they were anxious to make their mark.

The most obvious manifestation of this change was in the Department's rhetoric. In describing its purposes, the DIUS website stated that the Department will 'ensure the wider personal, community and cultural benefits of education and science are supported' and its mission statement included the role of 'Build[ing] social and community cohesion through improved social justice, civic participation and economic opportunity by raising aspirations and broadening participation, progression and achievement in learning and skills' (DIUS, 2007b).

In addition to a reinvigorated emphasis on social cohesion and inclusion, the government's response to Leitch (DIUS, 2007a) was presented as setting out the first steps on a journey rather than a definitive, inflexible, blueprint and moved away from the emphasis of the existing government's Skills Strategy – although in the case of one programme favoured by the Treasury, a Labour MP characterised the Train to Gain programme as being 'doomed to succeed regardless of cost'.[2] When it was published, the director of the National Institute of Adult Continuing Education gave the following reaction: 'This report is something of a relief. We were concerned that adult learning might be subsumed in an employer-led strategy, but congratulate the Government for deciding to focus on individuals' aspirations and ambitions' (NIACE, 2007).

In the opening chapter of the government's report (DIUS, 2007a; hereafter termed 'the plan') both the Leitch diagnosis and the medicine were endorsed without demur. The focus was on creating a supporting framework for implementation, setting out who was to do what to whom by when. Those elements of the Leitch review that might have discomforted or exposed the government were, effectively, ignored – with matters of migration and demography being cases in point. By being disciplined with words, the document threw a cloak of invisibility over untidy ideas that challenged the new orthodoxy by framing debate in a way that excluded or blunted the impact of Coffield (2007), Keep (2007), Unwin (2007) and others who came at the argument from inconvenient standpoints.

On the funding front, the plan endorsed the rebalancing of funding responsibilities between government, employers and individuals. Cynical commentators noted that employers' pounds appeared to have rather more value than individual learners' pounds but were relieved by the government's rejection (because of the risk of destabilising an already stretched system) of Lord Leitch's recommendation that the transition to a fully demand-led funding system could be put in place by 2010.

The direction of travel was, however, entirely clear – the employer-focused Train to Gain programme saw its projected funding (currently £440 million) rise to around £900 million by 2010/11. For individuals, the preferred way forward was identified as Skills Accounts, bringing funding together with a range of support and guidance linked to a learner record. These, the plan asserted, were to 'become the way into learning and upskilling for all those aged 19 or over' outside higher education (DIUS, 2007a, p 27).

The main change to the infrastructure of the sector was the establishment of a UK Commission for Employment and Skills, subsuming the Sector Skills Development Agency and the DWP's National Employers' Panel. In November 2007 it was announced that the chief executive of the Commission was to be Chris Humphries. As Mr Humphries had been an eloquent advocate and chair of the National Skills Task Force between 1997 and 2000, the announcement was neither unsurprising nor unwelcome. The only question was why the Prime Minister had needed seven years and his own review to act.

Although an earlier government-backed review of further education colleges (Foster, 2005) had criticised the number and complexity of infrastructural bodies in the sector, the plan did not take the opportunity to rationalise them. It did, however, begin to reshape the roles of SSCs and the LSC.

Lord Leitch's recommendation to support and empower SSCs was seen as either extremely visionary or foolhardy by commentators who drew attention to the fact that greatest reliance was to be placed on the newest, poorest, weakest and least experienced of the actors on the national skills stage. The government's plan appeared to acknowledge this by deciding to refocus their remit. This was to involve ensuring that employers retained a leading role in qualification development, raising employer ambition and investment in skills, and leading on sector labour market needs. Although shaking up the number and footprint of SSCs was not addressed, the decision to re-license each one did give the new Commission for Employment and Skills a flexibility to address the problems of certain SSCs' patchy performance if it so chose.

The plan's treatment of the future role of the LSC (a public body with a budget of £11.3 billion in 2007/08) was very cautious. With the greater part of its budget for 16- to 19-year-olds set to go to local authorities and with responsibility for adult work already being shared, in London, with the Mayor's office, a large question mark appeared over the future of the LSC. Although the plan confirmed that it was to 'have a central role to play in managing the transition' (DIUS, 2007a, p 49), its longer-term future was left in the air, with the government saying only 'we will consider and consult' (p 49).

Although not prescribed in the government's plan, encouragement was given to the establishment of Employment and Skills Boards (ESBs) (networks of local bodies similar to the London Skills and Employment Board): 'it will remain a matter for local partners to judge whether they wish to set up such a Board' (DIUS, 2007a, p 45). This permissive approach illustrated once again a desire to encourage alternatives to a silo culture in implementing policy and should be seen as complementary to a renewed recognition of the importance of place in policy making, apparent from the Treasury-commissioned *Review of Sub-National Regeneration and Development* (HM Treasury, 2007a). After leading within the Treasury on drafting that report, the minister concerned, John Healey, transferred in Gordon Brown's reshuffle to the Department for Communities and Local Government to implement the recommendations. What might be characterised as a 'new localism' was to feature in the DIUS agenda later in the year (see 'The emergence of an integrated employment and skills policy' at page 25 below).

Other areas covered in the plan included further details of the reform of vocational qualifications through the continued development of 14–19 Diplomas, Sector Qualification Strategies and the Qualifications Credit Framework.

Before moving on from the flurry of documents issued during Gordon Brown's first 30 days, mention should be made of another innovation – the 'draft Queen's Speech' (Office of the Leader of the House of Commons, 2007) in which the government gave advance notice of its draft legislative programme. This included details of a new Education and Skills Bill even as the Further Education and Training Bill was progressing through Parliament! Both Bills are reviewed in the section on 'Legislation' at page 30 below.

Comprehensive Spending Review and budgets for learning and skills

Following Parliament's summer break and the party conferences, one of the first major announcements of the autumn came on 9 October with the publication of the 2007 Pre-Budget Report and Comprehensive Spending Review, *Meeting the Aspirations of the British People* (HM Treasury, 2007b). With supporting documentation, this ran to some 600 pages and set out the government's forward spending plans to 2010-11.

The overall picture for spending by the new DIUS on higher education and adult skills was one of a rising budget set to increase from £14.2 billion in 2007/08 to £16.4 billion by 2010 (a rise of 2% in real terms). This was considered by many to be a good settlement for the sector and substantially greater than that of many other departments of state.

The Spending Review's supporting documents also set out 30 new Public Service Agreements (PSAs), the targets that the Treasury agrees with spending departments. These replaced the 110 PSAs from the previous spending round, which many believed were unhelpfully distorting decision making within the former Department for Education and Skills and the LSC and leading to tension between the priorities of the DWP and the former Department for Education and Skills. Of these new cross-governmental targets, no fewer than 12 had some relevance to adult learning in terms of inclusion and equity, regional and community policy as well as growth and productivity.

Once again, the need for all concerned with post-compulsory skills policy to think beyond their immediate silo was made by the Secretary of State for the DIUS, John Denham. Speaking to the Association of Colleges in November, he said:

> We need you to understand what we are trying to achieve and to join us in striving for the same demanding aims. Providers who do not listen and do not change with the times, you will lose funding to others who do. (Denham, 2007)

He went on to warn:

> As always, it is a matter of getting the balance right. We will always, with the LSC, try to get the targets right, the funding rules appropriate and the guidance clear. But they will never be perfect and where they are not, the prizes will not go to the people who chase a perverse incentive but to those who work to deliver the overall vision. (Denham, 2007)

A week before that speech, Mr Denham had, with Children's Secretary Ed Balls, given the further education sector a sense of how the government intended to prioritise spending for the year ahead (Denham and Balls, 2007). As well as its annual grant letter to the LSC the government issued a short paper, *Adult Learning and Skills: Investing in the First Steps* (DIUS, 2007c), and the LSC issued its own statement of priorities (LSC, 2007a). On first reading these documents appeared to promise a fresh approach with a Skills Strategy far more sensitive than in the past to social inclusion. They contained new proposals for adult apprenticeships, more details of the adult careers service, more coherent first-steps provisions and the expansion of Skills Accounts.

In addition, the budgets were, undeniably, rising. The LSC (2007a, p 33) proudly announced that 'Government funding for learning and skills has increased from £6.5 billion in 2001-02 to £11.2 billion in 2007-08'. Overall participation budgets for adults were set to rise too – from £3.063 billion in 2007/08 to £3.599 billion in 2010/11.

But although the words were warm, the numbers (in relation to both budgets and planned volumes of learners) painted a very different picture. The investment from the DIUS was, overwhelmingly, in 'Employer responsive' provision and many of the new initiatives were to be paid for not from new money but from reprioritisation of funds already in the system. Table 1.1 (which has stripped out DCFS grants to the LSC and excludes capital and administration spending) shows this clearly.

Of these budgets, the flatlining of 'Adult Safeguarded Learning' (in effect a cut, given inflation) came as no surprise but far more depressing to many practitioners was the fall in 'Developmental Learning' under the 'Adult learner responsive' budget. Since this line had not appeared in previous grant letters, it was not until reading the footnotes that readers discovered that this covered 'below level 2 learning outside the national qualifications framework and learning above level 3' (Denham and Balls, 2007, p 14) and that it was to decline by more than 44% from £385,850,000 to £106,222,000! At the same time, expenditure on the employer-focused Train to Gain programme, relatively unproven and representing uncertain value for money, was to almost double from £520,527,000 to £1,0233,240,000 in a breathtaking leap of faith!

In terms of learner numbers (see Table 1.2), the volume of 'Adult learner responsive' places was budgeted to fall by 381,000 places and in Safeguarded Learning (previously known as Personal and Community Development Learning) the projected fall was from 630,000 to 585,000. Once again, the overall total was expected to rise because of the number of 'Employer responsive' places, but the expenditure budgets were felt by many to risk decimating classes that adults choose for themselves rather than ones that government or employers want them to take, thus distorting the idea of a demand-led system by jeopardising a whole area of successful public provision that responds to real demand.

It would be unfair to hold the current Secretary of State personally responsible for these figures since they were almost certainly signed off by his predecessor. Mr Denham has said, however, at a meeting with the All-Party Parliamentary Group for Further Education and Lifelong Learning (27 November 2007) that 'there is a lot of money that can be used imaginatively in the system'.[2] This left many providers wondering anxiously just how much imagination and creativity the LSC would allow.

Table 1.1: LSC budget lines for adult participation, 2007–10

Budget line	Financial years			
	2007-08	2008-09	2009-10	2010-11
	£000s	£000s	£000s	£000s
Block A – **participation**				
Adult learner **responsive**				
19+ further education	1,612,655	1,576,452	1,504,867	1,510,199
Ufi/learndirect	113,625	122,100	122,000	122,000
Employability learning	24,409	29,102	35,529	41,770
Adult learner **responsive** **subtotal**	1,750,689	1,727,653	1,662,396	1,673,968
Of which for planning purposes:				
Foundation learning tier		243,262	274,962	289,738
Skills for life		568,337	590,037	606,114
Full Level 2		217,064	233,293	259,521
Full Level 3		313,141	372,842	412,374
Developmental learning		385,850	191,263	106,222
Employer **responsive**				
Employer-based NVQs	194,287	208,275	214,352	230,559
Apprenticeships and work-based learning	275,010	290,068	317,024	333,646
Train to Gain	520,527	657,073	777,287	1,023,240
Employer **responsive** **subtotal**	989,824	1,155,416	1,308,663	1,587,445
Of which for planning purposes:				
Foundation Learning tier		15,515	14,718	14,681
Skills for Life		51,794	56,994	61,997

Table 1.1 (continued)

Budget line	Financial years			
	2007-08	2008-09	2009-10	2010-11
	£000s	£000s	£000s	£000s
Full Level 2		669,969	769,563	834,683
Full Level 3		142,531	167,659	362,081
Apprenticeships (excluding Skills for Life)		269,715	297,286	313,795
Developmental Learning		8,893	2,443	208
Adult Safeguarded Learning (PCDL)	210,000	210,000	210,000	210,000
Offender Learning & Skills Service	113,038	122,203	124,770	127,933
Total adult participation (DIUS)	3,063,551	3,215,272	3,305,830	3,599,346

Note: PCDL = Personal and Community Development Learning; Ufi = University for Industry.

Source: Extracted from Denham and Balls (2007)

Table 1.2: LSC planned output volumes (selected)

Total Adult Learner Responsive volumes	Academic year		
	2008-09	**2009-10**	**2010-11**
Totals	**1,600,000**	**1,335,000**	**1,343,000**
Of which for planning purposes:			
Foundation Learning Tier	368,000	372,000	374,000
Skills for Life	923,000	914,000	904,000
Full Level 2	133,000	143,000	161,000
Full Level 3	137,000	157,000	165,000
Development Learning	497,000	216,000	116,000

Source: Extracted from Denham and Balls (2007)

The emergence of an integrated employment and skills policy

The autumn also saw evidence of the convergence of priorities between the DIUS and the DWP and the emergence of a more integrated employment and skills policy intended to help the government towards its goal of an 80% employment rate. On 26 November, the two Departments issued *Opportunity, Employment and Progression: Making Skills Work* (DWP/DIUS, 2007). This White Paper focused on the relationship between welfare and skills reform and signalled a new collaboration between the new adult careers service and the DWP agency Jobcentre Plus in working with welfare recipients.

It set out a belief that welfare-to-work policies should be about 'not just jobs, but jobs that pay and offer retention and progression' (p 8). Because of this concern for sustainable work the government believed that:

> [W]e need a new emphasis on skills as the key to sustainable employment, so that there is a focus on retention and progression not just job entry. With an emphasis on sustaining work we will create a seamless journey from benefits into work and into in-work training, career progression and more rewarding lives. (p 8)

In re-emphasising the government's requirement that rights should be matched by obligations and personal responsibility the White Paper demonstrated a continuity of policy thinking with earlier New Deals and the welfare policies advanced during the 1990s in the US under President Clinton, as an illustration from page 6 of the White Paper demonstrates: 'When skills needs are identified we will expect people to undertake the training necessary to meet them and when job opportunities are available we will expect people to take them'.

The White Paper went on to call for a major culture change, boosting individual and employer commitment to, and investment in, learning and higher skills, breaking the 'revolving door syndrome' of people alternating between periods of unemployment and insecure low-skill, low-wage employment by offering responsive, flexible and personalised support services from information and advice through to training.

Box 1.2: Principles of the welfare reform set out in *Opportunity, Employment and Progression* (DWP/DIUS, 2007)

A stronger framework of rights and responsibilities
Benefit claimants to have access to the necessary support, but also a clear responsibility to take the opportunities that exist to find a job and gain skills.

A personalised, responsive and more effective approach
Greater flexibility for Jobcentre Plus advisers and a greater role for private and third sector providers.

Sustainable employment
A new focus on retention and progression, not just job entry.

Partnership – the private, public and third sectors working together
The future commissioning strategy will maximise innovation in all sectors, driving improvements and leading to better and more sustainable outcomes.

Targeting areas of high worklessness by devolving and empowering communities
Areas with the greatest employment and skills needs will be offered assistance by funding and supporting communities to find innovative local solutions to local problems and by rewarding success.

Local Area Agreements and Local Strategic Partnerships will become the focus for the voluntary, private and public sector to work together to increase sustainable employment – thus reinforcing the direction of travel set out in the subnational review and emphasising the rehabilitation of local authorities as significant stakeholders in skills debates.

The delivery mechanism for the new services was identified as being the new adult careers service (described in other places as an advancement and careers service (John Denham, in *Hansard*, HoC, 26 November 2007) and as an employment and skills service (DIUS, 2007a, p 25). Something of this sort had been recommended by Lord Leitch and endorsed by the implementation plan. Although the White Paper refers to the integration of employment and skills services, it is clear that what is proposed at least initially is close, seamless coordination of what will remain separate services (Jobcentre Plus and LSC-funded Next Step services).

The new service is conceived of as being universal – for people in work as well as those on benefits. This is clear from page 13 of the White Paper, which makes a 'commitment to helping individuals in work to continue to train and gain new qualifications so that they can progress to better-paid and rewarded employment and achieve more for themselves and their families'.

Although the service may be open to all, it will also be mandatory for some. The association of the new service with compulsion has been a cause of misgivings among some advice providers but two quotations from page 16 make the direction very clear:

> [I]t is right, in line with our principle that employment support is based on rights and responsibilities, that those on out of work benefits should at appropriate points in their claim be expected to engage with the advancement service if they have skills needs preventing them from finding work and we will enforce this where necessary and appropriate.

> Where skills gaps could be a major barrier to finding employment customers will be encouraged to attend a full Skills Health Check. The results of the Skills Health Check will inform personal advisers' decisions about whether the claimant needs to be referred to work-focused training in order to enhance their prospects of finding work.

It is envisaged that what people will find on accessing the service will be a joined-up advice service, covering issues such as housing, employment rights, in-work benefits and childcare as well as continuing training and education and jobs.

Some of the services or products available through the service are seen as universal, others as being more tightly targeted. Skills Accounts, intended to enable individuals to take control of their learning, are conceived of as being for all. Page 24 of the White Paper says: 'Skills Accounts will last a lifetime and will be offered to all adults – in or out of work, whatever their skills level'. The accounts, designed to avoid the problems that brought down the previous scheme of Individual Learning Accounts, would put purchasing power into an individual's hands, offering a virtual voucher of state funding, according to a person's entitlement, to purchase relevant learning at an accredited, quality-assured provider of their choice.

The intention here is to promote a cultural change. As the White Paper puts it:

> [S]kills must not simply be the next step in our pursuit of a more effective welfare to work system, or an additional workplace responsibility of employer and employee. Lifelong learning must become the culture that informs our schools and colleges, our workplaces and our communities. We must each take responsibility for our own skills and development throughout our lives, and seek to create opportunities for others to realise their abilities. (p 29)

On the other hand, an entitlement to a free Skills Health Check, to identify an individual's skill needs and strengths (a recommendation from the Leitch review), appears to have been watered down to more targeted provision. As page 23 of the White Paper says:

> Our aim is for the full service in England from 2010-11 to deliver Skills Health Checks and action plans for up to half a million workless people and a further half a million adults in work, targeting those with low skills or who need to retrain to progress.

The intention of the White Paper is that all new claimants will be signposted to the adult advancement and careers service and new Jobseeker's Allowance (JSA) claimants will be subject to a skills screen when they start their claim in order to identify those with obvious basic skills needs. Where skill gaps could be a major barrier to finding employment claimants will be encouraged to attend a full Skills Health Check. New claimants for the Employment and Support Allowance (the new benefit replacing Incapacity Benefits) will have a similar screening regime to those claiming JSA and, where appropriate, a mandatory Skills Health Check at a later point in their claim. This may include improved specialist support for people with mental health problems.

Similar focused support is proposed for lone parents alongside proposals to limit eligibility to Income Support to those whose youngest child is age 12 (in 2008) and age 7 (by 2010) rather than age 16 as at present. Parents with children under the age of five may be offered access to Skills for Parents intervention through Sure Start Children's Centres. Further evidence of a holistic approach and of the increasing role of local authorities came in the White Paper's recognition of the new duty placed on local authorities to secure sufficient childcare for working parents and for those looking for work, the intention being to ensure that an absence of sufficient childcare could no longer be used as a reason for not working. Local authorities would now provide a systematic assessment of childcare needs and work to meet them in partnership with local childcare providers, Jobcentre Plus and local training providers.

Other changes outlined in the White Paper reformed the so-called '16-hour rule' (allowing benefit claimants to study under specific conditions) and put in place arrangements to ensure that longer-term JSA claimants would have the opportunity to undertake intensive training without jeopardising their income. In addition, the government announced its intention to remove the '16-hour rule' in Housing Benefit completely for short-term recipients of Incapacity Benefit, so that they, like long-term Incapacity Benefit claimants, could take up training necessary for them to return to work.

A further feature of the White Paper is its attempt to build employers into the integrated system. It repeats and develops statements in earlier documents, setting out their input into the new Commission for Employment and Skills, a continued central role in SSCs, and the expansion of apprenticeship programmes, including mature apprenticeships. In addition, Local Employment Partnerships are identified as having a key role in the future – bringing together employers and public agencies to match up new job opportunities with people at most disadvantage in the labour market by linking up pre-employment and in-employment training to try and create sustainable work.

In a separate document published in November, the LSC (2007b) set out reforms to increase flexibility in the Train to Gain programme and address some of the criticisms directed towards it. Among the changes was an abandonment of the prohibition of funding being used to support a second Level 2 and even a second Level 3 qualification in some cases where employers were prepared to make a substantial contribution towards the cost. Given that, earlier in the autumn, the government had announced its intention to reallocate £100 million of public funding used by higher education institutions to meet the cost of students studying for qualifications equivalent to or lower than the one they already hold, this decision highlighted some of the discontinuities between further and higher education in contributing to the skills agenda.

Legislation

During 2007, there were two pieces of government legislation affecting post-compulsory learning – the Bill that became the 2007 Further Education and Training Act and the 2007 Education and Skills Bill.

Of these, the former was something of a curiosity. Introduced to Parliament on 20 November 2006, just two weeks before the Leitch review, the Bill did not pretend to have any 'big vision' and was simply a collection of modest but useful piecemeal reforms. These included structural reforms to the LSC, the most significant of which was to give the Mayor's office in London a role in the shaping of the capital's adult skills budget. It also placed a new duty on the LSC to consult with learners and potential learners as well as employers on the funding and provision of learning and also made changes to college governance. More controversially, it proposed to give the Privy Council the enabling power to grant foundation degree-awarding powers to further education colleges rather than having them validated by a university. This was resisted, unsuccessfully, by the higher education sector.

The second piece of legislation flagged up in the 'draft Queen's Speech' was an Education and Skills Bill, which received its first reading on 28 November. The major features of this Bill included tackling the problem of NEETS (young people Not in Employment, Education or Training) by raising the minimum education or training leaving age to 17 by 2013 and to 18 by 2015, the aim of this being to ensure that every young person would be in some kind of recognised education or training until they were 19 years old. No young person would be forced to stay at school and there would be a range of opportunities including new diplomas, part-time training alongside employment, work-based learning and apprenticeships.

The Bill also included proposals for adult learners including the granting of a statutory right to basic and intermediate skills and enabling the benefits of adult skills to be measured. The LSC was to be given a duty to ensure the proper provision of free courses for basic literacy and numeracy programmes and courses leading to a first full Level 2 qualification. Nineteen- to 25-year-olds undertaking their first full Level 3 qualification would also not have to pay tuition fees. The Bill also proposed to give the Qualifications and Curriculum Authority additional powers to enable it to recognise and accredit awarding bodies (which might in future include colleges and employers), thereby reducing bureaucracy and increasing the transparency of the accreditation process.

On information, advice and guidance the Bill proposed that local authorities be required to have regard to the Quality Standards for Information, Advice and Guidance, which were published at the end of October, and placed a duty on schools to provide impartial careers education to help pupils to make the most appropriate future learning and career choices.

The Second Reading of the Bill was scheduled for January 2008.

Conclusion

The final policy-relevant document of the year ended 2007 on a gloomy note. On 18 December, the LSC issued a statistical first release on learner numbers for 2006/07. This revealed that 700,000 learners had been lost to publicly funded adult education over the course of the year. The BBC (2007) news report of this stated:

> [T]he National Institute of Adult Continuing Education [NIACE] pointed out that this year's fall, added to the drop the previous year, represented an overall decrease of 1.4 million. It contrasted this with the LSC's forecast that just 200,000 learners would be lost over the two years.

It went on to report:

> NIACE Director Alan Tuckett said: 'These are increasingly desperate times for adult education. It is of course the government's prerogative to set priorities and the modest gains in workplace learning highlighted here are welcome. But the loss of 1,400,000 learners from publicly-funded adult education in just two years comes at a very high price for social cohesion, for community well-being and for older people in particular, for civic engagement'.

Notes

[1] Seminars organised under Chatham House rule by the Centre for Excellence and Leadership held in London on 11 July and 9 October 2007.

[2] Private conversation.

References

BBC (2007) *Fewer adults in evening classes*, see: http://news.bbc.co.uk/1/hi/education/7154398.stm [accessed 21 December 2007].

Brown, G. (2007) Ministerial statement recorded in the Official Report, *Hansard*, 28 June, London: House of Commons.

Coffield, F. (2007) 'Are we on the right road?' *Adults Learning*, vol 18, no 6, pp 8–14.

DCSF (Department for Children, Schools and Families) (2007) *The Children's Plan – Building Brighter Futures*, Cm 7280, London: The Stationery Office.

Denham, J. (2004) 'Making work work: creating chances across the labour market', Lecture to the Fabian Society, 17 May, see: www.centreforexcellence.org.uk/UsersDoc/MakingWorkWork.pdf [accessed 17 December 2007].

Denham, J. (2007) Speech to the Association of Colleges, 22 November, see: www.dius.gov.uk/speeches/denham_association_of_colleges_221107.html [accessed 17 December 2007].

Denham, J. and Balls, E. (2007) Letter to the Chairman of the Learning and Skills Council ('LSC Grant Letter 2008-09'), 16 November, see: www.dius.gov.uk/publications/LSC-Grant-Letter-2008-09.pdf [accessed 17 December 2007].

DIUS (Department for Innovation, Universities and Skills) (2007a) *World Class Skills: Implementing the Leitch Review of Skills in England*, Cm 7181, London: The Stationery Office.

DIUS (2007b) www.dius.gov.uk/functions.html and www.dius.gov.uk/mission.html [accessed 17 December 2007].

DIUS (2007c) *Adult Learning and Skills: Investing in the First Steps* (publication reference 284656), London: DIUS.

DWP/DIUS (Department for Work and Pensions/Department for Innovation, Universities and Skills) (2007) *Opportunity, Employment and Progression: Making Skills Work*, Cm 7288, London: The Stationery Office.

Foster, A. (2005) *Realising the Potential: A Review of the Future Role of Further Education Colleges*, Nottingham: Department for Education and Skills.

Gove, M. (2007) 'Gordon Brown faces backwards', *Daily Telegraph*, 16 December.

Guardian, The (2007) Leader column, 12 December.

HM Treasury (2007a) *Review of Sub-National Regeneration and Development*, London: HM Treasury.

HM Treasury (2007b) *Meeting the Aspirations of the British People*, Cm 7227, London: The Stationery Office.

Keep, E. (2007) 'Both Leitch and Gordon Brown are over-optimistic about what skills and education alone can deliver', *Adults Learning*, vol 18, no 5, p 15.

Leitch, A. (2006) *Prosperity for All in the Global Economy: World Class Skills*, London: HM Treasury.

LSC (Learning and Skills Council) (2007a) *Our Statement of Priorities: Better Skills, Better Jobs, Better Lives*, Coventry: LSC.

LSC (2007b) *Train to Gain – A Plan for Growth*, Coventry: LSC.

National Skills Task Force (2000) *Skills for All – Proposals for a National Skills Agenda*, London: Department for Education and Employment.

NIACE (National Institute of Adult Continuing Education) (2007) 'NIACE welcomes government's Leitch implementation plan', see: www.niace.org.uk/news/archives/Jul07.htm [accessed 17 December 2007].

Office of the Leader of the House of Commons (2007) *The Governance of Britain – The Government's Draft Legislative Programme*, Cm 7175, London: The Stationery Office.

Unwin, L. (2007) 'Why don't we question the Leitch report more?', *The Guardian*, 8 May.

TWO

Planning for infrastructure and housing – is sustainable development a dream?

Roberta Blackman-Woods

Why is planning important for social policy?

This chapter is very much my own reflection on the current state of play with regard to government policy on the built environment in England. I have written it from the perspective of a Labour Member of Parliament (MP), a legislator and a representative of the people of my constituency, but also as someone who until a few years ago was a practising social policy academic. With two major Bills, one on housing and regeneration and the other on town and country planning, being considered in the current session of Parliament (2007/08), it seems an opportune time to think about what Labour's policy direction is in this area.

In a recent debate in the House of Commons on new planning legislation, what struck me was the number of MPs who stressed the importance of the built environment. There was recognition of the huge significance that planning plays as a lever of public policy that can shape and reshape communities, add to our heritage or detract from it, and create literally the shape of the world around us. This is especially the case because of the durability of much of the built environment; so planning decisions taken now affect the nature and form of buildings that exist for many years to come.

Perhaps it is not a surprise to have the importance of planning mentioned, especially in a debate about new planning, but its potential role in reducing social injustice, improving the quality of life in our neighbourhoods and tackling climate change can easily be understated by those not familiar with the power of planning legislation. Indeed, to a large extent planning decisions will dictate whether we promote and live in socially mixed rather than segregated communities, the extent to which different lifestyles and housing are tolerated, and whether we live in gated communities with a clear emphasis on keeping 'outsiders' out.

I wanted to write about planning because the way in which land is zoned, what is put on it, and for whom, has huge implications for social policy. Indeed, planning is intricately linked with the quality of our lives and what has become known as 'liveability'. Examples of this include access to shops, general practitioners (GPs) and housing, access to public transport and where jobs are located.

It is also a field of policy where the contestation brought about by the conflicting requirements and aspirations of individuals and communities is played out on a daily basis in local council development control committees, planning inspectorate decisions and public inquiries. Conflicting priorities in health, for example, are not so clearly seen or rehearsed in public. Much of the academic literature about planning examines whether the planning approval system is an effective neutral arbiter between conflicting demands or whether the system is in fact heavily weighted in favour of developers (see, for example, Healey, 1997). I will come back to this later in the chapter in relation to current legislative proposals.

What has Labour's record been so far?

Since the Labour government came to power in 1997, it has done nothing more than tinker with the planning and housing system in an incremental way. There were, however, significant policy changes introduced in the first term of the Labour government (1997–2001) relating to regeneration and to communities that were considered to be 'socially excluded'. Legislation relating to planning per se took longer but the 2004 Planning and Compulsory Purchase Act sought a more flexible and simpler system of constructing local plans. It ushered in Local Development Frameworks to replace local plans, created a system of regional planning and guidance, including giving new planning powers to Regional Assemblies, and provided financial support for 'Planning Aid', so that these services could develop a greater community voice in the planning system. The usual drive for efficiency was there too, with targets for speeding up the determination of applications and penalties for missing them.

This 2004 Act followed earlier attempts, primarily through a revision of planning guidance, to reform the planning system to make it more responsive to demands and with clear statements about the importance of community consultation. Little, if anything, was said about the need to improve the quality of decision making in planning and fundamental change was simply not on the cards at this time.

A large part of the incremental changes to the planning system made by consecutive governments has been implemented through alterations and additions to national planning policy guidance (PPG) and, more recently, through the introduction of Planning Policy Statements (PPSs) and the development of regional planning guidance. PPSs have replaced PPG and are issued by government following a period of public consultation. Their purpose is to provide further explanation of legislation and give guidance to local planning departments and others on how planning policy affects the planning system. Local authorities must take these national policies and guidance into account when preparing their local plans and in the determination of planning applications and appeals.

To date, PPSs have been issued for:

- Delivering Sustainable Development (PPS 1, February 2005);
- Housing (PPS 3, November 2006);
- Planning for Town Centres (PPS 6, March 2005);
- Sustainable Development in Rural Areas (PPS 7, 2004);
- Biodiversity and Geological Conservation (PPS 9, August 2005);
- Planning for Sustainable Waste Management (PPS 10, July 2005);
- Regional Spatial Strategies (PPS 11, 2004);
- Local Development Frameworks (PPS 12, September 2004);
- Renewable Energy (PPS 22, November 2004);
- Planning and Pollution Control (PPS 23, November 2004);
- Development and Flood Risk (PPS 25, December 2006).

Those that have remained unchanged as planning guidance are:

- PPG 2 Greenbelts (1995);
- PPG 4 Industrial Commercial Development and Small Firms (1992);
- PPG 8 Telecommunications (2001);
- PPG 13 Transport (2001);
- PPG 14 Development on Unstable Land (1990);
- PPG 15 Planning and the Historic Environment (1994);
- PPG 17 Planning for Open Space, Sport and Recreation (2002);
- PPG 24 Planning and Noise (1994).

The reason for listing the changes is to demonstrate the large amount and range of guidance and policy that is in existence. PPSs can be more than 100 pages long. Most changes to the guidance in terms of the conversion to PPSS has happened since 2004, reflecting a need that had been gradually building for some time for guidance to be updated to reflect changing circumstances and concerns. Increased attention to waste management and renewable energy are examples.

The overall impact of PPSs on the lived experience of the built environment is variable. Some PPSs have been very significant indeed. PPS 12 sets out the new system for compiling Local Development Frameworks. PPS 3 establishes a new approach to providing housing in mixed communities, with emphasis placed on the need for providing family housing. But perhaps the most noteworthy is PPS 1 on sustainable development, signalling as it does the government's policy direction of putting sustainability at the heart of the planning regime.

PPS 1 seeks to link economic development, including planning for infrastructure improvements, with good design and the protection of personal well-being and social progress. It states its aim as:

> ... ensuring that development supports existing communities and contributes to the creation of safe, sustainable, liveable and mixed communities with good access to jobs and key services for all members of the community. (PPS 1, p 2)

This statement sets out an approach to the development of national planning policies that is based on an integration of environmental, economic and social objectives in an overall framework of inclusivity, good design and addressing the causes and potential impacts of climate change. PPS 1 therefore is certainly aspirational and sees planning as a necessary tool if social inequality is to be addressed (PPS 1, p 7). The question is: does this mean anything in reality? Is it possible to reconcile the conflicting demands of economic development, the increasing need for housing and infrastructure development and measures to protect the social and physical fabric of communities while protecting heritage, wildlife, the physical environment and open space at the same time? It is a classic Labour 'third way' question: can we have sustainable development and economic growth?

This inherent tension in the planning system is of course what led to the commissioning of the Barker and Eddington reviews in 2005 (published in 2006) to consider changes that might be needed to land use and transport planning. A lack of responsiveness to the needs of the economy in the planning system was considered a possible impediment to economic growth, which is needed if the UK is to stay globally competitive. This will be discussed later following a brief examination of housing and regeneration policy as it relates to planning.

Housing and regeneration

During the Labour administration, housing legislation has also been fairly thin on the ground. Before the 2004 Housing Act, which brought in a new 'decent homes' quality standard and new powers to license houses in multiple occupation, previous Housing Acts had mostly related to community care, energy conservation or homelessness. Broadly speaking, policy particularly towards housing provision was much the same as with the previous Conservative government, although with the notable exception of bringing all social rented housing and much private rented housing up to the new 'decency' quality standard. Councils were strongly discouraged from building or providing council houses. Registered Social Landlords were the preferred providers of social housing but within a policy framework that saw home ownership as the tenure of choice. Investment in raising the quality of existing social housing was to be through Registered Social Landlords and the transfer of council stock to them. With some concessions relating to equity shares and the building of cheaper homes for key workers, the market was pretty much left to get on with it in terms of new supply. Even the major renewal programmes organised through the New Deal for Communities (NDC) and particularly the Housing Market Renewal initiative conceptualised the issue as one of needing to achieve sustainable housing markets rather than new supply (in fact, these programmes have funded significant demolition).

Investing in the quality of neighbourhoods was a much-needed approach, even if supply became a neglected issue. Regenerating impoverished neighbourhoods has been a key priority of the recent Labour administrations. While much attention has concentrated on anti-crime initiatives and tackling anti-social behaviour, policy initiatives have not all been about Anti-Social Behaviour Orders and crime rates. Indeed, some recent reports from the London School of Economics and Political Science have pointed to the strength and success of Labour's Neighbourhood Renewal Strategy in addressing multiple community needs (Paskell and Power, 2005; Power, 2007). There is, however, also recognition by Power and others that the process of regeneration has not yet been completed.

The approach of the Neighbourhood Renewal Unit was informed by the early work of the Social Exclusion Unit (SEU) and Policy Action Teams (PATs) (SEU, 2000a, 2000b, 2001), which were set up in the first term of the Labour government. The policy of the SEU was of course not exclusively area based but nevertheless much of the detailed analysis carried out by the PATs focused on the spatially concentrated nature of deprivation and the need to regenerate particular geographical communities. This strong area-based focus underpinned the setting up of the NDC programme. This involved setting up 17 Pathfinder partnerships followed by a further 22 partnerships in 1999. The aim of the NDC emphasises its spatial and multidimensional focus:

> New Deal for Communities (NDC) is a key programme in the government's strategy to tackle multiple deprivation in the most deprived neighbourhoods in the country, giving some of our poorest communities the resources to tackle their problems in an intensive and co-ordinated way. The aim is to bridge the gap between these neighbourhoods and the rest of England. (DCLG website: www.dclg.gov.uk)

Each NDC partnership was charged with tackling five key themes in each area:

* poor job prospects;
* high levels of crime;
* educational underachievement;
* poor health; and
* problems with housing and the physical environment.

Paskell and Power (2005) stress that in seeking to regenerate the poorest wards in the country the government was not only concerned with improving socioeconomic conditions, it also wanted to enhance the quality of the built environment, from raising the standard of housing to the upkeep of parks and green spaces.

This report analysed how 12 of the neighbourhoods fared in the process of regeneration. Its conclusion was that strategies in combination were more effective than single approaches, even if single issues were tackled on a larger scale. Interestingly at the time of the research in 2004/05, little improvement in the physical state of the housing stock was evident. The greatest achievement appeared to be that the attention paid to such communities in seeking to turn them from areas of decline had given the areas a newfound confidence and hope for the future. Progress with improving the housing stock had to wait for the requirement that social rented housing meet the decent homes standard to start having an impact on the ground.

The whole of the NDC programme was subject to evaluation. The first report from the Pathfinder areas reported progress (ODPM, 2004). The project team concluded that after two years most areas had established credible partnerships, which combined service provider and community representation. Information sharing and communication among key agencies and the community had also improved. Modest improvements to some services were noted and factors relating to liveability showed the greatest momentum in terms of actual change.

The NDC programme was complemented by the Neighbourhood Renewal Fund (NRF), which has invested additional resources in England's most deprived local authority areas. The NRF has now been merged with the Department for Work and Pensions' Deprived Areas Fund to create a new Working Neighbourhoods Fund. The focus of the new fund is to develop more concentrated and community-led approaches to supporting people from the most disadvantaged areas into employment. The focus on improving neighbourhoods and enhancing general liveability seems to have disappeared from the NRF element of this fund. Like much of the planning system itself it is being refocused to concentrate primarily on economic issues.

A shift in focus to growth – city regions?

In the latter stages of the Labour government's second term, a new concept of 'city regions' became fashionable and was used to shape the content of the new Regional Spatial Strategies introduced by the 2004 Planning and Compulsory Purchase Act. As a concept, it has been around for a long time (see Ravetz, 2000) but its rediscovery by Labour brought it centre stage in discussions about where economic development interventions should be focused. It also ushered in a new agreement with the 'city' and its capacity to engender growth in surrounding areas.

David Miliband, when Communities Minister at the Office of the Deputy Prime Minister (ODPM) (now Department for Communities and Local Government; DCLG), and Ruth Kelly, when Secretary of State at the DCLG, picked up the concept as a central tenet of government policy relating to regeneration. The Centre for Sustainable Urban and Regional Futures (SURF) at the University of Salford was commissioned by the ODPM to develop the potential of the approach. Ruth Kelly, in a speech in 2006, commented that:

> Indeed it is city-regions – that is, the wider economy of cities – that have generally led regional growth in the last decade…. If we are to compete as a nation we must have cities that can hold their own on the global stage. (Speech to Core Cities Summit, Bristol, February 2006).

Regional Spatial Strategies produced in draft at the end of 2006/early 2007 did reflect this focus on city regions as the driver for economic change. MPs in rural hinterlands were nervous but a policy focus on the city seemed set to remain, backed up by the new Regional Spatial Strategies to be implemented from 2009. However, the Treasury and the ODPM were also developing a parallel process that led to planning and housing becoming centre stage in the first Brown government.

In 2005 the Treasury and the ODPM commissioned Kate Barker to undertake a review of land use planning (Barker, 2006), and the Treasury and the Department for Transport commissioned Sir Ron Eddington to undertake a review of transport (Eddington, 2006). These two reviews have heralded the biggest change to land use planning of recent decades.

The reports were commissioned because of two main concerns being voiced by the Treasury. The first of these was the concern that growth in the economy was being stunted by delays to infrastructure improvement, most notably in roads, airports and energy installations. The second concern was the lack of progress on increasing the supply of housing. This was not only creating house prices beyond the reach of many, but MPs even in northern cities were reporting major problems of undersupply, particularly in the provision of social housing and the building of too many non-family properties to meet a demand (although sometimes overstated) for executive flats.

Kate Barker's report is often accused of being too economistic, with a lack of concern for wider issues of climate change, community involvement and environmental protection. Given the involvement of the Treasury in the commissioning of the report, and the underlying objective it set for the planning system of improving economic prosperity and competitiveness, this is hardly surprising. The terms of reference in addition to the above asked that consideration be given to ways of increasing the flexibility, transparency and predictability that enterprise requires, alongside ways of improving the efficiency and speed of the system. The relationship between the planning process and productivity, and the delivery of sustainable development goals, were also to be considered.

Barker made 15 key recommendations (Barker, 2006, p 6), most of which saw their way into the 2007 Planning Bill. There are a set of proposals that relate to:

- streamlining the planning system, reducing the amount of guidance and speeding up the process of developing local plans;
- ensuring that PPS 4 is rewritten to reflect a greater role for the market and acknowledgement of price signals;
- a reduction in form filling and a proportionate approach to regulation;
- enhancing efficiencies in processing applications by making greater use of partnership working;
- removing the need for minor commercial developments that have little wider impact to require planning permission; and
- speeding up the appeals system.

There are also some proposals that relate to:

- the application of land use policies such as enhancing fiscal incentives to ensure more efficient use of land;
- supporting the town centre first policy; and
- enabling local authorities to share in the profits of local economic growth.

Those recommendations that are considered to be the most controversial relate to the suggestions that:

- large-scale infrastructure projects should be based on national statements of strategic direction and determined by an Independent Planning Commission;
- there should be a presumption in favour of approving planning applications unless there are clear economic, social and environmental factors that clearly outweigh any possible benefits;
- the Secretary of State should focus on the strategic issues with reduced use of call-ins; and
- planning bodies should be encouraged to review their greenbelt boundaries and take a more positive approach to applications that will enhance the quality of the greenbelt.

Not surprisingly, the suggestion that greenbelt areas should not be sacrosanct and that major planning applications for infrastructure development should be moved to a planning quango, the Infrastructure Planning Commission, caused the greatest stir. There was also great unease about the general direction in favour of development and concern that enabling local government to benefit more from planning gain would lead to a huge bias in favour of developers in the determination of planning applications.

The planning legislation following Barker has not introduced measures to relax the greenbelt. A Planning Gain Supplement Bill that was designed to tax the 'betterment' of sites has been ditched in favour of measures in the current Planning Bill to allow a Community Infrastructure Levy to be raised instead.

Turning to Sir Ron Eddington's (2006) report, this reviewed the role that transport should play in maintaining the UK's productivity and competitiveness. The following quotation summarises this perfectly:

> There is clear evidence that a comprehensive and high-performing transport system is an important enabler of sustained economic prosperity: a 5 per cent reduction in travel time for all business and freight travel on the roads could generate around £2.5bn of cost-savings – some 0.2 per cent of GDP.... Transport Corridors are the arteries of domestic and international trade, boosting the effectiveness of the British Economy. (Eddington, 2006, p 1)

Eddington's recommendations focus on the need for the government to show foresight in the investment in transport by improving the performance of transport networks that are important for the UK's economic success; the need to reduce congestion in city catchments, key urban corridors and international gateways as these are economically the most significant; and the need for a 'sophisticated policy mix to meet both economic and environmental goals' (p 1). This means a careful assessment of congestion charging as well as targeted infrastructure investment. Lastly, there is a warning about government needing to be ready to meet future challenges and that in order to deliver major transport infrastructure improvements it is necessary to speed up the assessment of planning applications and have major strategic projects dealt with by an Infrastructure Planning Commission.

Both the Eddington and Barker reports make reference to the Stern (2006) report on the economics of failing to tackle climate change. Both refer to the need for planning to focus on sustained development including providing for renewable energy and reducing pollution and harmful emissions.

The Planning White Paper – sustainable communities?

The Barker and Eddington reports informed the content of the Planning White Paper issued in May 2007. As if to underline the role that planning should play in shaping a more all-encompassing sustainable vision for the future, the Planning White Paper, *Planning for a Sustainable Future* (DCLG et al, 2007a), was presented to Parliament on behalf of four Secretaries of State – for Communities and Local Government; Environment, Food and Rural Affairs; Trade and Industry; and Transport.

The content of the White Paper was not new. Most of its key arguments and provisions had been rehearsed in earlier reports. It was, however, important in signalling those areas where the government was taking a different or more cautious approach than those outlined by Barker or Eddington. Primarily this related to suggestions on the greenbelt, congestion charging and taxing betterment. It also tells us about the things the government thinks it has done well in planning terms. It highlighted its achievements as: speeding up planning decision making by applying determination time targets; the provision of planning portals to give information on applications; and increasing the number of planners. It also increased the use of brownfield sites (for an explanation of this concept see Roberts et al, 2002) and added to the supply of housing. Also, more emphasis was placed on good design.

But it is the outline of challenges that remain that are contained in the White Paper that is really interesting. These are listed as:

• meeting the challenge of climate change;
• supporting sustainable economic development;
• increasing the supply of housing;
• protecting and enhancing the environment and natural resources;
• improving our local and national infrastructure; and
• maintaining security of energy supply.

This list would suggest that sustainability needs to cover a wide range of factors that could easily conflict in practice, making the role of planning in balancing competing interests more difficult. Brown and Duhr (2002) draw attention to the woolly and wide-ranging nature of the concept of sustainability whereby it often changes its meaning to meet a particular context. They also point out that government use of the concept has changed over time. In the early revisions of PPG and the national statement in 1999 (DETR, 1999), emphasis was placed on environmental sustainability. Over the years the need to employ a more interdisciplinary concept that can embrace social and economic objectives as well has been employed, and this is evidenced in the latest PPS 1 statement on sustainability discussed earlier.

The White Paper makes it clear that the concept of sustainability underpinning it is based on integrating its economic, social and environmental objectives: 'In order to properly integrate our economic, social and environmental objectives, we need clear and up-to-date policy frameworks which can inform decision making at every level' (DCLG et al, 2007, p 19).

Much of the White Paper sets out the reasons for moving to a new set of national statements that would establish the case for nationally significant infrastructure development. It also deals with changes to the current operation of the planning system primarily to make it easier for householders to install small micro-generation mechanisms. It expresses the desirability of greater community consultation at all levels of plan making, although this latter objective seems to sit ill at ease with proposals to remove the determination of large infrastructure planning applications from elected local authorities. A great deal of attention is also paid to generally making the planning system more open, transparent and accountable.

Not surprisingly, the White Paper also focuses on the key role local authorities have in the planning process. To that end, the Sustainable Community Strategy, which authorities are required to undertake, is to be streamlined with the Local Development Framework core strategy. This is seen as being necessary to bring about culture change in planning so that spatial planning and sustainable planning are intrinsically linked. The government is also keen that local authorities have a greater role to play in 'place shaping', essentially to encourage them to be more effective leaders in shaping the nature of their localities. This is of course being proposed while at the same time removing substantial planning determination powers from them with regard to nationally significant infrastructure schemes. So the government is encouraging local authorities to do more but within a reduced footprint.

The White Paper is particularly informative with regard to current government thinking on planning because unlike Bills it tells us about what has influenced policy development. But nevertheless it is to the Planning Bill and the Housing and Regeneration Bill that I now turn.

Planning for the future – where are we now?

Given the evolution and gradual refining of policy development relating to the Planning Bill it is pretty much as expected. Its main provisions cover the setting up and remit of the Infrastructure Planning Commission; the development of national policy statements; what counts as national infrastructure projects; and how these applications will be determined. Changes to existing planning regimes cover alterations in respect of the development plan. There are to be new rules for delegated decisions (where officers make the decisions) and how these can be appealed, and a relaxing of permitted development rights (where planning permission is not needed) within certain limits and criteria.

The Bill also includes the setting up of the Community Infrastructure Levy, which aims, according to the explanatory notes, 'to ensure that costs incurred in providing infrastructure to support the development of an area can be met' by landowners who have benefited from the rise in value of their land as a result of planning permission being granted. For the time being the Community Infrastructure Levy is replacing the idea of planning gain supplements.

Objections seem to be threefold. First, that the setting up of the Infrastructure Planning Commission is undemocratic and reduces local accountability; second, there is an argument that there will be insufficient parliamentary scrutiny of national policy statements on infrastructure projects; and, third, that there is not enough detail about how the Community Infrastructure Levy will operate. The Second Reading Debate (see *Hansard*, 2007) also shows that there is some concern by a number of MPs about the capacity of the planning system to deal with such significant change. There is therefore also a recognition that the planning profession itself may need further investment in terms of their training and future supply.

The Planning Bill is moving through the parliamentary process just slightly behind the 2007 Housing and Regeneration Bill. The Housing and Regeneration Bill allows for the setting up of the Homes and Communities Agency that is tasked with improving the supply and quality of housing; securing the regeneration of development land or infrastructure; and supporting the general improvement and well-being of communities. The other significant policy shift is establishing a new system for regulating social housing and providing a new watchdog for tenants. The Bill is intended to enable the government to work towards its target of delivering three million new homes by 2020.

Clearly, the emphases both Bills place on new development, whether in infrastructure or in housing, are going to place strains on their ability to deliver sustainable communities and sustainable development generally. If the development and sustainability juggernauts are not to collide disastrously then preventive action will need to be taken. This will mean testing infrastructure developments against emissions targets and turning down development that would lead to a lack of control of carbon emissions, as well as prioritising renewable energy and developing it on a scale not yet seen. It would also mean ensuring that new homes are not only well designed but are built to the highest standards of energy conservation and are carbon neutral. Infrastructure projects supporting them such as new schools or GP centres would need to be built in a similar vein.

While the rhetoric of sustainability is there, as are the policy statements to support it, I am not yet convinced that delivery mechanisms are in place to produce such a significant change to what is built, how it is built and where.

PPS 3 outlines a view of communities that is not significantly different from the utopian vision of new towns espoused in the 1940s. The emphasis is on housing mix, balance and making sure that infrastructure such as schools, shops, green spaces and leisure opportunities are in place to support new housing developments. This universal approach to developing communities is to be welcomed but the government must answer the question of what has happened to regenerating disadvantaged neighbourhoods now that Neighbourhood Renewal Funding has gone.

The government is not likely to face difficulty getting both Bills passed in Parliament. The challenge will be delivering national infrastructure improvements and building three million more homes without demolishing its own sustainability framework. It will also be necessary to ensure that decisions taken by local authorities do not derail the central policy planks of improving the quality and supply of housing and creating the infrastructure to support it. Sustainable communities need to be created and maintained. The Infrastructure Planning Commission has yet to be tested in terms of delivering the nationally significant infrastructure needed for economic growth but local authorities can and do have their own agendas that differ significantly to that of central government. Getting them to align their local policies and delivery frameworks with those of central government in the contentious field of planning will be a challenge indeed.

References

Barker, K. (2006) *Barker Review of Land Use Planning: Final Report – Recommendations*, London: HMSO.

Brown, C. and Duhr, S. (2002) 'Understanding sustainability and planning in England: an exploration of the sustainability content of planning policy at the national, regional and local levels', in V. Rydin and A. Thornley (eds) *Planning in the UK: Agendas for the New Millennium*, Aldershot: Ashgate.

DCLG (Department for Communities and Local Government), Department for the Environment and Rural Affairs, Department of Trade and Industry and Department for Transport (2007) *Planning for a Sustainable Future: White Paper*, Cm 7120, London: The Stationery Office.

DETR (Department of the Environment, Transport and the Regions) (1999) *A Better Quality of Life: A Strategy for Sustainable Development in the UK*, Cm 4345, London: The Stationery Office.

Eddington, R. (2006) *The Eddington Transport Study*, London: HMSO.

Hansard (2007) Parliamentary debates, 10 December, vol 469, no 20, pp 26-135, London: House of Commons.

Healey, P. (1997) *Collaborative Planning; Shaping Places in Fragmented Societies*, London: Macmillan.

Housing and Regeneration Bill (2007) Bill 8, 54/3, London: The Stationery Office.

ODPM (Office of the Deputy Prime Minister) (2004) *National Management Pathfinder Programme National Evaluation: Annual Review 2003/4 Key Findings*, London: Neighbourhood Renewal Unit.

Paskell, C. and Power, A. (2005) *'The Future's Changed': Local Impacts of Housing, Environment and Regeneration Policy since 1997. A Report from CASE's Areas Study*, London: London School of Economics and Political Science.

Planning Bill (2007) Bill 11, 54/3, London: The Stationery Office.

Power, A. (2007) *Tenants and their Communities: Summary Report to the Department for Communities and Local Government on the Consultation with Tenants at Trafford Hall on the Future Roles of Social Housing*, London: London School of Economics and Political Science.

Ravetz, J. (2000) *City Region 2020*, London: Earthscan.

Roberts, P., Joy, V. and Jones, G. (2002) 'Brownfield sites: problems of definition, identification and the evaluation of potential', in V. Rydin and A. Thornley (eds) *Planning in the UK: Agendas for the New Millennium*, Aldershot: Ashgate.

SEU (Social Exclusion Unit) (2000a) *National Strategy for Neighbourhood Renewal: A Framework for Consultation*, London: SEU.

SEU (2000b) *Policy Action Team Report Summaries: A Compendium*, London: SEU.

SEU (2001) *A New Commitment to Neighbourhood Renewal: National Strategy Action Plan*, London: SEU.

Stern, N. (2006) *The Economics of Climate Change*, Cambridge: Cambridge University Press.

THREE

Towards a new pension settlement? Recent pension reform in the UK

Debora Price

Introduction

In December 2002, the Labour government announced the formation of the Pensions Commission (DWP, 2002). In 2005, the Commission published comprehensive proposals for pension reform in their second report, *A New Pension Settlement for the Twenty-First Century* (Pensions Commission, 2005). In a remarkable achievement, the proposals gained broad acceptance from government and opposition parties, trades unions, employer organisations, occupational schemes, the insurance industry, special interest groups and the voluntary sector. In November 2006, the reform packages began to crystallise with the introduction of the first Pensions Bill, described by then Secretary of State for Pensions, John Hutton, as 'a landmark settlement for future generations' (DWP press release, 29 November 2006). The Bill uneventfully became law, as the 2007 Pensions Act, securing major reforms to the state system to take effect from 2010. In December 2007, the government published the second Pensions Bill, which will reform the private and occupational pension system, to take effect from 2012. Although this Bill may attract more controversy, there is again substantial political and stakeholder consensus for the broad content. All reforms are incremental to the existing system, yet the reform package has the capability to alter the pension landscape dramatically.

The pension reforms have been designed to address a number of identified problems with the UK pension regime. The state pension system needs to be politically and fiscally sustainable as the population ages and the baby boomers begin to retire. This is a challenge facing all countries, but in the UK the challenge has taken a particular form. First, the state system was designed not to cause rises in taxes or National Insurance contributions as the proportions of older people in the population grew, but this necessarily implies widespread increases in poverty as the population ages. Second, the state pensions provide such low income that without a private pension people risk poverty in later life. Third, there are substantial inequalities in private pension provision along many dimensions, which have resulted in large proportions of disadvantaged older people facing poverty in old age. Fourth, UK policies for poverty prevention in old age focus on means-tested provision targeted at those most in need. This confluence of policies – low state pensions, inadequate private pensions and means-tested income for poverty prevention – means that without reform, it was anticipated that by 2050 three quarters of the pensioner population would be entitled to means-tested benefits (Pensions Commission, 2004).

Means testing has been seen as a critical problem for two reasons. First, it creates disincentives to save with resulting moral hazard – if no one saves because they perceive that they will not benefit because of the means-tested system, then means testing must be maintained to avoid poverty. Second, significant minorities of older people do not claim means-tested benefits to which they are entitled, for complex and well-researched reasons (Barnard and Pettigrew, 2003; ONS, 2003; Sykes and Hedges, 2005). Currently, somewhere between 30% and 40% of pensioners who are entitled to Pension Credit (the principal means-tested benefit for pensioners) do not claim their entitlement, and this includes between 20% and 30% of pensioners who are entitled to the Guarantee Credit – the 'breadline' element of this means-tested system (DWP, 2007a). The Pension Service considers that no more can be done to improve take-up (Pension Service, 2007).

In the light of these difficulties, this chapter reviews the 2007 developments, assessing the extent to which three crucial aims of the reforms have been met:

- Has the spread of means testing in old age been reversed?
- Will people save more into pensions?
- Will it pay them to save?

Political and institutional legacies: background to the reforms

Our current pension system is bewildering, as decades of reforms have been layered one after another upon previous systems (Pemberton,

2006).Yet despite its complexity, the system reflects long-standing core principles of liberalism, voluntarism, choice and autonomy (Taylor-Gooby, 2005). Throughout the period of the modern welfare state successive governments, Labour and Conservative, have sustained an ideological commitment to a contribution-based minimalist basic state pension with individuals making additional pension provision for themselves and their families via the workplace and the market. Apart from a few years in the late 1970s/early 1980s, since its inception in 1948, the basic state pension has always remained well below subsistence levels. This has been coupled with a minimal role for the state in providing earnings-related pension provision (Glennerster, 2006; Pemberton, 2006; Thane, 2006). From 1921 successive governments created and sustained fiscal incentives for occupational and private pensions (Glennerster, 2006; Harris, 2006; Whiteside, 2006). The politics of pensions and institutions that have developed around decades of a voluntarist approach have ensured that employers and the financial services sector have substantial power in negotiating pension reforms (Whiteside, 2006).

By 1967, 53% of the working population was covered by occupational pensions (Pemberton, 2006). This was the heyday of voluntary private provision. As the century closed, so did increasing numbers of occupational and private pensions in the private sector, especially defined benefit schemes. Closures were driven by increasing longevity, changed tax treatment of pension funds, regulations requiring accounting transparency, 'herd' behaviour of employers and the diminishing power of trades unions. The value of equities dropped, leaving occupational pensions with dramatic pension deficits and investment losses for private pensions. Scandals and governance failures continued to destabilise the private pension sector, and a series of employer and pension fund insolvencies led to tens of thousands of workers losing their lifetime pension savings, many with no apparent redress (Pensions Commission, 2004, 2005; Bridgen and Meyer, 2005; Taylor-Gooby, 2005; Pemberton, 2006; PPI, 2007a). The proportions of pensioners whose incomes were insufficient to avoid poverty in old age continued to grow so that in 2005/06, about half the pensioner population was entitled to means-tested benefits (DWP, 2007a).

Despite the empirical picture, in setting up the Pensions Commission in 2002, government hoped to limit the scope of the pensions debate to policy interventions that might stimulate private long-term savings (DWP, 2002). The interaction of the low basic state pension with patchy private sector provision and means testing in old age meant, however, that the Commission persuaded the government that it was not possible to analyse the non-state pension sector in isolation (Pensions Commission, 2004).

The existing system and the 'pays to save' problem

Under the current system a full basic state pension is worth £87.30 per week for a single person, or about 16% of average earnings, well below the poverty line of £145 per week in 2005/06[1] (IFS, 2006; HBAI, 2007). Accrual depends on a relatively full working life of contributions or credits.[2] For paid workers earning above the 'lower earnings limit' of £87 per week, there is a compulsory second pension system, although individuals can participate in this via a state system, an occupational pension or a private pension (each with its own micro-system). For those in the state system for second pensions, there are three different state earnings-related pensions – two legacy systems[3] and the current system, the State Second Pension. The State Second Pension is earnings related (although redistributive to low earners), but designed to slowly become flat-rate by about 2050. The design of the State Second Pensions is such that it is currently not possible for any individual to predict, even in today's terms, what their combined state second pension entitlement will be on retirement (DWP, 2007b, pp 125-6).

Income from the state remains the main source of income for older people, especially women (Ginn, 2008: forthcoming), with a fifth of single pensioners deriving all of their income from the state (DWP, 2007c, Table 3.1, p 28). Yet only 35% of women and 85% of men reaching state pension age are entitled to a full basic state pension (DWP, 2007d), and amounts accrued in the various state second pension systems are low. In November 2006, the average amount of all state pensions combined paid to pensioners was just £87 per week.[4]

Apart from the state system, voluntary provision in occupational and private pensions operates through tax concessions and National Insurance rebates. This mostly takes the form of trust or insurance-based occupational pensions of various types, or individuals may have personal pensions (again, of various types). Occupational final salary pensions can and have always been able to opt out of the state earnings-related schemes, with another complex system of rebates and guarantees operating if they do. Since 1988, occupational money purchase schemes and individuals have also been able to opt out of the state earnings-related schemes into private schemes.

For those who do not amass sufficient contribution-based state provision and private provision over their working life, there is a means-tested system in later life, known as Pension Credit. This system is also bewilderingly complex. Guarantee Credit provides a minimum weekly income to all pensioners, currently £119.05 for single people and £181.70 for a couple. If pensioners have some pension income or income from modest savings, then they may get Savings Credit as well, which is a tapered benefit, or they might receive just Savings Credit. Many low-income pensioners will also be entitled to means-tested Council Tax Benefit and Housing Benefit. The means-tested system is so complicated that it is difficult even for advisers to predict whether pensioners will qualify, and for which system. Many pensioners fall into the 'pensions poverty trap' – they may find any income from their pension or savings withdrawn at rates varying from 40% to 100%. In other words it may not pay them to save.

The 'does it pay to save?' problem is acute for those who will retire at the lower end of the earnings distribution. The guaranteed minimum element of Pension Credit is indexed to average earnings,[5] but the basic state pension is indexed to prices.[6] This means that the problem of the 'gap' between state pension accrual and the minimum guarantee is growing – the pension poverty trap is getting worse. One way of addressing this would be to cut the levels of means-tested benefits, but reducing the level of the minimum income guarantee would result in substantial growth in pensioner poverty (Brewer et al, 2007).

The reforms

The reforms will apply to future generations of pensioners only, with the transitions to the new system beginning in 2010. Retirement age will be extended between 2024 and 2068 to 68 for men and women. At some point between 2012 and 2015, the long-standing decline in the value of the basic state pension relative to average earnings will be halted. Moreover, for those retiring after 2010 only 30 years of either contributions or credits will be needed over the working life to receive a full basic state pension. The government predicts that by 2025, 90% of men and women will have a full basic state pension (DWP, 2007d).

In addition, the government will finally abandon its relatively weak attempts to provide a state earnings-related pension: the existing State Second Pension will be converted to a flat-rate pension by about 2030. We will by then have a flat-rate state pension split into two parts. The basic state pension will be virtually universal, at about 13% of average earnings (IFS, 2006). The second state pension will be contributory, and a full State Second Pension will be worth about 17% of average earnings in today's terms. It will require work-based contributions or credits over a full working life from age 16 to state retirement age (which will gradually increase to 68) to accrue a full state second pension. Approved occupational defined benefit schemes will still be able to opt out of the State Second Pension.

Credits will be given into both elements of the state pension for low earners earning within a designated band,[7] for parental childcare of children under 12, to carers caring for more than 20 hours a week for a severely disabled person, and to those with disabilities. Once in retirement, the annual uprating of the basic state pension will be linked to earnings, but the state second pension will be linked to prices.

The combined state pensions are designed to provide a maximum income of around £160 a week in today's terms, with most people expected to accrue no more than £145 a week – around 43 years of contributions or credits (DWP, 2007b, p 20), equivalent to the current poverty line (HBAI, 2007). For adequate replacement rates, an earnings-related element of pensions is needed.

Earnings-related pension: continuing a voluntarist approach

The Pensions Commission (2005) concluded that the institutional legacies, political histories and political risks were such that a state earnings-related scheme was not viable, particularly as this might threaten the more important principle that the basic state pension must be improved; further, any additional earnings-related private pension should be voluntary, with the rhetoric of choice, autonomy and responsibility pervading the Pensions Commission's reasoning throughout its second report.

Accordingly, a new system of Personal Accounts will be created by the Bill currently going through Parliament. Employers must auto-enrol employees who are aged between 22 and state pension age and earning between about £5,000 and £33,500 (band earnings) into a qualifying occupational scheme or Personal Account. Employees can opt out, but if they remain in the scheme, then they must contribute at least 4% of band earnings, employers must contribute 3%, and 1% will be contributed through tax relief. Those earning under £5,000 can opt in to the scheme but *will not* attract an employer's contribution; and those under 22 or between state pension age and 75 can opt in and *will* attract an employer contribution. There will be an annual cap on contributions of £3,600, except in the initial year, expected to be 2012, when savings of £10,000 can be transferred. No transfers will be allowed into or out of the scheme.[8] These reforms are particularly important for women since 80% of female employees earn less than £25,000 a year (compared with 55% of men) (DWP, 2007d), but the majority of those earning under £5,000, who are excluded from auto-enrolment and the employer contribution, will also be women.

The rationale for Personal Accounts is that pure voluntarism has failed, and the insurance market has simply failed to provide a low-cost product for workers who do not have access to a 'good' occupational scheme. Auto-enrolment is the means to overcome the inertia that people exhibit about pension saving. Insurance-based pension products available on the market typically have administration charges of more than 1.5% of funds, and compare poorly with the 0.3% to 0.5% typically incurred in large trust-based occupational pension schemes. Economies of scale and diminished regulatory burden should be achievable with a scaled-up system. The proposed scheme will be a trust-based defined contribution funded scheme, run by the Personal Accounts Delivery Authority. Trustees will offer a range of investment options, which will have different risk profiles. A default equity fund will exist for those not wishing to exercise 'choice'.

The ambition for Personal Accounts is impressive. The Government (DWP, 2007e) estimates that between 9 and 11 million people are eligible for auto-enrolment because they are not currently in an employer pension scheme (8–9 million) or they are but their employer contributes less than 3% of pay (1 million). Between 6 and 9 million are predicted to save more in workplace provision, including about 3.5–6.5 million in Personal Accounts. From the 17.5 million self-employed, economically inactive, unemployed or excluded, who could all opt in and take advantage of the low-charging regime, the government estimates that about half a million will do so.

With low opt-out rates the scheme will be regarded as a success, but for people to remain in the scheme it needs to be appropriate for their needs. Auto-enrolment in an overarching pension system where it may not 'pay to save' is complex, as is auto-enrolment into a risky investment. The government wants the scheme to succeed, have low costs and little regulation, and to launch and maintain it with a strong message that it will deliver returns. How can that message be delivered to those for whom remaining in the scheme might be a poor decision, because they are unlikely to see a reasonable return for their investment, or for other reasons related to their personal circumstances? This is an issue of moral responsibility because those at whom the scheme is aimed are low to moderate earners, who cannot afford to lose money or make bad choices.

Vulnerabilities in the reformed system

Despite its undoubted potential, the reformed system has a number of vulnerabilities, and the risks of these fall unevenly. First, the state second pension will remain contribution based. Few people are expected to accrue a full 52 years of contributions or credits, and differentials will remain for those with very different life courses. Second, together in full, the two state pensions will provide only a base level of income. A substantial minority are still not expected to accrue sufficient income in later life to avoid means-tested benefits. Third, by relying on a voluntary system for earnings-related provision, the future benefits of the pension system become uncertain. Outcomes will depend on employer responses to the reforms, on whether an effective enforcement regime can be devised in a voluntary system, and on which employees opt out of the Personal Account scheme. The financially stretched are the most likely to opt out – including low earners, lone mothers and people struggling with debt, all part of the target group for the new reforms.

The reforms *aim* to solve all three identified problems: halt and reverse the spread of means testing; ensure that people save more into pensions; and ensure that it pays them to save. It is not inevitable that they will succeed.

Reversing the spread of means testing

The basic state pension will be improved, but not enough to end means testing in retirement for millions of pensioners, even in the very long term. First, no current pensioners will share in the improvements. There are about 11 million pensioners, of whom over 1.4 million older women and 825,000 men live below the poverty line (HBAI, 2007). Many of these cohorts will remain in the pensioner population for decades to come, creating institutional age divisions in our older population. Even so, many in later cohorts will retire on means-tested benefits or become entitled to means-tested benefits as they age.

By the middle of the century, we will have over 17 million pensioners. Even government predictions are that 30% of the pensioner population – over five million people – will be entitled to means-tested Pension Credit in 2050 (DWP, 2007f); the Pensions Policy Institute (PPI, 2006) models indicate that this might be as high as 45%. This will not only be an issue for the older old – one in four of those within five years of state pension age will still qualify (DWP, 2007f). Around 6% of pensioners will be entitled to Guarantee Credit alone. This means that even when the reforms have had time to play out fully in the population, more than a million pensioners will at some point suffer a risk of up to a 100% withdrawal rate on income from pensions, savings and other sources. A further four million or so pensioners who are entitled to Guarantee and Savings Credit or Savings Credit alone, and potentially other means-tested benefits, will suffer a withdrawal rate somewhere between 40% and 100% on any income. The risks again fall unevenly – on government estimates, around two thirds of those entitled to Pension Credit in 2050 will be single women (DWP, 2007d, p 20). While it is no longer the case that three quarters of the pensioner population will be entitled to means-tested benefits, the extent of the remaining problem is not trivial.

The government has cited resource constraints as the reason for not providing a better basic state pension, making improvements retrospective for existing pensioners or bringing in the reforms earlier. The Pensions Commission (2005) assessed a range of projected pension expenditure of between 7.5% and 8% of Gross Domestic Product (GDP) on state pensions as politically achievable. The total spending on the government's reform package will rise from 6.2% to 7.3% of GDP over the period 2010 to 2050, squarely within this range. A higher basic state pension with more universal coverage would undoubtedly cost, but the failure to grasp this reform leaves individuals at risk of poverty and at risk of having made poor financial decisions. It is notable that even in the year 2000, before baby boomer retirement and further anticipated increases in longevity, in the EU15 only Britain and Ireland spent less than 7% of GDP on state pensions, with other European countries spending between 7.4% and 15% (Pensions Commission, 2004, Appendix D, p 107, Table D.7).

To a large extent the reforms to the basic state pension can be counted as successful. The spread of means testing has been halted, at least from 2010 onwards. Spending on Pension Credit is forecast to reduce from 0.6% of GDP today to 0.1% in 2050 (DWP, 2007b). Under the reformed proposals, most pensioners will be better off than they would otherwise have been, but millions will suffer withdrawal rates of between 40% and 100% on income from pensions, savings or other sources. Those caught in the pension poverty trap and most at risk of having made savings or pension provision during the working life that provide no or little return are women; those who live alone; the divorced, separated and never married; the older old; those who are disabled or carers; and those who rent in retirement (DWP, 2007b). These are also the groups who are more likely to be poor in old age, since means testing is a flawed system for reaching those in need, with multiple complex barriers to claiming.

Ensuring that more people save more into pensions

The second fundamental aim of the reforms is to ensure that more people save more into pensions. It may seem axiomatic that this will happen if almost all employees will be automatically enrolled into a new system with an employer contribution, but this is a surprisingly difficult question.

The powerful employer and financial services sectors have secured agreement that this scheme will only be aimed at the low paid – not part of their own target market. There are several features of the scheme that act against the interests of the target market to protect existing providers and the existing industry. The Pensions Policy Institute (PPI, 2007b) has argued that the two aims of increasing the numbers of people saving for a pension yet for Personal Accounts not to compete with existing provision creates tensions, and that most policy options involve a trade-off between the two.

This lobby has secured a number of important elements to the reforms. All workers earning less than £5,000 per annum (most are women) are excluded, and even if they opt in to Personal Accounts they will not attract an employer's contribution. The 3% employer contribution has been written into primary legislation and annual uprating to the band has been left to the discretion of the Secretary of State. Those offering occupational schemes with more than a 3% contribution can auto-enrol employees into their existing scheme and do not have to offer Personal Accounts. Yet even good defined benefit occupational schemes offer poor value for money to an employee who will spend only a short time in the scheme and then become a deferred member for many years (more likely to be women: DWP, 2007d, p 39). This is particularly so since a proposed change in the pension regulatory regime will permit schemes to restrict the revaluation of deferred members' pensions to the higher of inflation or 2.5% (DWP, 2007g, p 8). Transfers into the scheme from other pensions or lump-sum payments will not be allowed even though if the scheme achieves charge rates in the region of 0.3% to 0.5% it may be the best place for a low-paid employee to invest their pension. The maximum that can be paid into the scheme in any year will be £3,600, regardless of lifetime accumulation in the scheme, and there will be no financial advice associated with Personal Accounts.

With these restrictions on the table, securing the agreement of employers' representatives and the financial services sector to these proposals has been surprisingly straightforward, despite the addition to the wage bill of the employer contribution. Ultimately, these contributions will be passed on through lower wages and/or higher prices and are unlikely to affect employers much, particularly if the Personal Accounts administration is efficient. Alternatively, those employers who currently offer good-quality schemes with contributions higher than 3% might close down or reduce their contributions to those schemes to pay for the higher expected participation rates with auto-enrolment. This has become known as the 'levelling-down' problem, and it is a particularly unpredictable element of the proposed pension system.

The Pensions Policy Institute (PPI, 2007b) has produced an analysis of the scenarios that may unfold. If no employer decides to pass on the costs of the reforms by reducing their pension contributions (a very unlikely scenario) then the reforms could increase annual saving by £10 billion. But at the other extreme, if no employer offers more than the minimum 3% contribution, then annual pension savings will *decrease* by £10 billion per annum. On average, people could be saving much less than they are currently, rather than more.

In a recent survey, more than seven in ten employers were unaware of the proposed reforms (DWP, 2006). Securing their cooperation may be difficult or impossible. The scheme is voluntary, and so enforcement cannot be triggered simply because employees are not members. There will be no way to prevent employers pressurising employees not to enrol, or even collusion between employers and employees to sustain higher wages in exchange for not remaining in the scheme. Employees most likely to suffer this problem are those on low wages who are in a weak bargaining position, and those working for small employers. These are most likely to be women.

Employer behavioural responses are crucial, but so are the responses of employees. Even if no employer offers more than the minimum, this will still bring about seven million employees into a work-based pension scheme, and there is an argument that it is better to have more people saving a little than the particularly uneven pattern of savings that exists now. But this analysis assumes that all employees participate. It seems unduly optimistic that savings might increase overnight by £8–£10 billion per annum, and then remain at that level. Some of those who are auto-enrolled will simply cease contributions to other pensions or savings such as personal pensions, building society accounts, ISAs and so on. No attempt has been made to estimate *net* savings as a result of these reforms. Further, a number of employees will not participate. Affordability concerns and lack of trust in providers are important reasons for not saving, and consumer debt is at an all-time high (PPI, 2007b).

Opt-out rates may also be influenced by investment returns, not considered in the debate so far. The word 'risk' has barely featured in the seminars and consultations that have accompanied the new policies, yet with the structure of the Personal Account as a direct contribution-funded scheme, all risk of investment returns and interest rates falls on individuals. The default fund will be equity based, as will almost all of the other funds on offer. Equity markets are volatile. Presumably, even in a lightly regulated regime, the Personal Accounts trustees will be required to communicate each year to individuals how much they have contributed so far and how much their investment is now worth, remind individuals that investments can go up as well as down, and that the government is giving no guarantees against poor returns. Low-paid individuals are least able to take risks with their money and one year of poor returns may have a substantial impact on how keen people are to remain in the fund.

There is no precedent for considering long-term opt-out rates for a national auto-enrolled pension scheme that includes reluctant employers and low-paid employees. Existing research in the US and UK tends to show much higher participation rates with auto-enrolment than with no auto-enrolment, with participation rates in the region of 85%, compared with about 60% for opt-in schemes (Pensions Commission, 2004, 2005). But as the Pensions Policy Institute (PPI, 2007b) has pointed out, this may reflect more proactive and more generous employers, where there is a culture of encouraging people to join the scheme. As many as nine million might participate if opt-out rates are only 20% and large numbers of the self-employed and others with no employer contribution join. If only 50% join and fewer 'others' then this figure may reduce below four million, not all of whom will be new savers (PPI, 2007b).

The upshot of this is that the reforms may come at the expense of reduced overall saving into pensions, potentially in large order of billions of pounds per year, because of employer responses. This may not matter if the goal is to bring at least some saving to the vast majority of paid workers, but if these are the very people at high risk of low or poor returns to their savings in retirement, then the issue becomes problematic. Being a private-funded, equity-based system means that individuals who may be poorly placed to take risks with their long-term investments are being incentivised to do so.

'Pays to save', auto-enrolment and generic advice

There is no research that attempts to estimate the numbers of those in paid work who potentially should opt out of Personal Accounts because they are likely to see little or no return for their money in retirement, or because their financial circumstances would suggest that pension saving is inappropriate for other reasons.

We know that the numbers of people who are still likely to be caught by poverty traps associated with means-tested benefits in later life are considerable: as noted above, 30% of pensioners are projected to be entitled to Pension Credit in 2050, and more will be entitled to Housing Benefit and Council Tax Benefit. Almost all pensioners in 2050 will have been of working age at the start of the new system in 2012, and so this suggests a large-scale problem. Without knowing the path of the life course, it is very difficult to predict for any one individual how risky it is for them to save in a Personal Account. The Pensions Policy Institute (PPI, 2007c) showed that a number of groups were at medium risk of low returns on their investments, and others at high risk of having no or negative returns on their investments. The medium risk categories included various groups who in 2012 will be in their twenties, forties and fifties. At high risk are those who are likely to rent in retirement.

A substantial minority of older people rent in retirement: one third of people over 75, and almost a quarter (23%) of people aged 65 to 74, with fairly similar proportions of 45- to 64-year-olds (22%) (DCLG, 2007). If those who will rent in retirement are at high risk of poor returns from Personal Accounts, then this too is a problem potentially affecting millions of people.

There are other reasons why it may not be appropriate to save into a pension. If a household is paying off debt at high rates of interest, it would often make more sense to commit current income to debt reduction rather than to saving. It may be more important to build up a fund of ready cash for emergencies or to save towards a house than to contribute to a pension, where cash is locked in until retirement. The insurance industry is heavily regulated to try to ensure that people are given appropriate tailored advice before signing up to a pension.

These problems of potentially inappropriate saving are more likely to apply in the target group for Personal Accounts of low to moderate earners. Yet there will be no advice associated with the decision to stay opted in or to opt out of Personal Accounts. The rationale for this is that costs must be kept as low as possible in the Personal Account scheme and giving any advice would undermine this, but the Thoreson Review (HM Treasury, 2007, p 83) has noted that industry stakeholders objected in principle to the funding of advice for Personal Accounts.

Otto Thoreson, chief executive of Aegon UK, is currently undertaking a review of 'generic financial advice' for the Treasury Financial Capability strategy. The interim report (HM Treasury, 2007) advised that a national generic advice service should be established to assist people with generic financial strategies. The Thoreson Review will remain in close contact with the Department for Work and Pensions and the Personal Accounts Delivery Authority as the Personal Account strategy unfolds, but it has been made clear that the sort of detailed advice pertaining to their individual circumstances that might assist individuals at risk of bad decisions will not be forthcoming, for example whether individual circumstances and trajectories make people high or low risk for wasting their money or investing it suboptimally; or the level of financial risk that it is sensible for someone in that individual's position to be taking. Presumably no 'generic' advice service could afford exposure to the legal liabilities that would ensue if advice were personalised. The imperative seems to be to present an optimistic account, encouraging people to stay in Personal Accounts, and not to take any steps that might shake confidence in the new system.

Towards a new pension settlement?

The Pensions Commission accepted that there were few economic reasons for preferring a private system to a public system for earnings-related provision. It argued that in the UK a good-quality earnings-related private system has never worked because it has never gained political consensus or public buy-in enabling it to be sustained through decades of political change. It is more politically acceptable to create a 'tax' through the wage packet than through an improved National Insurance system. The abandoning of support for the public earnings-related system is a fundamental ideological commitment to the private sector, and means that what may have been the last opportunity to engender middle-class buy-in for compulsory state-supported or state-provided earnings-related provision has passed. Legacy, liberal ideology and the bargaining strength of the financial services sector have prevented the resurgence of a state earnings-related scheme in favour of another voluntarist private sector approach. The power of the financial services sector to influence the shape of the new Personal Account scheme is evident in its many restrictive features, and through targeting only those on low and moderate pay. The risk of investments and interest rates falls entirely on individuals little able to absorb losses and poor returns.

Personal Accounts have the ability to transform retirement, forcing many employers who would otherwise never have contemplated doing so to contribute at least 3% of wages to an employee pension. But the success of the reforms will depend crucially on the behavioural responses of employers and employees, as well as on investment returns. Employers have the ability to undermine the system considerably, and the risk of 'levelling down' may mean that over time much less money goes into the pension system than hoped for. Opt-out rates of employees will need to be closely monitored and understood if the system is to succeed.

While moving in a welcome direction the reforms have failed to ensure one crucially important element – the virtual eradication of means testing from the retirement system. The reformed state pension, far from being radical, looks fairly similar to structures that we have seen in the past. The abandonment of a state earnings-related pension and combining the two state pensions into effectively one flat-rate system means we are left with something similar to Beveridge's original idea of a single flat-rate pension at subsistence level to which voluntary savings could be added. The state pension reforms do much to reverse the disastrous trajectory of the current basic state pension, but its value has been left very low and the second tier of the state pension remains contributions based. The basic state pension is insufficient to ensure that pensioners escape poverty in future, and means testing remains an important element in the reformed system.

Means testing creates perverse incentives – not to save – which sit uneasily with a new system of national Personal Accounts, into which people will be encouraged to save through auto-enrolment. Unlike their wealthier counterparts, the 'target group' for Personal Accounts – the low paid and those with weak or intermittent labour market positions – will not be given tailored advice. This is to preserve low costs in the Personal Account system but there will be no way to protect people from making 'bad' decisions about their pensions, and no redress if they do. Indeed, there is a risk that the new arrangements will encourage low earners to do so.

We are likely to see growing inequalities in public and private sector pension provision, and increasing political tensions relating to the cost and fiscal burden of public sector pension promises. Reliance on private provision for replacement income in later life continues neoliberal policies that have in the past led to gender, class and ethnic inequalities in pension provision, and despite radical improvements via the greater universality of the state pensions and the auto-enrolment scheme, such structural differences are likely to continue.

Notes

[1] 60% of median equivalised income for a single person with no children before housing costs.

[2] Currently 44 years for men and 39 for women; the state pension age is 65 for men, 60 for women. Both are being equalised by 2020. Those earning below the Lower Earnings Limit of £87 per week do not participate in the basic state pension.

[3] Graduated Retirement Benefit and the State Earnings Related Pension. The 2007 Pensions Bill contains proposals to simplify the three State Second Pensions.

[4] Calculated using the DWP Resource Centre Tabulation Tool at: www.dwp.gov.uk/resourcecentre/

[5] By the 2007 Pensions Act.

[6] On occasions uprating has exceeded the RPI (Retail Price Index).

[7] Between the Lower Earnings Limit and the Lower Earnings threshold, currently between £87 and £100 a week.

[8] A special regime will be created for pension sharing on divorce.

References

Barnard, H. and Pettigrew, N. (2003) *Delivering Benefits and Services for Black and Ethnic Minority Older People*, DWP Research Report No. 201, London: Department for Work and Pensions.

Brewer, M., Browne, J., Emmerson, C., Goodman, A., Muriel, A. and Tetlow, G. (2007) *Pensioner Poverty over the Next Decade: What Role for Tax and Benefit Reform?*, London: Institute for Fiscal Studies.

Bridgen, P. and Meyer, T. (2005) 'When do benevolent capitalists change their mind? Explaining the retrenchment of defined-benefit pensions in Britain', *Social Policy & Administration*, vol 39, no 7, pp 764-85.

DCLG (Department for Communities and Local Government) (2007) *Housing in England 2005/6: A Report Principally from the 2005/06 Survey of English Housing*, London: DCLG.

DWP (Department for Work and Pensions) (2002) *Simplicity, Security and Choice: Working and Saving for Retirement: Action on Occupational Pensions*, Cm 5677, London: DWP.

DWP (2006) *Employer Attitudes to Personal Accounts: A Report of a Quantitative Survey*, DWP Research Report No. 397, London: DWP.

DWP (2007a) *Pension Credit Estimates of Take-up in 2005/6*, London: DWP.

DWP (2007b) *Pensions Bill – Impact Assessment*, London: DWP.

DWP (2007c) *Pensioners Incomes Series 2005/06 (Revised)*, London: DWP.

DWP (2007d) *Gender Impact of Pension Reform: Pensions Bill 2007*, London: DWP.

DWP (2007e) *People Benefiting from Private Pension Reform: Explanation of Participation Estimates*, London: DWP.

DWP (2007f) *Projections of Pension Credit Entitlement*, London: DWP.

DWP (2007g) *Deregulatory Review of Private Pensions: Government Response*, London: DWP.

Ginn, J. (2008: forthcoming) 'Poverty and financial inequality in later life', in T. Ridge and S. Wright (eds) *Understanding Inequality, Poverty and Wealth: Policies and Prospects*, Bristol: The Policy Press.

Glennerster, H. (2006) 'Why so different? Why so bad a future?', in H. Pemberton, P. Thane and N. Whiteside (eds) *Britain's Pensions Crisis: History and Politics*, London: The British Academy.

Harris, J. (2006) 'The roots of public pensions provision: social insurance and the Beveridge plan', in H. Pemberton, P. Thane and N. Whiteside (eds) *Britain's Pensions Crisis: History and Politics*, London: The British Academy.

HBAI (Households Below Average Income) (2007) *Households Below Average Income 1994/5 to 2005/6*, London: DWP.

HM Treasury (2007) *Thoresen Review of Generic Financial Advice: Interim Report*, London: HM Treasury.

IFS (Institute of Fiscal Studies) (2006) *An Initial Response to the White Paper*, London: IFS.

ONS (Office for National Statistics) (2003) *Entitled but not Claiming? Pensioners, the MIG and Pension Credit*, London: ONS.

Pemberton, H. (2006) 'Politics and pensions in post-war Britain', in H. Pemberton, P. Thane and N. Whiteside (eds) *Britain's Pensions Crisis: History and Politics*, London: The British Academy.

Pension Service (2007) *The Pension Service Annual Report and Accounts, 2006/07*, London: The Stationery Office.

Pensions Commission (2004) *Pensions: Challenges and Choices: The First Report of the Pensions Commission*, London: The Stationery Office.

Pensions Commission (2005) *A New Pension Settlement for the Twenty-First Century: The Second Report of the Pensions Commission*, London: The Stationery Office.

PPI (Pensions Policy Institute) (2006) *An Evaluation of the White Paper State Pension Reform Proposals*, London: PPI.

PPI (2007a) *The Changing Landscape for Private Sector Defined Benefit Pension Schemes*, London: PPI.

PPI (2007b) *Will Personal Accounts Increase Pension Saving?*, London: PPI.

PPI (2007c) *Incentives to Save and Means Tested Benefits*, London: PPI.

Sykes, W. and Hedges, A. (2005) *Understanding the Service Needs of Vulnerable Pensioners: Disability, Ill-health and Access to The Pension Service*, DWP Research Report No 263, London: DWP.

Taylor-Gooby, P. (2005) 'UK pension reform: a test case for a liberal welfare state', in G. Bonoli and T. Shinkawa (eds) *Ageing and Pension Reform around the World: Evidence from 11 Countries*, Cheltenham: Edward Elgar.

Thane, P. (2006) 'The "scandal" of women's pensions in Britain: how did it come about?', in H. Pemberton, P. Thane and N. Whiteside (eds) *Britain's Pensions Crisis: History and Politics*, London: The British Academy.

Whiteside, N. (2006) 'Occupational pensions and the search for security', in H. Pemberton, P. Thane and N. Whiteside (eds) *Britain's Pensions Crisis: History and Politics*, London: The British Academy.

FOUR

Climate change and climate change policy in the UK 2006–07

Carolyn Snell

Introduction

In a year when the Nobel Peace Prize was jointly awarded to climate change campaigner Al Gore and to the UN's Intergovernmental Panel on Climate Change (IPCC), climate change appears to be rising up the policy agenda. Climate change is a complex and contested issue, both in terms of the scientific understanding of the problem and the range of policy solutions available. As with many environmental problems, the human activities associated with climate change produce relatively invisible outputs; for example, carbon dioxide (CO_2) emissions from a car are not visible and produce no smell. Emissions are also transboundary in nature – there are high levels of inequality between those who feel the benefits associated with CO_2-emitting activities (such as energy and transport use) and those who feel the effects of climate change, such as those living in low-lying countries with limited capacity to protect against rising sea levels. As a result, UK policy on climate change occurs at a range of policy levels, and falls under the remit of a number of governmental departments.

This chapter outlines some of the key international, European and domestic climate change targets before discussing the developments in 2006–07, focusing on recent policy changes. The most notable areas of policy development are the 2006 Climate Change Programme, which sets out the overall governmental climate change strategy, and contains core elements such as the European Union Emissions Trading Scheme (EU ETS); the 2007 Climate Change Bill; and the 2007 Energy White Paper *Meeting the Energy Challenge* (DTI, 2007). An assessment of key policy direction is offered, and the chapter concludes by assessing current UK progress, questioning whether the recent policy proposals do enough to address climate change.

However, prior to this we first discuss the nature of climate change as a policy problem, and the G8 summit and Stern Review that have in many respects precipitated the current policy climate.

Climate change as a policy problem

It is not the purpose of this chapter to enter into a debate about the scientific case for anthropogenic climate change, nor to explore in depth scientific arguments about carrying capacity and acceptable limits to greenhouse gas (GHG) emissions.[1] However, it is important to understand the nature of climate change as a policy problem, and the science–policy relationship, and this section briefly considers these issues.

Climate change

The nature of the problem is best described in the words of the experts:

> Warming of the climate is unequivocal, as is now evident from observations of increases in global average air and ocean temperatures, widespread melting of snow and ice, and rising average sea level. (IPCC, 2007, p 5)

> Global atmospheric concentrations of carbon dioxide, methane and nitrous oxide have increased markedly as a result of human activities since 1750 and now far exceed pre-industrial values determined from ice cores spanning many thousands of years. (IPCC, 2007, p 2)

> The understanding of anthropogenic warming and cooling influences on climate has improved since the Third Assessment Report leading to very high confidence (90%) that the global average net effect of human activities since 1750 has been one of warming. (IPCC, 2007, p 3)

Debating the evidence

Oreskes (2004) reminds us that absolute proof is rare in the environmental sciences. Instead, as the body of evidence grows consensus is reached. However, consensus does not mean that everyone agrees, and there will always be those who hold different views based on conflicting evidence or on their own constructions of what that evidence means. Scientific knowledge also changes over time as new evidence comes to light, breaking down old paradigms and creating new ones. There are those, such as Bjørn Lomborg, author of *The Sceptical Environmentalist* (2001), who argue that since much of our scientific knowledge on the environment is uncertain and unproven it should not form the basis of any policy decisions taken concerning the environment. On the other hand, there are others who are concerned that waiting for indisputable proof may delay action to prevent irreversible damage. Indeed, the 'precautionary principle', formulated in the 1992 Rio Declaration on Environment and Development, called for action in the face of serious environmental risks even in the absence of full scientific certainty. The precautionary principle has now become a mainstay in international policy making, appearing in numerous international agreements.

Despite this, scientific uncertainty has often played a key role in climate change policy debates, prompting calls for more research and more evidence before any decisions are made. Discussing proposed EU policies to protect species and ecosystems from climate change, Lawton predicts that:

> In the horse-trading that will go on within and among Member States to turn the Commission's proposed policies into reality ... these scientific uncertainties will be used by those ideologically opposed to anything that might put a brake on economic growth. (Lawton, 2007, p 471)

Likewise, as he discusses policies that might minimise the impact of CO_2 emissions on oceans, 'the pessimist in me says that it may be all too easy to use the uncertainties as an excuse for doing nothing' (Lawton, 2007, p 471).

Recent policy background – the G8 summit and Stern Review

The G8 summit

On 6-8 July 2005, the Group of Eight industrialised nations (G8) met at Gleneagles, Scotland. Prior to the summit there were hopes that it would represent a clear turning point in combating climate change; however, 'the outcome ... left most observers somewhere between disillusion and cautious optimism' (Butler and Schiermeier, 2005, p 156). Changes in wording between draft and final statements allowed sufficient question to hang over scientific evidence to allow governments once again to commission more research rather than to plan any definitive course of action (Walther et al, 2005, p 648). The lack of a discussion concerning stabilisation levels for GHG concentrations, and subsequent setting of targets for emission reductions, was also criticised (May, 2005).

However, key positive outputs included: the agreement by all G8 leaders (including the US, a first during the Bush administration) that human activity is a major contributory factor to climate change; the production of an action plan 'Climate Change, Clean Energy and Sustainable Development'; and a 'Dialogue on Climate Change, Clean Energy and Sustainable Development'.

The Stern Review

The Stern Review (Stern, 2006) was commissioned by Gordon Brown as part of the G8 Dialogue on Climate Change. What set it aside from other reviews and recommendations was the focus on the economic impact of climate change. While there have been other economic assessments, the Stern Review was labelled as the most comprehensive view of the economics of climate change ever produced (Jordan and Lorenzoni, 2007, p 311). One of the most notable arguments of the review was that:

> [I]f we don't act, the overall costs and risks of climate change will be equivalent to losing at least 5% of global GDP each year, now and forever. If a wider range of risks and impacts is taken into account, the estimates of damage could rise to 20% of GDP or more. In contrast, the costs of action – reducing greenhouse gas emissions to avoid the worst impacts of climate change – can be limited to around 1% of global GDP each year. (Stern, 2006, p vi)

The review is not without its critics. The assumptions and subsequent recommendations made within the report have been questioned by a number of critics (see, for example, Mendelsohn, 2007). It is not within the remit of this chapter to explore the merits and limitations of the Stern Review; however, the review is relevant here because it has played a role in influencing recent policy developments in the UK. The key areas of action recommended are: carbon pricing implemented through tax, trading or regulation; policies to support innovation and low-carbon technologies; and the removal of barriers to energy efficiency and the encouragement of individual action on climate change (Stern, 2006, p viii).

UK commitments

International commitments and policy mechanisms

The most significant commitment is the Kyoto Protocol, agreed in 1997 and ratified in 2005. Annex One countries (developed countries) committed to reducing emissions from a basket of six GHGs by at least 5.2% below 1990 levels between 2008 and 2012. While the EU15 member states adopted the overall target of an 8% reduction, this varied state by state, with the UK being committed to a 12.5% reduction. Further action at the international scale has been encouraged by the UK government – 'The G8 +5 dialogue which was started at Gleneagles ... is an excellent forum in which new broad principles for an international framework can be agreed' (DEFRA, 2007a, p 18) – and indeed the UK has a reputation for being a driver of international climate change policy (even if this enthusiasm is not matched domestically).

A number of mechanisms exist at the European level to support the delivery of the Kyoto targets. The European Climate Change Programme has developed a number of directives, including the EU ETS, and directives on the promotion of electricity from renewable energy sources, on the energy performance of buildings, and on the promotion of biofuels (DEFRA, 2006, p 20). Over and above this, the European Council met in March 2007 and made the following statement:

> Until a global and comprehensive post-2012 agreement is concluded, and without prejudice to its position in international negotiations, the EU makes a firm independent commitment to achieve at least a 20% reduction of greenhouse gas emissions by 2020 compared to 1990. (Council of the European Union, 2007, p 12).

This commitment was to be increased to a 30% reduction as part of international agreements.

National commitments

Aside from Kyoto, the UK also has domestic targets to reduce emissions. By 2010 CO_2 emissions are to be reduced by 20% below 1990 levels. Further into the future the aim is to 'ensure that the UK can make the real progress by 2020 towards the long-term goal to reduce CO_2 emissions by some 60% by about 2050' (DEFRA, 2006, p 3).

However, it must be noted here that while the UK is on target to meet the Kyoto reduction levels, Carter and Ockwell (2007, p 11) note that 'this achievement is largely the fortuitous result of the switch from coal to gas for power generation during the early 1990s rather than a deliberate Government emissions reduction policy'. They suggest that the domestic goals of reduced CO_2 emissions by 20% below base levels by 2010 are likely to be missed, and that these trends are of concern for the longer-term 2020 and 2050 goals (2007, p 71).

UK policy

This section focuses on the main areas of action in 2006–07, but also outlines previous areas of action that these developments have built upon. Current UK action on climate change comprises a number of activities, and many of these activities overlap in a range of policy documents.

The UK Climate Change Programme

The UK Climate Change Programme was launched in 2006, following the 2004 review of the original Climate Change Programme of 2000. The Programme sets out the overall governmental climate change strategy. The Programme details UK plans to deliver its Kyoto target and how it intends to move towards its domestic goals. The first annual report was delivered in July 2007 and described the action taken by the government to reduce CO_2 emissions, and to consider the implications of the Stern Review. The Climate Change Programme brings together a number of areas of action, and Table 4.1 demonstrates the predicted impact of existing policy measures while Table 4.2 demonstrates the predicted impact of new measures. Within both the previous and the new incarnation of the Programme there were a number of actions set out to reduce CO_2 emissions. Those flagged as significant by the Department for the Environment, Food and Rural Affairs (DEFRA) are the climate change levy[2] and climate change agreements[3] (both introduced in 2001), and the Renewables Obligation[4] and Energy Efficiency Commitment[5] (both introduced in 2002).

Table 4.1: Existing measures and carbon savings

Existing measures	Carbon savings in 2010 (million tonnes of carbon)
Energy supply	
Renewables Obligation	2.5
Business	
Climate change levy	3.7
UK emissions trading scheme	0.3
Carbon Trust	1.1
Building Regulations 2002	0.4
Building Regulations 2005	0.2
Climate change agreements	2.9
Transport	
Voluntary Agreements package, including reform of company car taxation and graduated VED	2.3
Wider transport measures	0.8
Sustainable distribution in Scotland and Wales	0.1
Fuel duty escalator	1.9
Domestic	
Energy Efficiency Commitment (EEC) (2002–05)	0.4
Energy Efficiency Commitment (EEC) (2005–08)	0.6
Energy Efficiency Commitment (EEC) (2008–11)	0.6
Building Regulations 2002	0.7
Building Regulations 2006 including 2005 condensing boilers update	0.8
Warm Front and fuel poverty programmes	0.4
Market transformation including appliance standards and labelling	0.2
Agriculture	
Woodlands Grants Scheme (England)	0.2
Woodland planting since 1990 (Scotland)	0.5
Public sector	
Central government, NHS, UK universities and English schools including Carbon Trust activities	0.2
TOTAL	17.13

Source: DEFRA (2006, p 124)

Table 4.2: New measures and carbon savings

Additional measures	Carbon savings in 2010 (million tonnes of carbon)
Energy supply	
Subsidy for biomass heat	0.1
Second phase of EU ETS	3.0–8.0
Business	
Carbon Trust support for investment in energy efficiency in SMEs	0.1
Measures to encourage or assist SMEs to take up energy-saving opportunities	0.1
Transport	
Renewable Transport Fuel Obligation	1.6
Future voluntary agreement with car manufacturers to reduce CO_2 emissions from new cars	0.1
Domestic	
Increased activity in Energy Efficiency Commitment (2008–11)	0.5
Provision of advice to stimulate early replacement of inefficient boilers and implementation of the Energy Performance of Buildings Directive	0.2
Package of measures to improve energy efficiency in buildings	0.1
Better billing and metering	0.2
Products Policy: consumer information and standards for lights and other energy-using products	0.2
Agriculture	
Strategy for non-food crops	0.1
Public sector	
Additional effort by local authorities	0.2
Revolving loan fund for the public sector	0.1
Actions by devolved administrations	0.3
Other measures	0.1
TOTAL	7.0–12.0

Note: SME = small and medium-sized enterprise.

Source: DEFRA (2006, p 124)

EU ETS

As is clear from Table 4.2, the most significant new measure is the second phase of the EU ETS. The Trading Scheme is a market-based approach that sets a cap on total CO_2 emissions from European industries. Allocations are divided between the relevant industries, and firms emitting less than their allocations can sell on unused permits. The UK's allocations were approved by the European Commission in November 2006 and were subsequently published in the National Allocation Plan in March 2007 (DEFRA, 2007f). The National Allocation Plan aims to save up to eight million tonnes of carbon per year.

The EU ETS features as a significant component of the 2007 Energy White Paper (DTI, 2007), the Climate Change Programme and also the Climate Change Bill. There has been little assessment of the second phase of the EU ETS simply because it is very much under development and review. However, a review of the criticisms of the first phase allows some indication of the strength of the second, and implications for the third.

There are a number of issues regarding the way in which the scheme has been developed and key elements defined. The Environmental Audit Committee, chaired by MP Tim Yeo, raised a number of concerns in October 2007 (House of Commons Environmental Audit Committee, 2007). First, it is argued that the impact of the scheme is at worst overestimated, and at least unclear and insufficiently transparent. For example, the government has compared the impact of the scheme with a 'business as usual' scenario. Thus the eight million tonnes of carbon figure in Table 4.2 is said to reflect a cut on future emissions projections rather than on 1990 emissions levels (Carter and Ockwell, 2007, p 84), which has clear implications for the actual effectiveness of the scheme. The Environmental Audit Committee has described this is a 'counterfactual exercise' since it is difficult to be certain about how emissions in a 'business as usual' scenario would have actually increased. It is argued that greater clarity and transparency about the mechanisms of the Trading Scheme will improve confidence in it (House of Commons Environmental Audit Committee, 2007).

There are a number of criticisms about the precise details of the scheme's operation. The caps placed on EU states have been heavily criticised:

[T]he key weakness of the scheme to date [is] that the cap was not set sufficiently tightly to generate a price of carbon that incentivises real emissions reductions and abatement investment. With six months of the first Phase remaining, EUAs[6] have become virtually worthless. (DEFRA, 2007c, p 2)

Initially this problem looked like it would be repeated as member states requested overgenerous allocations. However, all but two initial National Allocation Plans were rejected on these grounds. Uncertainty about the long-term 'rules' are also said to have hampered a more effective Trading Scheme. The initial results of the European Commission Directorate General for Environment (2005) review of the EU ETS indicate that a lack of clear long-term 'rules' of the scheme are affecting the liquidity of the CO_2 allowance market. The review argues that:

> [S]ome companies fear that emission reduction efforts could be sanctioned [by possible changes] in the next allocation plan, so they refrain from reducing emissions in the current period. This impacts liquidity in the CO_2 market negatively. (European Commission Directorate General for Environment, 2005, p 2)

There are also recommendations about the way in which allocations are distributed; prior to the first phase there was debate as to whether governments would sell emission allowances rather than giving them out. It was decided by the European Parliament that governments could auction up to 5% of allowances in phase one and up to 10% in phase two (Hepburn et al, 2006, p 137). However, some non-governmental organisations (NGOs) are calling for 100% of allowances to be auctioned.

It is also argued that many member states have actually seen an increase in emissions in covered sectors in the first phase, despite the need to reduce them in line with Kyoto targets (see, for example, Egenhofer et al, 2006). The second phase of the EU ETS runs alongside the first reporting period of the Kyoto Protocol, and the emission reduction efforts required of member states for this period are more clearly defined. However, various NGOs and pressure groups have argued that caps for the third phase should be clearly linked to the EU emissions reduction targets, such as the 30% target by 2020.

The coverage of the EU ETS has also caused debate. As noted above, allocations to the aviation and surface transport sector are notable by their absence, especially given their contribution towards CO_2 emissions. Currently, determining how to measure emissions from international aviation and allocate them to a particular country is proving to be a barrier to including this sector, although DEFRA comments that they would like to see aviation included by the end of the second phase (DEFRA, 2007d). The issue of surface transport is more complex, with both DEFRA and a consortium of interest groups preferring these to be omitted from the EU ETS and instead covered through fiscal and information-based policy instruments.

The Climate Change Bill

Following the publication of the 2006 Climate Change Programme, the draft Climate Change Bill was published for consultation in March 2007. The consultation phase ended in June 2007, and the Government published its response to this in the Command Paper *Taking Forward the UK Climate Change Bill* (HM Government, 2007a). The Bill was introduced in the House of Lords on 14 November 2007 with the aim of receiving Royal Assent in the first half of 2008. The Command Paper notes that around 17,000 individuals and organisations responded to the draft Bill (HM Government, 2007a), and as a result a number of alterations were made (HM Government, 2007b). Table 4.3 outlines both the key original proposals and subsequent changes to them. Criticisms of the Bill can be divided into three main themes: first, the scientific robustness of the proposals; second, the coverage of the Bill; and, third, the capacity of the Bill to deliver. While many of these concerns were raised during the consultation phase of the Bill, the revised version demonstrates that a number of concerns have not been fully addressed. It has to be noted here that this is not a comprehensive review; indeed, at the time of writing, the Bill is entering a new stage of development, and it is impossible to capture all criticisms of it at this stage.

Scientific robustness of the proposals

As noted earlier in this chapter, there is a degree of uncertainty associated with the science of climate change. There is overwhelming evidence to support the idea that human activity is contributing towards climate change, but greater levels of uncertainty about exact impacts both of GHG emissions and of GHG emission reductions. In the past the 'need for more evidence' has sometimes prevented policy action. This issue is relevant here; in a number of responses to the draft Bill, concerns were expressed about the 2050 reduction target of 60%. There is no global consensus on how to delineate dangerous from acceptable climate change, but EU leaders have outlined a commitment to constraining

Table 4.3: Key components of the 2007 Climate Change Bill

Area	Components	Key changes post-consultation
Targets and budgeting	**Key statutory targets** • Put into statute the UK's targets to reduce CO_2 emissions through domestic and international action by 60% by 2050 and 26%-32% by 2020 against a 1990 baseline • Consider including reductions in aviation and shipping emissions should the international climate policy climate change • A focus on CO_2 as this is the most prevalent GHG • A move towards lower carbon technologies throughout the economy	**Increasing the strength of the UK's carbon management framework** Climate Change Committee to report on: • whether the 60% figure should be even stronger • implications of including other GHGs in targets • implications of including international aviation and shipping emissions within targets
	Carbon budgeting • 5-year 'carbon budgets' (limits to total carbon emissions over a specified period of time) from the beginning of 2008 • Period 1 2008–12 will run concurrently with the first Kyoto commitment, and the second phase of the EU ETS. This will help provide a trajectory to meeting the 2020 interim target and main 2050 target	The government will press for the inclusion of aviation in the EU ETS **Strengthening the role and independence of the Climate Change Committee** Setting requirements for the government to seek the Committee's advice before: • amending the 2050/2020 targets • introducing regulations on the use of carbon credits • establishing trading schemes

	Reviewing targets
	• Kyoto targets are only binding until 2012; negotiations will need to be ended and targets agreed by 2009
	• Statutory targets and carbon budgets should be flexible ahead of this date
	• The 2050 and 2020 targets should only be adjusted within limited circumstances:
	  o scientific evidence
	  o international law and policy
	• Review of carbon budgets to ensure that environmental goals are being achieved in the most proportionate way. Changes should only be made where there are significant changes in circumstances (such as the inclusion of CO_2 from aviation within the EU ETS)
		Increasing the transparency and accountability of the UK's carbon management framework
		
		Strengthening transparency and accountability by:
		• requiring the Committee on Climate Change to publish its analysis and advice to government and minutes of its meetings
		• requiring the government to explain to Parliament if it does not accept the Committee's advice

Table 4.3 (continued)

Area	Components	Key changes post-consultation
Targets and budgeting	Overseas credits towards budgets and targets • EU ETS and Kyoto flexible mechanisms allow carbon trading. The Bill requires the government to set regulations over the types of overseas credits that can count towards the UK carbon budget and emissions reduction targets, and the amount of reductions that each type of credit represents	• rationalising and increasing coherence of current reporting requirements on emissions • reporting annually to Parliament on emissions from international aviation and shipping in line with UNFCCC practice **Ensuring greater impact on the UK's emissions**
	Banking and borrowing • Emissions reductions that exceed those budgeted for can be banked for the next budget period • A limited quantity of emissions can be borrowed from a subsequent period where necessary	Use of the Bill to: • implement Carbon Reduction Commitment • pilot local authority incentives for household waste and minimisation
	Compliance • Legal duty to meet targets. Failure would be open to a judicial review	**Adapting to the consequences of climate change**
Committee on climate change	To set up an independent, non-departmental public body to independently assess how the UK can achieve its emission reduction goals	The Bill will require the government to assess the risks to the UK and to report these to Parliament
Enabling powers	To ensure enabling powers to make it easier to implement trading schemes	
Reporting	Annual reporting on progress towards budgets and targets by the Committee on Climate Change with an annual response by government	

Sources: Left and middle columns: HM Government (2007a, pp 13–46); right column: HM Government (2007b, pp 7-8)

global warming to no more than 2°C, a target also cited in UK governmental policy (Anderson and Bows, 2007, p 1). However, whether the 60% target will limit warming to 2°C is questioned by a number of critics. The Royal Society recommends 'that the Bill identifies the overall goal that the 60% cut in emissions is aiming to achieve … without this it is not possible to determine whether the 60% cut is appropriate' (2007, p 1). Equally, Anderson and Bows comment that 'even with the Bill's current neglect of aviation and shipping, the emission pathway it describes correlates approximately with an 80-60% chance of exceeding 2° to 3°C warming respectively' (2007, p 1).

This criticism has led a diverse range of individuals and organisations to call for a higher reduction target of 70%–80%. Among politicians, Conservative MP and Shadow Environment Secretary Greg Barker argued for a more ambitious Bill, pointing out that scientific evidence now suggests that a 60% cut in emissions will not go far enough. Similarly, Green Party principal speaker Dr Derek Wall advocates more stringent cuts of 6%–9% in a year, and Green MEP Caroline Lucas has argued that the 60% target 'flies in the face of science…. Creating a legal framework for tackling CO_2 emissions in the UK is a massive opportunity, but to start with the wrong target is to fall at the first hurdle' (Politics.co.uk, 2007). Such criticisms are echoed by a range of NGOs including Tearfund and the World Wildlife Fund who both argue for an 80% 2050 target with a reduction in emissions by 3% a year in order to stabilise warming at 2°C (Tearfund, 2007; WWF, 2007). Indeed, Nicholas Stern, writing in *The Guardian* in advance of the Bali summit on climate change, argues that 'even a minimal view of equity demands that rich countries' reductions should be at least 80%' (Stern, 2007, p 42).

While the Bill has been revised and additional flexibility has been built in to allow for changes to the targets, they currently remain the same. The director of the World Development Movement argues that 'The government's proposed "review" of the target, after it has become law, looks like a delaying tactic in the face of compelling scientific evidence on the need for greater emissions cuts' (World Development Movement, 2007).

Coverage of the Bill

The coverage of the Bill has been criticised quite heavily, and while some amendments have been made to the language of the Bill, in essence a number of the criticisms remain valid. Scientific bodies, NGOs and political parties all comment on the omission of a broader range of

GHGs, and the exclusion of aviation and shipping emissions. As The Royal Society (2007, p 1) argues, 'we note the emphasis of the proposed framework is on the reduction of CO_2 emissions and recommend that this be extended to include the other greenhouse gases, aviation and shipping emissions'. Indeed, the three Parliamentary Committees that examined the draft Bill all noted the weakness of excluding aviation and shipping emissions given their impact on CO_2 emissions.

Capacity of the Bill to deliver

A number of concerns have been raised about the capacity of the Bill to actually deliver on the targets. While some changes and alterations have been made to address these concerns, it is not clear whether these are sufficient. For example, critics have questioned the power and authority of the Climate Change Committee, both in terms of its neutrality and its technical ability. The Liberal Democrats' environment spokesman Chris Huhne has argued that the Climate Change Committee is open to political interference (Politics.co.uk, 2007) and both The Royal Society and the Royal Society of Chemists (RSC, 2007) have queried the role of technical expertise on the committee, with the RSC arguing that:

> The RSC recommends the experts serving on the Committee each be advised by a shadow stakeholder group that will comprise experts covering the key aspects of the topic so that the Committee member can present balanced unbiased advice. (RSC, 2007, p 8).

It is also argued by some that the five-year reporting period proposed by the Bill is insufficient, especially as the first reporting period will not occur within the term of the current Parliament. Critics argue instead for an annual reporting system to ensure that progress is sufficiently monitored.

Energy and planning

A number of plans and papers relating to energy and planning were published in 2007, and links between these and climate change objectives are clearly made. The main areas of action relate to energy efficiency, housing, planning and energy.

One of the principal aims of the UK Energy Efficiency Action Plan (DEFRA, 2007e) is to support the government's ambition to deliver zero-carbon homes by 2016. The plan outlines a range of measures to improve the energy efficiency of households, along with knowledge about energy efficiency (DEFRA, 2007e, p 6). The plan also outlines the role of the EU ETS, the climate change levy and agreements in reducing emissions in energy-intensive industrial sectors. Closely related to this, the 2007 Green Paper *Homes for the Future: More Affordable, More Sustainable* (DCLG, 2007) was presented to Parliament by the Department for Communities and Local Government in July, and made numerous references to climate change, especially through the links made to the Code for Sustainable Homes (DCLG, 2006). The White Paper *Planning for a Sustainable Future* (HM Government, 2007c) was published in May 2007, and was informed by both the Barker and Eddington reviews (Barker, 2006; Eddington, 2006). The Paper proposed the production of 'national policy statements to ensure that there is a clear policy framework for nationally significant infrastructure which integrates environmental, economic and social objectives to deliver sustainable development' (HM Government, 2007c, p 24). In this context, nationally significant infrastructure refers in part to new power-generating facilities and facilities 'critical to energy security'. As Carter and Ockwell (2007, p 66) comment, this includes a number of types of facility ranging from nuclear power stations to wind farms. At a more individual level, the Paper proposes that a variety of different forms of household microgeneration of energy be allowed exemption from planning permission.

The development with the most direct relevance to climate change policy, however, is the Energy Review, 'The Energy Challenge', which was released in July 2006 (DTI, 2006), and the subsequent White Paper *Meeting the Energy Challenge*, published in May 2007 (DTI, 2007). The White Paper intended to put the results of the review into action. Key aims of the Paper are outlined in Table 4.4.

Energy policy has not been without controversy in the last 18 months, especially as the UK lags behind other EU countries in terms of its share of energy generated by renewables (Carter and Ockwell, 2007, p 81) and the government's own target of having 10% of energy generated from renewable sources by 2010 is unlikely to be met. The planning process for onshore wind farms is described as long and fraught, with a high proportion of schemes failing to win planning approval. Offshore wind farms are now regarded as a more acceptable alternative, but cost and global markets are thought to have delayed the development of these (Carter and Ockwell, 2007, p 79).

Table 4.4: Key components of the 2007 Energy White Paper

Component	Description
Establish an international framework to tackle climate change	This should include a shared vision for stabilising the concentration of greenhouse gases in the atmosphere. We also want a strengthened EU Emissions Trading Scheme (EU ETS) to deliver a market price for carbon and to be the basis for a global carbon market. This will enable carbon emissions to be reduced in the most cost-effective way
Provide legally binding carbon targets for the whole UK economy, progressively reducing emissions	The draft Climate Change Bill creates a new legal framework for the UK achieving its targets through domestic and international action. There is provision in the draft Bill for the targets to be amended in light of significant developments in climate science or in international law or policy
Make further progress in achieving fully competitive and transparent international markets	This will enable companies to get fair access to the energy resources we need. Effective markets will ensure that the world's finite resources are used in the most efficient way and ensure that we make the transition to a low carbon economy at least cost. Further liberalisation of EU energy markets is an important part of this
Encourage more energy saving through better information, incentives and regulation	By removing barriers to the take-up of cost-effective energy efficiency measures, all of us can take steps to reduce emissions and our energy dependence.
Provide more support for low carbon technologies	This White Paper describes how public–private sector collaboration and increased international collaboration can address this
Ensure the right conditions for investment	We need a clear and stable regulatory regime, including for valuing carbon, to reduce uncertainty for business, and help to ensure sufficient, timely investment. Our improved framework will help businesses, individuals and the government deliver more energy-saving, cleaner energy supplies and timely energy investments

Source: Adapted from DTI (2007, pp 8-9)

Also, as a result of a legal challenge by Greenpeace, the 2006 Energy Review and 2007 White Paper were delayed. Concerns about the speed and focus of the consultation – even voiced by bodies such as the Trade and Industry Committee who might be considered as more sympathetic to the case for nuclear power – culminated in a successful legal action against the Department of Trade and Industry. Greenpeace (2007, p 2) argued that:

> It looked as though the Government had already made up its mind on the issue of nuclear power and the consultation was window dressing ... fundamentally the process was not viewed as the 'fullest public consultation' which the Government had previously promised to conduct in 2003 before giving the go-ahead on new nuclear power.

The consultation phase of the review was ruled by Mr Justice Sullivan to be 'misleading', 'seriously flawed' and 'procedurally unfair' (BBC, 2007a).

The renewed interest in nuclear power as a means of reducing CO_2 emissions is indicated in current policy proposals, and the Planning White Paper (HM Government, 2007c) may speed up the development of nuclear sites. However, the long time frame required to develop a new generation of nuclear power stations limits the contribution that this will have to short- to mid-term emission reduction targets. Carter and Ockwell (2007, p 83) conclude that 'as radical new energy policies will be needed to achieve these [2020] targets anyway, a wise Government would surely focus on ... securing greater energy efficiency and massively expanding the renewables sector'. This sentiment is echoed by a number of NGOs, and also the Liberal Democrats. On the other hand, as Shadow Trade and Industry Secretary Alan Duncan argues: 'whatever the rhetoric, there is nothing in this White Paper that will guarantee that a single nuclear power station will be built' (BBC, 2007a).

Areas not covered by this review

There are a couple of policy developments beyond the scope of this review; while it is not possible here to evaluate the effectiveness of these schemes it is worth outlining two further areas of action.

First, a number of campaigns to raise public awareness have been launched by the government. In March 2007 the government launched the 'Act on CO_2 campaign', and as part of this a public web-based

CO_2 calculator was unveiled in June 2007. The Climate Change Communication Initiative, led by DEFRA in partnership with the Environment Agency, the Carbon Trust and the Energy Saving Trust, has launched a range of initiatives including the Climate Challenge Fund. This Fund supported 53 projects in 2006, including 'the Scouts, who will be encouraging members to "Be Prepared for the Future", whilst the Women's Institute will develop EcoTeams to help bring home the realities of climate change' (DEFRA, 2007g). The effectiveness of these initiatives is yet to be assessed, with DEFRA currently calling for bids to review the effectiveness of these projects.

Transport is a policy area highly relevant to climate change; however, there have been few policy changes in the past year other than fiscal measures outlined in the 2006 and 2007 Budgets. These included an increase of fuel duty of 2 pence per litre from 1 October 2007, an increase in car vehicle excise duty rates for the most polluting cars, and reduced rates for the cleanest. The 2007 Budget also announced a review of vehicle and fuel technologies, which over the next 25 years could help decarbonise road transport (DEFRA, 2007a, pp 15-16).

Conclusions

This chapter began by outlining the nature of climate change as a policy problem and the role of risk and uncertainty in policy discourse. The various agreements, reviews, policies and targets discussed within this chapter have all been subject to criticism either through methodological approach or scientific uncertainty, especially when dealing with long-term predictions. However, what is clear and has become acknowledged by world leaders is the link between human activities and climate change and the need for action. The Stern Review suggested three areas of action: carbon pricing, support for policy innovation and the deployment of low carbon technologies, and support for individual action. There is evidence of activity in all three areas in current governmental policy and proposals (the third of these has been neglected in this chapter due to lack of space and evidence). However, the effectiveness of these is more questionable.

Current developments in governmental policy send mixed messages. The Climate Change Bill demonstrates international leadership on climate change, and indeed, at the international level, the UK has often been a lead state in negotiations. However, the change in policy direction between the 2003 and 2007 Energy White Papers (DTI, 2003; DTI, 2007) has been heralded by critics as a missed opportunity; the change in focus to include the potential development of a new generation of nuclear power stations may undermine the development of other low carbon technologies. While a continued programme of nuclear power may help to reduce CO_2 emissions, the broader environmental risks are much higher when compared with other forms of low carbon technologies.

The methodologies and targets developed within both the EU ETS and the Climate Change Bill have also sparked criticism. Whether the EU ETS is an effective market-based approach that is capable of reducing emissions sufficiently has been questioned, and until the third phase of the scheme is developed this will still be unclear. Equally, given debates about critical thresholds, whether the targets within the Climate Change Bill are sufficient is still keenly debated, with Nicholas Stern (2007) arguing for higher targets than those suggested in the Bill. Even if these targets are accepted, capacity and accountability have also been raised as problematic; whether the reporting periods set out within the Climate Change Bill are sufficiently challenging is currently debatable.

In summary, it has been a busy year in this policy area. Clearly the UK has made some progress, but whether the evidence base for the proposed targets and strategies is sufficient is unclear, and this may limit the effectiveness of climate change mitigation policies.

Notes

[1] It should be noted here that CO_2 is one of a number of GHGs that are associated with anthropogenic climate change. While it is not the most harmful gas it is the one that is most prevalent, which is why many policies focus solely on its reduction.

[2] The climate change levy is a tax on the use of energy in industry, commerce and the public sector, with offsetting cuts in employers' National Insurance contributions (DEFRA, 2007b).

[3] Given the energy usage of *energy-intensive* industries the government has provided an 80% discount from the levy for those sectors that agree challenging targets for improving their energy efficiency or reducing carbon emissions (DEFRA, 2007b).

[4] The Renewables Obligation is the government's main mechanism for supporting generation of renewable electricity.

[5] Under the Energy Efficiency Commitment electricity and gas suppliers are required to achieve targets for the promotion of improvements in domestic energy efficiency (DEFRA, 2007b).

[6] Each allowance is equal to one unit of CO_2 emitted (1 tonne CO_2e). This is termed an EU allowance (EUA).

References

Anderson, K. and Bows, A. (2007) *A Response to the Draft Climate Change Bill's Carbon Reduction Targets*, Tyndall Centre Briefing Note 17, Norwich: Tyndall Centre for Climate Change Research.

Barker, K. (2006) *Barker Review of Land Use Planning Final Report – Recommendations*, Norwich: The Stationery Office.

BBC (2007a) 'Nuclear review "was misleading"', *BBC News*, 15 February, available at: http://news.bbc.co.uk/1/hi/uk_politics/6364281.stm [accessed 24 November 2007].

BBC (2007b) 'Nuclear power "must be on agenda"', *BBC News*, 24 May, available at: http://news.bbc.co.uk/1/hi/uk_politics/6681377. stm [accessed 24 November 2007].

Butler, D. and Schiermeier, Q. (2005) 'Grim but determined – the G8 reaches accord on Africa and climate', *Nature*, vol 436, no 7048, pp 156-7.

Carter, N. and Ockwell, D. (2007) *New Labour, New Environment: An Analysis of the Labour Government's Policy on Climate Change and Biodiversity Loss*, A report commissioned by Friends of the Earth, July, available at: www.york.ac.uk/res/celp/webpages/projects/projects. htm [accessed March 2008].

Council of The European Union (2007) *Presidency Conclusions*, available at: www.consilium.europa.eu/ueDocs/cms_Data/docs/pressData/en/ ec/93135.pdf [accessed 19 November 2007].

DCLG (Department for Communities and Local Government) (2006) *Code for Sustainable Homes: A Step-Change in Sustainable Home Building Practice*, London: DCLG.

DCLG (2007) *Homes for the Future: More Affordable, More Sustainable*, Green Paper, Cm 7191, London: The Stationery Office.

DEFRA (Department for Environment, Food and Rural Affairs) (2006) *Climate Change: The UK Programme*, London: The Stationery Office.

DEFRA (2007a) *The Government's Response to the Better Regulation Commission's Report: Regulating to Mitigate Climate Change, a Response to the Stern Review*, London: DEFRA.

DEFRA (2007b) *Climate Change Agreements*, available at: www.defra.gov. uk/environment/climatechange/uk/business/ccl/intro.htm [accessed 23 November 2007].

DEFRA (2007c) *Analysis Paper on EU Emissions Trading Scheme Review options*, September 2007, London: DEFRA.

DEFRA (2007d) *Including Aviation and Surface Transport in the EU ETS*, available at: www.defra.gov.uk/environment/climatechange/trading/ eu/future/aviation.htm [accessed 23 November 2007].

DEFRA (2007e) *UK Energy Efficiency Action Plan*, London: The Stationery Office.

DEFRA (2007f) *EU Emissions Trading Scheme: Approved Phase II National Allocation Plan 2008-2012*, London: DEFRA.

DEFRA (2007g) *Government Opens New Front in Climate Campaign: Climate Challenge Fund Winners Announced*, available at: www.defra.gov. uk/news/2006/060616a.htm [accessed 23 November 2007].

DTI (Department of Trade and Industry) (2003) *Our Energy Future: Creating a Low Carbon Economy*, Cm 5761, London, The Stationery Office.

DTI (2006) *The Energy Challenge: Energy Review Report 2006*, Cm 6887, London, The Stationery Office.

DTI (2007) *Meeting the Energy Challenge: A White Paper on Energy*, White Paper, Cm 7124, London: The Stationery Office.

Eddington, R. (2006) *The Eddington Transport Study*, London: HMSO.

Egenhofer, C., Fujiwara, N., Åhman, M. and Zetterberg, L. (2006) *The EU ETS: Taking Stock and Looking Ahead*, European Climate Platform Background Paper No. 3, available at: www.ceps.be/files/ECP_ETS_Fin_draftBGP3_Mar06.pdf [accessed 20 October 2007].

European Commission Directorate General for Environment (2005) *Review of the EU Emission Trading Scheme, November 2005*, available at: http://ec.europa.eu/environment/climat/pdf/highlights_ets_en.pdf [accessed 21 October 2007].

Greenpeace (2007) *The 2007 Energy White Paper – Media Briefing*, available at: www.greenpeace.org.uk/files/pdfs/climate/energywhitepaper_briefing2.pdf [accessed 2 November 2007].

Hepburn, C., Grubb, M., Neuhoff, K., Matthes, F. and Tse, M. (2006) 'Auctioning of EU ETS phase II allowances: how and why?', *Climate Policy*, vol 6, no 1, pp 137-60.

HM Government (2006) *The Eddington Transport Study: The Case for Action*, London: The Stationery Office.

HM Government (2007a) *Taking Forward the UK Climate Change Bill: The Government Response to Pre-Legislative Scrutiny and Public Consultation*, Cm 7225, London: The Stationery Office.

HM Government (2007b) *Draft Climate Change Bill*, London: The Stationery Office.

HM Government (2007c) *Planning for a Sustainable Future*, White Paper, Cm 7120, London: The Stationery Office.

House of Commons Environmental Audit Committee (2007) *Emissions Trading: Government Response to the Committee's Second Report of Session 2006–07 on the EU ETS Eighth Report of Session 2006–07*, London: The Stationery Office.

IPCC (Intergovernmental Panel on Climate Change) (2007) *Climate Change 2007 – The Physical Science Basis: Contribution of Working Group I to the Fourth Assessment Report of the IPCC*, available at: www.ipcc. ch/ipccreports/ar4-wg1.htm [accessed 1 October 2007].

Jordan, A. and Lorenzoni, I. (2007) 'Is there now a political climate for policy change/policy and politics after the Stern Review', *The Political Quarterly*, vol 78, no 2, pp 310-19.

Lawton, J. H. (2007) 'Ecology, politics and policy (presidential address)', *Journal of Applied Ecology*, vol 44, no 3, pp 465-74.

Lomborg, B. (2001) *The Sceptical Environmentalist*, Cambridge: Cambridge University Press.

May, R. (2005) 'Open letter to Margaret Beckett and other G8 energy and environment ministers', *Royal Society News*, available at: www. royalsoc.ac.uk/page.asp?id=3834 [accessed 23 October 2007].

Mendelsohn, R. O. (2007) 'A critique of the Stern Report', *Regulation*, vol 29, no 4, pp 42-6.

Oreskes, N. (2004) 'Science and public policy: what's proof got to do with it?', *Environmental Science and Policy*, vol 7, no 5, pp 369-83.

Politics.co.uk (2007) 'In-Focus: Climate Change Bill: towards a low carbon future', *Politics.co.uk*, 5 June, available at: www.politics.co.uk/in-focus-main/domestic-policy/environment/climate-change/climate-change-bill-towards-low-carbon-future-$474383.htm [accessed 21 November 2007].

RSC (Royal Society of Chemists) (2007) *RSC Response to Draft Climate Change Bill*, available at: www.rsc.org/ScienceAndTechnology/Policy/Documents/draftClimateChangeBill.asp [accessed 1 November 2007].

Stern, N. (2006) *The Economics of Climate Change: The Stern Review*, Cambridge: Cambridge University Press.

Stern, N. (2007) 'Bali: now the rich must pay', *The Guardian*, 30 November.

Tearfund (2007) *Tearfund Briefing on the Climate Change Bill 23 August 2007*, available at: www.tearfund.org/webdocs/Website/Campaigning/Tearfund_Briefing_on_Climate_Change_Bill.pdf [accessed 23 November 2007].

The Royal Society (2007) 'Royal Society response to the UK Climate Change Bill consultation', *The Royal Society*, available at: www.royalsoc.ac.uk/displaypagedoc.asp?id=26430 [accessed 1 October 2007].

Walther, G., Hughes, L., Vitousek, P. and Stenseth, N.C. (2005) 'Consensus on climate change', *Trends in Ecology and Evolution*, vol 20, no 12, pp 648-9.

World Development Movement (2007) *Climate Change Bill: Queen's Speech Response 6 November 2007*, available at: www.wdm.org.uk/news/queenspeechresponse06112007.htm [accessed 7 November 2007].

WWF (World Wildlife Fund) (2007) *Consultation on the Draft Climate Change Bill: Response by WWF-UK*, available at: www.wwf.org.uk/filelibrary/pdf/climate_bill_response.pdf [accessed 23 November 2007].

FIVE

Policy for older people in Wales

Gill Windle and Alison Porter

Introduction

Social policy in relation to older people is an area of increasing importance. This chapter looks at an innovative approach to using policy to improve older people's lives: the Strategy for Older People in Wales. This broad, high-level policy development takes a holistic approach to older people's lives, and places a great emphasis on engaging older people in the democratic process. The chapter takes a critical look at the implementation of the Strategy, and considers the particular challenges this presents to the process of evaluating policy innovation. It draws some comparisons with the Strategies of the devolved governments of Northern Ireland and Scotland. It concludes with some of the learning from the Strategy, highlights some of its limitations and considers how further evaluation may best be taken forward.

Background and context

Population ageing is emerging as a worldwide trend, reflecting improvements in health services, education and economic development, increases in life expectancy and falls in fertility. The oldest old (80 years and over) are the fastest growing segment in many nations (Kinsella and Velcoff, 2001). It is estimated that by 2021 this older age group will constitute almost 5% of the population in the UK (ONS, 1999). This demographic change emerged first in Europe, making this region unique in relation to the ageing world population (Scharf et al, 2003). The UK is regarded as being one of the world's 25 oldest countries, with 20.4% being aged 60 or over (Kinsella and Velcoff, 2001). It is estimated that by 2025 the number of people aged 65 and over in the UK will exceed the numbers aged under 16 by 1.6 million (ONS, 2003).

Such demographic changes present both opportunities and challenges for government policy. This is evidenced in the often-perceived increasing burden on pensions, and health and social care provision. Ageing can be accompanied by biological changes that increase the risk of illness, death or disability (ONS, 1999). Although life expectancy has increased, there is some debate as to whether there have also been improvements in morbidity in older age (ONS, 1999).

In addition to health, there are many other life events and changing circumstances that can be considered as potential threats to the well-being of older people. Bereavement, changes in financial situations and in social relationships also tend to be concentrated in later life. Hence there is concern within public policy and society as to how quality of life can be maintained and enhanced in older age and how people can be helped to positively respond to the various challenges of older age.

Wales, with its population of almost three million, provides a particularly interesting case study for policy making in relation to older people, for two reasons. First, the ageing population might be regarded as more of a pressing policy issue than in the UK as a whole, for the simple reason that there are, proportionately, more older people, and more of them are experiencing ill-health. Figures from the 2001 Census show that 22.66% of the Welsh population are over 60 (compared with 20.79% in the UK as a whole); an increase of 30% in the older population over the past 40 years. The numbers of those in Wales aged 85 and over increased from 15,450 in 1961 to 58,381 in 2001; this represents 2.10% of the total population, compared to the 1.91% of the population which the 85 and over age group make up in the UK as a whole. Although, compared to 20 years ago, life expectancy in Wales has risen by four years, the proportion of older people experiencing ill-health is higher than in England. Five out of ten Welsh people between the ages of 60 and 70, and seven out of ten people aged over 80 were reported in the 2001 Census as having a limiting long-term illness.

The second particular characteristic of Wales is the existence, since 1999, of devolved government. While not having the same tax-raising powers as the Scottish Parliament, the National Assembly for Wales and its executive body, the Welsh Assembly Government, have been granted control of policy over a wide range of issues. Among the devolved issues for which policy is made in Cardiff are social welfare, health and health services, housing, employment, education, local government and public administration. This provides some scope for the politicians and civil servants of Wales to devise appropriate responses to what they discern to be specifically Welsh needs. It also allows politicians to experiment and innovate by devising specifically Welsh responses to policy challenges.

A new approach to policy and older people: the Strategy for Older People in Wales

In response to the projected changes in the older population and the accompanying challenges, the Welsh Assembly Government introduced the Strategy for Older People in Wales in 2003. Underpinned by the United Nations Principles for Older People (independence, participation, care, self-fulfilment and dignity), the Strategy presents a vision for ageing in Wales, and was the first all-encompassing approach by a government towards ageing in the UK. Setting out a 10-year framework of action, the Strategy acknowledges that 'there is no quick fix to the challenges and opportunities presented by an ageing population' (WAG, 2003, p 12).

Nevertheless, it is ambitious in its aims, with objectives to improve quality of life in older age across a range of devolved and non-devolved issues such as age discrimination, the participation of older people, transport, education, employment, poverty, housing, health and social care. This approach to public policy development attempts to move away from current perspectives that often tend to portray older age as a problem and a burden. It challenges discrimination and negative stereotypes of ageing. It also reflects the more recent trend under the New Labour government for evidence-based policy making. This approach requires policy makers and those who implement policies to make use of the best available evidence from a wide range of sources, such as national statistics, academic research, economics, pilot projects, evaluation of previous policies, commissioned research and systematic consultation with service providers (Davies, 2004).

Initiated by the devolved Labour government of Wales, the Strategy's development was informed by consultation with a range of organisations representing older people, academic research, expert views and older people themselves. The Strategy aims to provide a structured basis for local and national government and the independent sector in Wales to be proactive and develop policies in response to the demographic changes. It has five key aims:

(1) To reflect the United Nations Principles for Older People, to tackle discrimination against older people wherever it occurs, promote positive images of ageing and give older people a stronger voice in society.

(2) To promote and develop older people's capacity to continue to work and learn for as long as they want and to make an active contribution once they retire.

(3) To promote and improve the health and well-being of older people through integrated planning and delivery frameworks and more responsive diagnostic and support services.

(4) To promote the provision of high-quality services and support which enable older people to live as independently as possible in a suitable and safe environment and ensure services are organised around and responsive to their needs.

(5) To implement the Strategy for Older People in Wales with support funding to ensure that it is a catalyst for change and innovation across all sectors, improves services for older people and provides the basis for effective planning for an ageing population.

To support the implementation of the Strategy, the Welsh Assembly Government committed £13 million over a five-year period from April 2003. This financial commitment was to a shorter period than the overall 10-year ambitions of the Strategy, a reflection of the pragmatic issues around re-election of the administration. The Welsh Assembly Government's role in implementation of the Strategy has been to provide strategic direction and leadership for local government and independent organisations who are directly involved in planning for an ageing population or are working with older people.

A National Partnership Forum for Older People in Wales was established through a process of public appointments. The Forum provides a source of advice to the Assembly, and a channel of communication from older people and their representatives to both local and national government. Underpinning this is an acknowledgement that there are differing needs across Wales, and that implementation needs to be driven from a local basis in order to meet those needs.

The Assembly recognises that local government in Wales is the hub of the development of the Strategy (WAG, 2007, p 8). Although responses tailored to local circumstances were encouraged, the Assembly put in place the same support structures and delivery mechanisms across the country. Guidance was provided to local authorities through a series of Welsh Health Circulars, setting out key areas for action, suggestions for projects and funding arrangements. Eighty per cent of all the funding for the Strategy was allocated to local authorities, amounting to £2.4 million a year after the initial start-up year. In each local authority area, £35,000 was designated for funding a local Strategy coordinator. Their role is to encourage new approaches to the development of policy and service development across other departments and agencies, local health boards and NHS trusts, local voluntary organisations and with older people. In addition, from the second year onwards, each local authority area received a sum to spend on implementing the Strategy in their area; this sum was based on the Standard Spending Assessment and varied, in 2004–05, from £35,000 in the lowest spending authority to £159,000 in the highest spending authority.

From the start of the Strategy, local authorities have been required to comply with an annual cycle of planning and reporting to the Welsh Assembly Government on their spending of Strategy funds. Detailed guidance to local authorities spelled out how consultation with older people and other partners should feed into those plans, and outlined the structure of the documents. Plans were to include assessment and analysis of need and an audit of existing provision, as well as aims and objectives, milestones and deadlines, spending proposals, systems for monitoring and evaluation, and performance measures.

The remaining 20% of Welsh Assembly Government spending on the Strategy went to four organisations working across Wales to support the implementation of the Strategy: the Beth Johnson Foundation, Better Government for Older People, Age Alliance Wales and the Welsh Institute of Health and Social Care. The role of these organisations will be discussed later in the chapter.

The challenge of evaluation

A commitment to an examination of the impact, process and outcomes of the implementation was outlined by the Welsh Assembly Government from the start. Specifically, the Strategy states that the Welsh Assembly Government would be:

> Commissioning an overarching evaluation which would: run alongside the implementation of the Strategy, inform development and implementation at key stages, and provide an analysis of the outcomes and impact of the Strategy. (WAG, 2003, p 30)

Evaluating the Strategy for Older People in Wales presents something of a challenge. Commenting on some of the difficulties posed in policy evaluation, Martin and Sanderson (1999) note that although the policy under investigation may produce some new initiatives, it is equally possible to misattribute effects to older initiatives. It is also difficult to disentangle the effects of policies that might have happened anyway, whether or not a strategic steer was put into place. The application of policy to a social situation is not a simple chain of cause and effect, since 'policy is implemented within a social and political context of ideology, commercial interests, resource constraints, media reports, pressure groups, lobbyists and public expectations, all of which skew its effects' (Harwood, 2007, p 483).

Nevertheless, during 2006 and 2007 the Welsh Assembly Government undertook a review of the first phase of the Strategy. This primarily involved examining progress made in its implementation and identifying priorities for the future. An advisory group was convened to hear evidence from a wide range of sources. These sources included a consultation exercise, the results of focus groups conducted across Wales by Age Concern and Help the Aged, research and policy briefings and a four-part interim review of the Strategy by the All Wales Alliance of Research and Development (AWARD) (Porter et al, 2007). This period concluded with the production of a report by the Advisory Group *Living Longer, Living Better* (WAG, 2007) to inform the planning of Phase 2.

Lessons from the implementation of the Strategy so far

Focusing service providers on older people's issues

Although there is new money attached to the Strategy, the amount available to each local authority is small compared with their overall budgets. One way in which the Strategy has had an impact is through local authorities using this money as a way to support the refocusing of statutory services on older people's issues (in their broadest sense). This more 'joined-up' approach to service planning has been achieved through two key roles in each local authority area: the Strategy coordinator and the 'Older People's champion'.

It is clear from the available evidence that the local coordinators are crucial to the effective implementation of the Strategy. However, both the interim review by AWARD (Porter et al, 2007) and the consultation exercise (WAG, 2007) suggest that the location of the coordinators needs further consideration. This is important as a prominent theme in the Strategy and other guidance is the need for 'joined-up working' in order to relate Strategy work to other strategic initiatives. The majority of coordinators are located in social services departments or similar, and some report concerns around marginalisation and the risk of being identified solely with health and social care issues (Porter et al, 2007). Those placed in corporate policy units indicated a number of advantages to this position, particularly its usefulness in facilitating a broad strategic remit across all departments. Given the similar broad remit of the Strategy, locating coordinators within a central office may be an effective way forward for Phase 2. This would have the advantage of integrating all of the strategic objectives on an equitable basis across all aspects of public policy. This need to 'mainstream' the Strategy is a key recommendation for Phase 2 (WAG, 2007).

Each local authority has also appointed an Older People's champion, mostly from within their local Cabinet, with the aim of ensuring that the issues of older people are kept at the forefront of policy and service development. Feedback from the consultation indicated that the appointment of Older People's champions was generally considered a positive step. However, it was felt that local authorities should have a clear specification of the role, remit and expectation of the champions (WAG, 2007). Interviews with coordinators indicate some concerns 'that the Champions – already busy people – simply did not have the time available to do the role justice' (Porter et al, 2007, p 17). If, in the long term, the Strategy is to be successfully mainstreamed across all policy areas for Phase 2 then the recommendation from *Living Longer, Living Better* (WAG, 2007) to issue guidance to local authorities outlining the role of the champion, should be fully endorsed. As with the Strategy coordinator, it may also necessitate that the remit of the champion has a wider departmental focus than social services.

Activity and change at the 'grass roots'

Through allocated Strategy money, all of the local authorities have funded individual projects to reflect the strategic objectives (WAG, 2006) and it was apparent from qualitative interviews carried out during the evaluation that there is considerable enthusiasm for the development and delivery of projects at the 'grass-roots' level (Porter et al, 2007). The limited scale of the funding reflects the fact that it was meant for experimental, pump-priming or pilot initiatives, although in some instances Strategy funds appeared to have been spent on services that might otherwise have been considered as core statutory provision. All local authorities had examples of projects that were considered innovative in that they reflected local development rather than part of a national programme and differed from existing services. Porter et al (2007) report that the funding of projects varied considerably, with some authorities focusing spending on a limited number of large projects, while others funded a larger number of small-scale projects. One local authority used Strategy funding as the seed for a successful bid to bring in a European Union (EU) grant of £1.6 million over two years (Porter et al, 2007).

However, what is not clear is how effective these projects have been, as little, if any, robust evaluation has been conducted. The interim review (Porter et al, 2007) reports that although the Assembly suggested that local authorities incorporate performance measures, they appear little used in the annual plans and reports. In addition, some wide disparities in reporting were found between and within these reports. The irregular and interchangeable use of terms such as 'outcomes' and 'objectives' indicate a lack of understanding of the Assembly's vision for change as set out in the Strategy. This also has implications for research and evaluation. Where reference to performance indicators appeared, it tended to reflect achievements that 'tick the box' such as 'report published by April 2005'.

It is, then, impossible to determine from the reporting of such outcomes the exact nature of the benefits from the money spent on a specific project. Likewise, the extent to which consideration has been given to the sustainability of some projects after Strategy money ceases was not always clear. Should the potentially good work that has been set to date be continued into the future, local authorities would be well advised to conduct a thorough review of effectiveness in order to leave them well placed to seek further, possibly external, funding. Calculating accurate 'baseline' data before an initiative is put in place, and taking the same measures after its completion, is an essential basic approach for any intervention.

Porter et al (2007) found that the project areas to receive most attention across Welsh local authorities tended to be those which reflected objectives prioritised by the Assembly (for example the engagement of older people), while other objectives (for example creating a network of community learning centres, increasing economic activity) had received far less attention. It is expected that in the next phase of the Strategy, those areas receiving least attention will be prioritised (WAG, 2007). Devolution also has a strong impact on the extent to which the Welsh Assembly Government can deliver some of the objectives of the Strategy. Although Wales now has devolved executive powers relating to issues such as health, local government, housing and the environment, the UK government and Parliament retain sole responsibility for other matters such as social security, pensions and the economy (Trench and

Jeffery, 2007), limiting the potential for change to critical issues, such as pensioner poverty.

The participation of older people

With a strong focus on citizenship and valuing older people, the Strategy is clear in its requirements for the meaningful engagement and participation of older people in society and at all levels of government. This objective reflects a growing interest in participatory approaches to research and evaluation, particularly in public and social policy areas (Kemshall and Littlechild, 2000). Across Wales, local authorities have used Strategy funding to work in partnership with voluntary organisations such as Age Concern, Help the Aged and local voluntary service councils to be actively involved in encouraging the participation of older people. In each area, a 50+ Forum (or set of Forums) acts as a formal structure for engagement with older people. In many instances this process has drawn on already established 50+ groups or 'Forums' or resulted in the formation of new forums.

In some areas there are core members of the 50+ Forum who are very active; they have considerable input into the Strategy and are regularly involved with local authorities as part of their planning and consultation processes. Forum members give their time voluntarily, although in virtually all areas there is a paid development worker to support their work, along with a budget for out-of-pocket expenses.

Many of the key stakeholders in the four local authority case study areas studied by AWARD (Porter et al, 2007) expressed positive opinions on the prospect for the forum to be a voice for older people. In each, all of the strategic planning groups had older lay members. However, the consultation (WAG, 2007) indicated that some forums felt that they were being used for consultation on specific local authority topics, but often they did not get feedback on their comments and confirmation that they were being heard. This view is echoed in the interim review report by AWARD, which states that:

> While mechanisms for gathering views and 'giving voice' to older people are widespread, concerns were expressed about how receptive organisations (at all levels) were to listening to those voices. (Porter et al, 2007, p 42)

As such the future phase of the Strategy will need to ensure that engagement is a two-way process.

The process of recruitment to forum membership has varied between local authority areas, but the underlying principle has generally been that anyone who wants to be a forum member can join a forum. Although many forum members are active in local community groups (running lunch clubs, local history societies and so on) and bring their concerns for those interests to the forum table, they are not formally 'representative' of those groups, nor are they elected through a democratic process. There is also a question about how representative they are of the wider population. In the four case study areas, typical forum members were highly motivated individuals, in many instances retired professionals active in their local communities. Although the Strategy targets those aged 50 and over, representation on forums of people below retirement age was low. Participation was also felt to be affected by a lack of awareness of forum activity and a general lack of interest from communities. Forum membership requires attendance at meetings, which can be problematic for people in rural areas who do not have their own transport (Porter et al, 2007). If the process of engagement is to continue it would appear that there is a need to develop some novel approaches towards including older people on the forum who are more representative of the wider population.

On the other hand, if the opinions of older people are sought through other means of engagement (for example community surveys) then the circle of inclusion is widened to those who might otherwise not view the forum as relevant, or find participation on the forum as too challenging. Porter et al (2007, p 123) suggest that the 'Forums should be assessed in terms of how effective they are as a process, not in terms of whether they provide a representative sample of older people to make decisions on behalf of all'. Following this rationale, as a process, there is, then, some indication of the success of the forum.

Welsh Assembly Government support structures

To ensure effective implementation, on a strategic level the Welsh Assembly Government has established a number of key structures and funded support organisations. A Deputy Minister with specific responsibility for older people was established in 2003. This has had the advantage of focusing the ageing agenda at ministerial level. In addition, an Assembly Cabinet sub-committee was established to ensure consistency across ministerial portfolios. The necessary legislation to establish the first Commissioner for Older People in Wales was passed through Parliament. This post is expected to be taken up in late 2007.

A National Partnership Forum for Older People in Wales was established through a process of public appointments. The Forum provides a source of advice to the Assembly, and a channel of communication from older people and their representatives to both local and national government. Funding under the Strategy has already gone to four independent organisations, each with a remit to drive forward one aspect of the Strategy in partnership with local authorities and other service providers. The Beth Johnson Foundation was funded to develop and implement a strategy for intergenerational practice in Wales. The Wales Centre for Intergenerational Practice was established at the University of Glamorgan. A partnership between the Welsh Local Government Association and the Assembly saw funding being provided to Better Government for Older People to develop a network in Wales to support local authorities' work on the Strategy and assist collaboration through networking and sharing information. The Welsh Institute of Health and Social Care (WIHSC) at the University of Glamorgan received funding to work with local authorities in developing understanding and knowledge about implementing evidence-based approaches to local networking and partnerships. For the voluntary sector, Age Alliance Wales was funded to develop a coordination and development unit to take projects forward.

The interim review (Porter et al, 2007) acknowledges a number of successes achieved by each of the support organisations. The Strategy consultation indicates general support for these organisations as a means to initially implement the Strategy. However the consultation also highlights some confusion around their operations, and queries their effectiveness and success (WAG, 2007). To some extent this was echoed in the interim review, which suggested that a review of the support organisations should be taken. The interim review goes further to highlight that there have been some considerable changes in the roles of the support bodies and in some instances there is some overlap. Also some coordinators expressed considerable dissatisfaction with one or more support organisations (Porter et al, 2007). Given the evidence it is likely that should the Assembly act on the recommendations of the Advisory Group report, a full review of the support bodies will be undertaken before the commencement of Phase 2.

Comparisons with Northern Ireland and Scotland

The Strategy for Older People in Wales was the first of its kind in the UK, reflecting an innovative and forward-thinking governmental approach. In

2007 Scotland introduced its own Strategy *All Our Futures: Planning for a Scotland with an Ageing Population* (Scottish Executive, 2007). Similar in content to the Welsh Strategy, it is underpinned by the United Nations Principles for Older People. It was developed through consultation with a wide range of groups and organisations, including focus groups, commissioned research, statistical evidence and an external Advisory Group representing a wide range of interests. However, where it differs is in its implementation. Although there is a strong emphasis on local government taking the Strategy forward, local authorities in Scotland did not receive dedicated funding for a Strategy coordinator.

The Strategy indicates an intention to establish a National Ageing Forum to monitor the development and implementation of ageing strategies across Scottish society. There is also a strong emphasis on intergenerational work, and the Strategy proposes the establishment of a Scottish Centre for Intergenerational Practice 'to help develop intergenerational work across Scotland' (Scottish Executive, 2007, p 14).

In Northern Ireland, *Ageing in an Inclusive Society* (Office of the First Minister and Deputy Minister, 2005) reflects the Northern Ireland government's overall anti-poverty strategy to develop an integrated approach to financial, economic and social exclusion. Again, this Strategy was developed through utilising research and undertaking consultation exercises, and a conference involving academics, Northern Ireland departments and public bodies, trades unions and employer representations debated the extent of the nature of poverty and social exclusion in older age. Its strategic vision is 'to ensure that age related policies and practices create an enabling environment, which offers everyone the opportunity to make informed choices so that they may pursue healthy, active and positive ageing' (Office of the First Minister and Deputy Minister, 2005, p 13). It shares some similar themes with its Welsh and Scottish counterparts, focusing on economics and lifelong learning, healthy ageing, housing, access to services, tackling ageism and partnership working. Again, this Strategy differs in its plan for implementation. The Strategy's action plan indicates that responsibility for specific actions would be led by specific departments. To ensure implementation, the coordination of the actions is placed with a senior civil servant who will be given the role of a champion for older people.

From the current findings from the Welsh Strategy interim review, there is a strong indication that its success to date has depended on the significant implementation plan and support structures put in place by the government. These are considerable in comparison with the Northern Irish and Scottish Strategies. In particular, much of the responsibility for implementation in Northern Ireland is focused on one person – the champion for older people.

Even with these supports in place in Wales, the interim review has indicated that a key area for concern is the opportunity to fully integrate the Strategy across all governmental departments. This has implications for the effectiveness of the Northern Irish and Scottish Strategies, which do not have this extensive support.

The Strategy in context: other Welsh Assembly Government policies and programmes

Since the implementation of the Strategy, a number of key policies and programmes have been developed that address some of its objectives:

• 'Designed for Life', a 10-year health and social care strategy for the NHS in Wales was launched in 2005.
• 'Fulfilled Lives, Supportive Communities', launched in 2007, is a 10-year strategy for improving social services.
• A 'National Service Framework for Older People', consisting of evidence-based standards for the access and delivery of quality healthcare in Wales, was launched in 2006.
• The 'Healthy Ageing Action Plan for Wales', regarded as a key element of the Strategy for Older People in Wales, was launched in 2005 and contains a number of key areas for the promotion of health and mental well-being and the reduction of illness.

As yet, the impact of these policies has not been evaluated. However, in many instances they are underpinned by quantitative evidence and they have defined operational targets that are amenable to future measurement.

In Wales, as in the rest of the UK, poverty is a key issue for many people. Decisions about pensions and the economy have not been devolved and are led by the UK government. However, assistance can be provided indirectly through other devolved issues. To help promote social inclusion and address low income, free bus travel was made available to all people aged 60 and over and a 60% increase in trips resulted (WAG, 2006). Although this programme was initiated in 2002 before the implementation of the Strategy, it closely reflects the Strategy objectives. A number of community transport projects have also been developed across Wales, although not all of these are specifically for older people (WAG, 2006). Free swimming has been introduced for those aged 60 and over. To help older people maximise their income, to increase benefit take-up and to improve access to and information on services for older people, 'one-stop' service centres have been tried out. The pilot programme 'Link-Age' was launched in 2005 and has tested out this approach in Wales, focusing on benefits. This initiative was led by the Department for Work and Pensions (DWP) in collaboration with the Welsh Assembly Government. Consultation on the initiative indicated considerable support (Pensions Service, 2005). However, as yet, no formal evaluation appears to have taken place.

Looking ahead: how will we know what difference the Strategy makes?

Policy evaluation is a complex task and most approaches now adopt a mixed method approach combining both quantitative and qualitative techniques. The Welsh Assembly Government appears to have taken on board some of the suggestions for evaluation as outlined in a detailed report by Walters (2005). As reported on in this chapter, an independent review at the end of the first phase of the Strategy was commissioned (Porter et al, 2007). This gave considerable attention to the implementation process, and provides a valuable insight into the national and local structures that were put in place to support this phase. Other sources of evidence summarised in the report *Living Longer, Living Better* (WAG, 2007) provide some further qualitative indication on how the Strategy has been perceived to date.

The nature of the evaluation process so far indicates that the Welsh Assembly Government is receptive to some of the more novel approaches to this topic, in particular the use of qualitative data. However, the 'snapshot' of opinion provided by individuals and organisations involved in the review indicates that this opinion, while informative, might not be wholly representative. In this instance, although the qualitative findings are valuable, they are only part of the picture. A robust quantitative inquiry is also necessary.

The latter is important, as what is less clear at this stage of the implementation process is to what extent the Strategy has changed the lives of older people in Wales for the better. The preliminary indications would suggest that there should be a positive impact. Further evaluation of individual-level outcomes could help support or refute this. As part of their review, Porter et al (2007) identified a range of performance measures that could be used to estimate the impact of the Strategy on the lives of older people.

These were drawn from existing, routinely collected data, some on an all-Wales level and some collected at a smaller scale, allowing comparison between areas in Wales. The suggested performance measures were based on those established by the DWP for measuring the impact of policies developed under 'Opportunity Age'. However, in contrast to the DWP, which suggests 33 indicators, only 12 indicators were proposed. These were selected by workshop delegates (Strategy coordinators, members of 50+ Forums, Older People's champions and other associated professionals) and represent those thought to be the most appropriate to measure in Wales. The measures (listed below) relate to the general aims of the Strategy and provide an objective perspective:

(1) Mental well-being
(2) Income
(3) Healthy life expectancy at age 65+
(4) Attendance/participation in sport or leisure activities
(5) Intensive support/help to live independently
(6) Community-based service/help to live independently
(7) Employment rate at age 50+
(8) Access to treatment
(9) Unfit/poor-quality housing
(10) Fear of crime
(11) Work-related education/training
(12) Access to goods and services using usual methods of transport.

However these indicators will not provide an in-depth understanding of an individual's economic, psychological, health and social aspects of the ageing process, and how these might change in response to the introduction of new policy initiatives. At this stage the Strategy lacks this aspect of evaluation. Defining the evaluation framework at the outset of the Strategy would have provided a clear focus from the start for what data needed to be collected. It would have provided the focus for an overall analysis plan that could extend across the key Strategy areas. Unfortunately to date there is no complete evaluation that has examined both the impact and outcomes of the Strategy, despite the development of the detailed framework for evaluation (Walters, 2005).

A clear challenge for further evaluation is to increase the representativeness of opinion and rigorously examine the effectiveness of individual programmes through good-quality study designs. In many instances quasi-experimental approaches could be extremely beneficial. As recommended by Walters (2005), existing sources of data should be utilised and explored. The framework for evaluation proposed in the report by Walters (2005) is a longitudinal study design with three main elements: the collection and analysis of existing statistical data, the collection and analysis of qualitative data and four local authority case studies to examine process change. The report suggests that these should be undertaken at baseline and at five-, seven- and ten-year intervals.

The identification of existing quantitative and qualitative data is proposed and the report presents a considerable number of questions to ask of the data relating to the main Strategy objectives.

In a longitudinal study, data are collected from the same participants at different periods in time. This provides a valuable opportunity to explore stability and change, the determinants of transitions, inter-individual differences and intra-individual differences (Rudinger and Rietz, 2001). This type of study design is now under way in England (ELSA; the English Longitudinal Study of Ageing). Using a range of standardised measures, ELSA examines the quality of life of people aged 50 and over. ELSA could be an inspiration to Wales to move towards creating its own interdisciplinary data source that would provide a valuable resource for evaluating policies such as the Strategy, and compare the effects with England and the rest of Europe.

Conclusion

The Strategy for Older People in Wales has been a bold and broad move by the Welsh Assembly Government to improve the health and well-being of the ageing population. However, its very broadness, encompassing all aspects of people's lives rather than just the traditional social policy concerns of health and social care, combined with its ambition of involving governance systems and service providers at all levels, presents considerable challenges for evaluation. Disentangling the pure effects of the Strategy from older initiatives, or those that would have happened anyway, will be a challenge. In addition, the slow process of social change, combined with the 10-year funding period allocated for the Strategy implementation, might not provide enough opportunity to be able to fully address the impact of the Strategy on individual lives. Nevertheless, it would appear that the general strategic objectives of implementation have been achieved and the launch of the second phase of the Strategy is due to commence in March 2008. Across Wales, the mechanisms have been put in place to facilitate change for devolved issues. A thorough investigation of its effectiveness on the quality of life of older people is now required.

References

Davies, P. (2004) *Policy Evaluation in the United Kingdom*, www.policyhub. gov.uk/docs/policy_evaluation_uk.pdf [accessed 17 January 2007].

Harwood, R.H. (2007) 'Evaluating the impact of the National Service Framework for Older People: qualitative science or populist propaganda?', *Age and Ageing*, vol 36, no 5, pp 483-5.

Kemshall, H. and Littlechild, R. (2000) (eds) *User Involvement and Participation in Social Care*, London: Jessica Kingsley.

Kinsella, K. and Velkoff, V. A. (2001) *An Aging World*, US Census Bureau, Series P95/01-1, Washington, DC: US Government Printing Office.

Martin, S. and Sanderson, I. (1999) 'Evaluating public policy experiments: measuring outcomes, monitoring processes or managing pilots', *Evaluation*, vol 5, no 3, pp 245-58.

Office of the First Minister and Deputy Minister (2005) *Ageing in an Inclusive Society*, www.ofmdfmni.gov.uk/ageing-strategy.pdf [accessed 17 January 2007].

ONS (Office for National Statistics) (1999) *Social Focus on Older People*, London: The Stationery Office.

ONS (2003) *Social Trends*, London: The Stationery Office.

Pensions Service (2005) *Joining up Services for Older People in Wales: Link-age Wales – The Consultation Report*, available at: http:\\wales.gov. uk/docrepos/40382/dhss/403821211/40382121/link-age-report-e.pdf?lang=cy [accessed December 2007].

Porter, A., Peconi, J., Evans, A., Seddon, D., Robinson, C., Perry, J., Windle, G. and Harper, G. (2007) *Strategy for Older People in Wales: An Interim Review*, http://new.wales.gov.uk/topics/olderpeople/strategy/ evaluation?lang=en [accessed 17 January 2008].

Rudinger, G. and Rietz, C. (2001) 'Structural equation modelling in longitudinal research on aging', in J. E. Birren and K. W. Schaie (eds) *Handbook of the Psychology of Aging* (5th edition), San Diego, CA: Academic Press.

Scharf, T., van der Meer, M. and Thissen, F. (2003) *Contextualising Adult Well-Being in Europe: Report on Socio-Cultural Differences in ESAW Nations*, www.bangor.ac.uk/esaw/summaries.htm [accessed 2 February, 2004].

Scottish Executive (2007) *All Our Futures: Planning for a Scotland with an Ageing Population*, www.scotland.gov.uk/Resource/ Doc/169342/0047172.pdf [accessed 17 January 2008].

Trench, A. and Jeffery, C. (2007) *Older People and Public Policy: The Impact of Devolution*, Cardiff: Age Concern, www.accymru.org.uk/files/Devolution%20report.pdf [accessed 17 January 2008].

WAG (Welsh Assembly Government) (2003) *The Strategy for Older People in Wales*, http://new.wales.gov.uk/topics/olderpeople/publications/strategy?lang=en [accessed 17 January 2008].

WAG (2006) *The Strategy for Older People in Wales: Annual Report 2005-2006*, Cardiff: Strategy for Older People Policy Unit, WAG.

WAG (2007) *Living Longer, Living Better: Report of an Advisory Group on the Strategy for Older People in Wales*, http://new.wales.gov.uk/topics/olderpeople/strategy/evaluation?lang=en [accessed 17 January 2008].

Walters, V. (2005) *The Strategy for Older People in Wales: A Framework for Evaluation*, Swansea: National Centre for Public Policy, University of Swansea.

Part Two
Current debates

Flexibility or flexploitation? Problems with work–life balance in a low-income neighbourhood

Hartley Dean

'Work–life balance' is a contested notion, involving conflicting interpretations of 'flexibility' in relation to employment and family commitments. It may be justified on the basis of a social case, a business case or the contemporary public policy compromise. In practice, however, people's capacity as employees and family members to achieve the kind of flexibility they want rests on their bargaining power. This chapter draws on findings from a small-scale qualitative investigation of work–life balance in a low-income neighbourhood in the UK. It discusses the issue of bargaining power in relation to employer practices, income maintenance and childcare arrangements. The chapter concludes by arguing that prevailing 'Third Way' public policy approaches favour forms of flexibility that can sometimes be exploitative. They need to be inflected towards an understanding of work–life balance that is premised more on the social than the business case.

Ideology and work–life balance

In debates about work–life balance, 'work' and 'life' are code for *wage labour* on the one hand and *familial caring* on the other and for the ways in which each may be 'flexibly' accommodated to the other. This chapter proceeds from the premise that our understandings of jobs or occupations on the one hand and of kinship ties and household arrangements on the other are historically contingent and socially constructed. Functionalist sociological orthodoxy envisages a narrative in which capitalist modernity swept aside the unity between work and life that (supposedly) once characterised feudal social relations. It reconstituted productive 'work' in terms of the wage relation and it transformed '*the* family' from a unit of economic production into a specialised unit of consumption and social reproduction (Morgan, 1975; Gittins, 1993). Industrial capitalism shifted work from the field to the factory and it kept the factory separate from the family. The modern welfare state played a critical part in mediating that separation (Titmuss, 1958; Pascall, 1997). Post-industrial capitalism now requires a more flexible relationship between the changing worlds of paid employment and family life. The re-evaluation of that relationship may be informed by competing ideological perspectives, reflecting different interpretations of the orthodox account.

Social welfare perspectives

What defines social welfare perspectives is a normative assumption that social policy intervention has not only been functionally necessary to the survival of capitalism, but also it was and remains morally necessary in order to ameliorate the adverse consequences of capitalism. It is an assumption that may assume a conservative or a reformist complexion.

Conservative versions fear the potentially corrosive implications that capitalism may have for the 'traditional' family. The imagined familial tradition that such perspectives seek to uphold is a social construction that may derive from the legacies of Catholic theology on the one hand or the middle-class moral-individualism of the 19th century on the other. Disparate elements of this perspective may be found in social conservative and Christian democratic approaches to family policy (Esping-Andersen, 1999), in left-wing critiques of neoliberalism (such as Halsey, 1993), or in the demands of 'welfare feminists' for social policies that celebrate the distinctive familial and caring roles characteristically performed by women (Williams, 1989, pp 49-52).

Reformist versions of the social welfare perspective are concerned more about the social injustices to which capitalism gives rise and the burdens placed on families – and particularly women – as a direct or indirect result of labour market exploitation. This has been the perspective of the social democratic left. It has been variously reflected in labour movement campaigns for a 'family wage', or, more radically, in policies – especially in Nordic countries – that promote equal participation by women in the labour market through universal childcare provision (Daly and Rake, 2003). It is reflected in the International Labour Organisation's *Workers with Family Responsibilities Convention* of 1981. The most radical reforms are demanded by those feminists who recognise that the capitalist welfare state and the pursuit of a family wage have perpetuated gender inequalities and patriarchal family forms (Pateman, 1989), and who seek not only equal treatment for women in the labour market but also equal sharing between men and women, particularly in relation to the performance of unpaid caring roles (Lewis, 2006). It is suggested that the work–life balance agenda might portend an opportunity to challenge the essentially masculine rights- and work-based ethics in favour of a feminist 'ethic of care' (Williams, 2001).

The precursor to the contemporary work–life balance policy agenda was the work–family reconciliation policy agenda espoused in the course of attempts to define the 'European Social Model'. In 1992 the Council of the European Union recommended that member states should 'enable women and men to reconcile their occupational, family and upbringing responsibilities arising from the care of children' (CEU, 1992, Article 1). In the course of the 1990s there followed a number of directives supporting forms of employment that could be flexible in terms of workers' needs and yet secure: requiring member states to legislate on maximum working hours, parental leave provision and for equal protection for part-time workers. This seemed to signal a shift in favour of a social welfare perspective that addressed not only economic disadvantages but also long-standing socially constructed inequalities (Hantrais, 2000). There was always, however, an ambiguity about the European Social Model. It bore the stamp of both conservative *and* reformist perspectives. The professed concern with gender equality entailed a conflation between elements of corporatist social protectionism, on the one hand, and social democratic demands for social justice, on the other. More recently, as the language of 'work–family reconciliation' seems to be giving way to that of 'work–life balance', the European Social Model appears – as we shall see – to be succumbing to influences from competing perspectives.

Liberal/business perspectives

The classical liberal perspective endorsed the separation of the factory from the family; of public affairs from private lives; of the sphere of the market and the state from that of hearth, home and family. Formal freedoms and equality under the law extended in the public sphere to workers and citizens, but the lives that people led privately were of little or no concern, precisely because people ought to be free to do as they please. In theory, therefore, classical liberals would brook no interference by the state in the free functioning of the labour market or in the private sphere of family life. In practice, utilitarian versions of liberalism have in the interests of the greater good not only countenanced but also promoted distinctly illiberal interventions directed primarily to the poor and calculated both to enforce labour market participation and to police dysfunctional families (King, 1999). Liberalism's priority was economic efficiency. And post-industrial capitalism in the age of the information economy requires new methods to ensure labour market efficiency. At the same time, liberalism's concern for formal equality has enlarged not so as to interfere in gender relations within the privacy of the home, but to advance sexual equality in the labour market.

The Keynesian economic orthodoxy that informed the emergence of different kinds of welfare regime in the post-Second World War period may have represented a strand of 'social' liberal thinking, but the welfare regimes that emerged were still capitalist (Esping-Andersen, 1990). They were still premised on a belief in market-making and the efficacy of markets. The 'crisis' of the capitalist welfare state in the 1970s (for example Mishra, 1984) coincided with a resurgence of classical liberalism, or 'neoliberalism', that was critical of the ways in which corporatist social protectionism and social democratic welfare universalism subverted market functioning. The neoliberal perspective sought to rein back social spending and to manage it in ways that promoted the efficiency of the economic supply-side. What came to be known as the 'New Right', while celebrating free-market economics, embraced a distinctly authoritarian, or 'neo-conservative', approach in relation to work and family (Gamble, 1988). At the same time, however, capitalism itself was changing. Business management was revolutionised and embraced new techniques for controlling highly dispersed and flexible production processes; imposing a performance-driven customer service orientation; and eliciting self-motivation and self-discipline among workers. The new managerialism embodied a doctrine that implicitly celebrated a liberal conception of the human individual as a utility-maximiser, whose performance could be fine-tuned through target-setting and personal incentives.

Paradoxically, while social policy in the post-Second World War era had tended to function with highly gendered assumptions about the family and tended to reinforce women's dependency within the family (Pascall, 1997), economic policy was ready to embrace the idea of sexual equality in the labour market. The 1957 Treaty of Rome – which established the 'common market' that would later develop into the European Union – included provision for equal pay for men and women (Article 119). Legislation to achieve this has generally been slow to develop and far from wholly effective. Nonetheless, the Treaty laid a foundation of sorts for equal opportunities programmes and gender equality policies. But the original motivation was a market-oriented concern to ensure a 'level playing field' within a common market. Potential workers – regardless of sex – should have access to a free labour market and such advantages or disadvantages as may accrue to individual businesses or nations should apply equally to all businesses and nations. Business seeks to maximise its access to labour power, or at least to avoid being undercut by competitors who can access potentially cheaper sources of labour power than they can.

Capitalist employers – unless prevented from doing so by legislation or trade union power – have always been willing to exploit women's labour as an underused resource. But in a post-industrial economy the new business managers recognise the importance of attracting and retaining the skills of women: or at least of those women with skills that are particularly valuable. There is a business case for promoting work–life balance (Employers for Work–Life Balance, 2006). From the employers' perspective, work–life balance may be seen as a means of maximising labour-force productivity (Bloom et al, 2006). In a competitive economic environment employers would like workers to be 'flexible' (which may entail part-time, irregular or anti-social working hours) and plentiful (because this helps keep wages low). To this extent, employers are likely to welcome anything that national governments do to help workers juggle their lives around their jobs or that enables those who might not otherwise have been able to work to do so. Such intervention assists the supply of low-skilled, low-paid labour required in service industries and throughout the labour market periphery. More particularly, however, in the high-skilled, high-paid core of the post-industrial economy, employers may be willing selectively to embrace the work–life balance agenda for themselves. Employers may be keen, for example, to offer concessions in order to retain the services of professionally skilled mothers, especially if the employer has previously invested in their training and careers. Employers may be willing to accommodate flexible working hours and pay generous childcare subsidies in the case of highly valued and highly productive technical and managerial staff. But such policies do not necessarily apply to lower-skilled or essentially expendable workers at operational or local branch level (Dean, 2002a).

The 'Third Way' public policy perspective

From a public policy perspective the work–family reconciliation or work–life balance agenda has become a more or less explicit component of a project to 'modernise' the capitalist welfare state. This applies not only within the 'Third Way' rhetoric that has characterised New Labour in the UK (Home Office, 1998; Blackman and Palmer, 1999), but also at the level of European policy (EC, 1997). One does not have to accept that there truly is a globally ascendant 'Third Way' combination of New Right and Old Left traditions (Giddens, 2001) in order to acknowledge that policy makers throughout the developed world are seeking to accommodate two kinds of secular trend: one economic; the other social.

On the economic front there is the process of economic globalisation, a process that has entailed a shift in global political and economic orthodoxies from a Keynesian demand-side approach to monetarist supply-side policies (Yeates, 2001). The promotion of work–life balance may be seen as a response to global pressures on the structure and functioning of labour markets. Potentially, it may increase both the quantity and quality of the labour supply and so, for example, enable countries better to compete for inward investment.

On the social front, developed countries have to varying degrees witnessed shifting patterns of household formation, in the age-mix of their populations and in the prevalence of social inequality (Scharpf and Schmidt, 2000). There has been a general trend towards a decline of the male breadwinner household and a corresponding rise in both dual-earner and lone-parent households. Such trends have challenged the assumptions on which social protection systems were once based, while also, in some countries, putting pressure on social spending. Associated with changes in the household economy and the composition of families have been demographic changes: declining fertility and increased longevity. These shifts result in population ageing and concerns about the sustainability of state pensions and health and social care systems. A key policy response has been to assert that work in itself is the best form of welfare so far as all working-age adults are concerned and that workers should be encouraged, so far as possible, to extend their working lives. In so far as it helps maximise labour-force participation, work–life balance becomes a relevant policy consideration, albeit that it must be accommodated to the fact that in post-industrial economies certain labour market sectors are characterised by work that is low paid and/or insecure. While it may therefore be necessary for policy makers to try and 'make work pay', they are prepared nonetheless to tolerate elements of the social inequality that accompanies economic competitiveness; provided, that is, inequality does not lead to 'social exclusion' (Levitas, 1996). Social exclusion, for these purposes, is directly equated with labour market exclusion in adulthood and with the underdevelopment of human capital during early childhood (Hills et al, 2002). Work–life balance policies may incidentally provide a framework that not only stimulates labour-force participation but also insinuates or extends childcare initiatives aimed particularly at early years childhood development among low-income working families in the hope of stimulating a virtuous circle of self-improvement and gains in economic productivity in later life (Moss, 2000; Huston, 2004).

In this context, work–life balance policies take on a complex array of social and economic justifications as social welfare provision adapts to the changing dynamics of the household economy (Esping-Andersen, 1999). In the UK the work–life balance policy agenda is intertwined with a set of initiatives, including:

- *Welfare-to-work*: policies to assist or compel working-age adults – including older unemployed workers, the partners of the registered unemployed, lone parents and disabled people – into economic activity.
- *Making work pay*: provision for a modest national minimum wage and the replacement of existing in-work means-tested benefits with a more extensive system of tax credits that supplement the incomes of low-paid workers and families with children.
- *Childcare strategy*: increased levels of daycare provision through an expansion of early years education, provision for after-school clubs and Childcare Tax Credits to offset the cost of private childcare provision; and special provision for young children in deprived areas.
- *Family-friendly employment*: legislative provision in cautious compliance with European Union (EU) directives for reduced working hours, enhanced maternity leave and pay, the introduction of paternity leave and a right to request parental leave, together with a national campaign to promote voluntary support for a work–life balance approach on the part of employers (Dean and Shah, 2002).

The thrust of policy discourse combines concern for the social welfare of 'hard-working families' (for example Labour Party, 2005) with declarations favouring the business case for work–life balance and the assertion that it offers a 'win-win' solution that benefits both families and businesses (DTI, 2001).

A matter of bargaining power?

The claim that work–life balance offers a 'win-win' solution may be plausible so far as workers at the leading edge of the information economy are concerned, but if the UK's approach were to be regarded as any sort of model there is an apparent tension between a social welfare perspective that entails a degree of selective paternalism so far as 'hard-working families' are concerned and a liberal/business perspective that entails a predominantly permissive approach to the management of the workplace.

This author has recently undertaken a study exploring what the residents of a low-income inner-London neighbourhood understood by, and expected from, 'work–life balance' (Dean and Coulter, 2006; Dean, 2007a, 2007b). The investigation entailed in-depth interviews with a purposive sample of 42 economically active working-age parents (mostly mothers – from a mixture of lone-parent and two-parent households). The interviews investigated the participants' experiences of work, benefits (including tax credits), childcare provision and other policy measures, but also their views on the importance and effectiveness of the facilities and services currently at their disposal. Participants generally supported the idea of work–life balance, but many were sceptical as to whether it could ever be achieved. Stress and long hours were unavoidable in some jobs, or else income and prospects had to be forgone in order to obtain 'family-friendly' working conditions. What the participants had in common was a certain powerlessness or lack of bargaining power that was exhibited in three specific dimensions.

Employer practices

First, participants lacked bargaining power against their employers. In some situations, participants blamed the inherent nature of the jobs they did:

> 'I should be able to finish at the dot of five o'clock and go home and forget all about my job ... but it would never happen with my job, 'cos it's the nature of it.' (Lone mother with seven-year-old son with special educational needs)

Others blamed their managers:

'There is special leave [for family emergencies]. However, it's got to go to the head person and it depends on what he deems as important. It's not worth applying for it.' (Lone mother with four children)

There appeared to be two salient factors. First, participants were seldom fully aware of their employment rights and even those who knew that they had a right, for example, at least to *request* a change of working hours or time off to care for young children, would often lack the confidence to ask:

'I don't really want to be doing things like that [asking for a change of hours] – making a fuss. I just get on and do my work.' (Partnered mother with three children)

Some participants were trade union members but none appeared to have received any clear advice or support from their trade union in relation to work–life balance issues. Most strikingly, one participant was herself a trade union shop steward, yet she confessed that:

'Easter's coming [and] I'm going to be in a bit of trouble. I'm even afraid to give my manager my leave card. The thing is, you know, it's the school holiday.' (Lone mother with two school-age children)

The other factor was the extent to which participants had managers whom they considered to be 'understanding'. But whether this could be relied on was a 'very hit and miss' affair. In a few instances, participants had managers who were clearly exemplary. But not all participants were so lucky:

'I think probably because [my boss] doesn't have any children, I think when it comes to like explaining that you can't come in because your children aren't well, she's not really that flexible.' (Lone mother with two young children)

Some participants were able to compare current with previous employment experiences. What clearly emerged was the startling variability of management standards, even sometimes within the same employing organisation. Several participants were working for employers, including public and voluntary sector agencies and organisations accredited under the Investors in People scheme, who paid 'lip service' to work–life balance principles, and yet line managers could exhibit a certain hypocrisy in terms of the kind of commitment they demanded from workers.

There was a sense of community in the neighbourhood where the study was conducted. A majority of the participants said they were happy living there and many reported engagement in local voluntary activities. But few had anything but the vaguest idea about where their neighbours or other members of the community might be working. There was no awareness among participants of where the economic foundations of that community might be located. Inner-urban neighbourhoods are not like mining villages or company towns where information about job opportunities and customary employment practices are exchanged by word of mouth. In this instance, there was a sense in which participants were disempowered by the sheer scale, diversity and unpredictability of the metropolitan labour market to which they sought access.

Income maintenance

Second, participants lacked bargaining power in relation to their incomes and living standards. None of the participants, when asked, considered that they were being paid what they were worth and all lived in households in receipt of some kind of state income maintenance – whether social security 'benefits' or 'tax credits'. All participants (or their partners) were receiving the universal Child Benefit (or, as some still call it, 'family allowance'). Most were receiving some other form of means-tested income maintenance although some who clearly were entitled to additional assistance – for example, through the Child Tax Credit – were not claiming it, often through ignorance although sometimes through choice.

Some participants, despite their earnings, were heavily dependent on state income maintenance:

> 'I wouldn't be able to survive without benefits, not on the wages I get. If I didn't have the Working Tax [Credit] and the Child Tax [Credit] and my family allowance I'd be stuck.' (Lone mother with one school-age child)

But, just as the participants had notably lacked awareness of their employment rights, they similarly lacked awareness of their rights to income maintenance. The level of their confusion was extraordinary.

Participants felt powerless in the face of the benefits/tax credits system. Almost all expressed uncertainty, if not bafflement, as to the rules and terminology attached to the array of benefits/credits provided for low-income working households, let alone the basis on which they might be entitled to them. Additionally, most of those who had claimed the new Child and Working Tax Credits had had adverse experiences, often entailing overpayment and subsequent recovery proceedings, and this was enough to discourage some from claiming:

'I mean, when it says it [Child Tax Credit] was awarded, I was like "ooh! I'm getting loads of money. I'm really cool. We're really much better off" and then they sent me a letter to say they'd overpaid me and I had to pay it back.... And then after a year I got another letter saying that I'll be getting £8 per week. [Laughs] It went from like a hundred and something pounds a week to £8, yeah.... [Question: *Do you think you're getting everything you're entitled to?*] I haven't got a clue.' (Lone mother with three children)

'I heard about this Family Tax Credit and people owing them instead of them giving this nice means of money and it doesn't work out and they have to end up paying all these debts back. I don't think I want to get involved in that, no thanks.' (Partnered mother with two school-age children)

While the initial administrative problems of the new tax credit systems may have been a transitory problem, several participants had at some stage in their lives had adverse experiences claiming other means-tested benefits and many expressed the view that they would prefer not to have to rely on state income maintenance payments at all:

'But I prefer to get my full wage than get more tax credit ... that way you don't have to declare anything to anyone.... If I was on Housing Benefit or Council Tax [Benefit], oh my God, it's just so – they just want to know everything.... Nothing's private.... When I reduced my hours, yes. I did actually fill out a form and all the rest of it [to claim extra benefit], but then I thought "They're getting all inquisitive again. I can't be arsed with this." I thought "No!" [Laughter]' (Lone mother with one school-age child)

'I get – I can't remember what it is. I don't get Working Tax [Credit]. I get, is it Child Tax Credit? Yes that's what I get, I think.... It does make a big difference ... that money helps me to be able to pay the approved carer [that is, it includes Childcare Tax Credit, which is in fact an element of the Working Tax Credit]....[Question: *Do you think you're getting everything you're entitled to?*] I don't know, I'd prefer not to get anything. I prefer to work and be paid a good wage.' (Partnered mother with school-age child and dependent disabled mother)

The tax credit system, which was supposed to make work pay, perpetuates what would seem for some to be an unwelcome degree of dependency on the state. Official estimates of caseload take-up during 2003/04, the first year of the new system's operation, indicate that while between 78% and 81% of eligible claimants received their entitlement to Child Tax Credit, only 54% to 58% of eligible claimants received their entitlement to Working Tax Credit (HM Revenue and Customs, 2006). While Child Tax Credit – which is targeted at both low- and middle-income households with children – appears to be reaching a substantial majority of those who are eligible, the Working Tax Credit – which is targeted more rigorously at low-income households in which one or more adult is in full-time work – is proving less effective. The in-work benefits that preceded the tax credit system had been administered as a part of the social security system and take-up levels had always been poor to moderate (Dean, 2002b). The hope had been that reconstituting the benefit as 'credits' paid by the tax authorities might diminish the stigma that was thought to be attached to the receipt of low-wage top-ups. Neither the official data nor the qualitative data from our small-scale study would suggest that this has yet happened so far as Working Tax Credit is concerned. Child Tax Credit and Working Tax Credit are equally complex and, certainly, no less complex than the benefits they replaced. But the fact that Child Tax Credit – paid to support children – is more successful than Working Tax Credit – paid to compensate for inadequate wages – would indicate that it is not only complexity that impairs take-up. The clear implication of what participants said was that they would prefer to be paid for the full value of their work. Participants were overwhelmingly committed to working and many said they enjoyed or even 'loved' their jobs. But despite the satisfaction they might obtain from working, some implicitly, or even explicitly, acknowledged that they were exploited. As one of the few fathers in the sample said, 'I just have to look at myself and value myself for what I'm worth'. Tax credits would not appear to assist in this.

Childcare arrangements

Third and finally, participants lacked bargaining power in relation to childcare providers. By and large participants did not wish to have to bargain over childcare. Most parents signalled a clear preference for self-provided or informal childcare and many expressed feelings of guilt about entrusting the care of their children to strangers. As one mother said, 'I didn't want to have children for other people to look after'. Some participants, because they were unable to find or unwilling to pay for strangers to look after young children, would resort to involving older siblings:

> 'He's only 13, do you know what I mean, and he's picking up his brother, he's cooking the dinner. He's got to do this and do that. I'll 'phone him up and give him instructions while I'm at work and it's a lot of responsibility for a 13-year-old to do. I just feel so guilty sometimes.... In an ideal world, people like my friend and grandmothers and people who look after children for you – I think that should be recognised and credits awarded to pay or help pay for that childcare. I don't see why we should be told who should look after our children.' (Lone mother with two school-age children)

This last remark is an allusion to the policy of restricting the payment of the Childcare Tax Credit element to cover the cost of approved or registered childminders or childcare providers, something several participants resented.

There were participants who asserted, for example, that 'I'm not one of those people who thinks staying at home makes you a better mother', and even those who were initially diffident about entrusting the care of their children to childminders, nurseries or after-school clubs were often comfortable and sometimes very satisfied with the outcomes. Problems could nonetheless arise with the standards of formal care. Participants did report instances of unreliability and even alleged ill-treatment on the part of carers, bullying by other children and accidents while children were in daycare. The cost and availability of childcare were also issues. There was particular resentment on the part of some participants at the fees charged by private childminders and nurseries – even though these could be partially offset through the Childcare Tax Credit element. Some participants were able to reflect on how childcare provision in the neighbourhood had improved in recent times, but this was often qualified by continuing uncertainties about how to access care and the difficulties of choosing between providers:

> 'There's help with childcare now, but back then I just had to stay at home with my kids. If I'd had help I would have liked to go back to work before.' (Partnered mother with two school-age children)

> 'There are more choices, I think. I mean ... there's the early years' nursery up the road.... It was there [before] but I don't think it was that easy to get a place. You know to get in. There was criteria I think. It just wasn't that easy. So that would've made it a bit different – I think. But you know, you just muddle along.' (Lone mother with two older children and a foster child)

> 'I put their names down, but the nursery that my two-year-old goes to, they only start from two, and she warmed to that nursery. She let go of my hand and ran off and felt more at home than at the nursery this little one [13-month-old daughter] goes to. So for me, the early years' nursery, their baby unit – I really love their baby unit, but I don't really like the looks and feel of their nursery for the after twos. I didn't like [it].... Hopefully, if they have a space over there, I will move her.' (Lone mother with four children)

There was little consensus among the participants as to the qualities they wanted from the various childcare facilities in the neighbourhood. There were competing moral considerations (see also Duncan and Irwin, 2004) as to whether the priority was to ensure the emotional security and well-being of the children or whether parents wanted forms of childcare with a developmental or educational function. There was one mother who insisted: 'I want to know that he's [her son] got a structured programme.... I don't want it to be just play, play, play, play'. However, most participants were less preoccupied with the developmental value of the childcare available to them and there was evidence of concern among some participants about the extent to which an informal economy of childcare within the neighbourhood was being superseded by a network of formal provision that was not only more highly commodified, but also increasingly professionalised, or at least 'a bit *too* structured'. One participant, who worked as a childminder herself, expressed concerns that the government-sponsored Sure Start centre established in the neighbourhood was promoting an essentially 'middle-class' approach to child-rearing while failing to engage with the needs of the poorest parents. Although this can be no more than an anecdotal observation it does chime with elements of the findings from a formal evaluation of Sure Start (National Evaluation of Sure Start, 2005).

While clearly there was some childcare on offer in the neighbourhood that was of a high standard, overall provision was fragmented and evidently failing to meet the needs or to engage the aspirations of every resident. None of the participants' employers was offering childcare facilities for employees.

Conclusions

The conclusion to be drawn is that in the tension between social welfare perspectives and liberal/business perspectives, it is the latter that are winning out. Work–life balance policies are, to an extent, closing the symbolic gap between factory and family – between the workplace and the household – but on terms that do not necessarily compensate working families for the consequences of a quest for global economic competitiveness. There is evidence of exemplary management, of income maintenance arrangements that do facilitate labour market engagement and high-quality childcare facilities. But under the UK's prevailing policy regime a satisfactory work–life balance is achievable only for some. Flexible working arrangements require trade-offs between employers and employees, but the indications from a sample of working parents from a low-income neighbourhood are that such trade-offs tend by and large to 'spill over' (Hyman et al, 2005) or encroach not so much on the nature of their work, as on the substance of their family life. State subvention intended to compensate for low pay is not working well, but it is workers who bear the cost of this failure, not employers (see also Lane and Wheatley, 2005). The provision of regulated and partly subsidised childcare is enabling some parents – especially mothers – to re-engage with the labour market, but provision can be fragmented and unreliable (see also Daycare Trust, 2005).

For employers, the issue of work–life balance has been presented as a straightforward contest between the 'win-win' theory espoused explicitly by the UK government and the case attributed to the European Social Model (Bloom et al, 2006): the former argues the business case for work–life balance, holding that it can increase productivity in a global free market; the latter argues that measures to promote work–life balance, even if they reduce productivity, represent a cost that should be borne to ameliorate the consequences of rampant economic competition. The 'win-win' or business case theory holds that flexible managers who accommodate workers' needs will get better results. Bloom et al's analysis, based on quantitative data, confirms the qualitative findings outlined above and suggests that good management does indeed lead to better work–life balance outcomes. However, they also present evidence that work–life balance does not of itself enhance productivity. Conversely, they demonstrate that, subject to good-quality management, neither does work–life balance harm productivity. From this we might infer that work–life balance would be best promoted on the basis of the social, not the business, case.

The thoroughgoing changes in the culture and dynamics of the workplace that might be entailed to ensure a satisfactory work–life balance for lower-paid and lower-skilled workers clearly would not bring short-term economic benefits for employers, but the case for doing so could be presented as an issue of corporate social responsibility, in the same way as it has in relation to the needs of disabled workers (Employers Forum for Disability, 2006).

From a classical liberal perspective, the development of tax credits as wage supplements might logically be supposed to be anathema. The original precedent for wage supplements had been the 'Speenhamland system' of poor relief introduced in parts of England in the late 18th century, but which was swept away under the Victorian Poor Law (de Schweinitz, 1961). That something like it should have become attractive to free-market liberals under post-industrial capitalism is indicative of a supply-side economic orthodoxy that no longer has need of a reserve army of labour to keep wages low and which assumes that low-paying employers must be enabled to compete in a global market economy. When a means-tested wage supplement (Family Income Supplement) was first reintroduced in the 1970s, the justification at the time was that as a solution to a growing problem of in-work poverty, a selective wage supplement was preferable to an increase in the universal family allowance (Dean, 2002b). It would seem that the same consideration continues to apply.

However, if the Speenhamland system had once been unacceptable from a liberal perspective as unwarranted interference in the functioning of a free labour market, its contemporary reincarnation might be regarded as unacceptable from a social welfare perspective, since it amounts to unwarranted state collusion in the exploitation of wage labour; to the promotion of 'flexploitation' (Gray, 2004). There are alternatives: increasing universal Child Benefit (Bennett and Dornan, 2006); in conjunction, possibly, with increasing the national minimum wage to something nearer a 'living wage' (for a critical discussion, see Grover, 2005).

From a classical liberal perspective, childcare is primarily a matter for parents, not employers or governments. And yet we have seen that in the name of liberalism governments may be prepared to assist poor parents to pay for childcare and/or to intervene in childcare provision in circumstances where it is supposed this might break a cycle of poverty or social exclusion. Notwithstanding certain variations of emphasis, such an approach provides the central elements of Third Way public policy. The outcome is not yet sufficient to provide the kind of childcare that can effectively ensure work–life balance for all working parents. One of the keys to effective childcare that is suggested by the study above is that parents must have trust in the provision that is made (see also Daycare Trust, 2004). While the UK government has lately announced an extension of its Sure Start programme, this will not of itself amount to anything approaching universal childcare provision. From a social welfare perspective there is a case for taking further steps towards a more integrated and integrative approach to early years childcare and education on a par, for example, with that which applies in certain Nordic countries and in New Zealand (Moss, 2004).

Work–life balance emerges as a complex issue, situated at the intersection of several overlapping policy agendas. The evidence from a low-income neighbourhood in the UK – where people lacked the bargaining power to secure the kind of flexibility that they would choose – suggests that present attempts by policy makers to address the issue lean too far towards the liberal or 'business case' perspective and are insufficiently holistic. The challenge – which should not be underestimated – is to incorporate more firmly elements from the 'social' case for work–life balance; to emphasise it as a corporate social responsibility issue, while working towards more universalistic forms of income maintenance and childcare provision.

Acknowledgements

The chapter is based on findings from a study funded by the Economic and Social Research Council, under Award Ref: RES-000-22-1491, whose support is gratefully acknowledged. The author is indebted to Alice Coulter, who undertook interviewing and preliminary data analysis.

References

Bennett, F. and Dornan, P. (2006) *Child Benefit: Fit for the Future*, London: Child Poverty Action Group.

Blackman, T. and Palmer, A. (1999) 'Continuity or modernisation? The emergence of New Labour's welfare state', in H. Dean and R. Woods (eds) *Social Policy Review 11*, Luton: Social Policy Association, pp 107-26.

Bloom, N., Kretschmer, T. and van Reenen, J. (2006) *Work–Life Balance, Management Practices and Productivity*, London: Centre for Economic Performance, London School of Economics.

CEU (Council of the European Union) (1992) *Recommendation 92/241/ EEC on Childcare*, Luxembourg: OOPEC.

Daly, M. and Rake, K. (2003) *Gender and the Welfare State*, Cambridge: Polity.

Daycare Trust (2004) *Talking about Childcare: Conversations with Parents and Children from Low-Income Families*, London: Daycare Trust.

Daycare Trust (2005) *Daycare Trust Annual Review*, London: Daycare Trust.

de Schweinitz, K. (1961) *England's Road to Social Security*, Pennsylvania, PA: Perpetua.

Dean, H. (2002a) 'Business versus families: whose side is New Labour on?', *Social Policy and Society*, vol 1, no 1, pp 3-10.

Dean, H. (2002b) *Welfare Rights and Social Policy*, Harlow: Prentice Hall.

Dean, H. (2007a) 'Tipping the balance: the problematic nature of work–life balance in a low-income neighbourhood', *Journal of Social Policy*, vol 36, no 4, pp 519-37.

Dean, H. (2007b) 'Poor parents? The realities of work–life balance in a low-income neighbourhood', *Benefits: The Journal of Poverty and Social Justice*, vol 15, no 3, pp 271-82.

Dean, H. and Coulter, A. (2006) *Work–Life Balance in a Low-Income Neighbourhood*, CASEpaper 114, London: London School of Economics.

Dean, H. and Shah, A. (2002) 'Insecure families and low-paying labour markets: comments on the British experience', *Journal of Social Policy*, vol 31, no 1, pp 61-80.

DTI (Department of Trade and Industry) (2001) *The Essential Guide to Work–Life Balance*, London: DTI.

Duncan, S. and Irwin, S. (2004) 'The social patterning of values and rationalities: mothers' choices in combining caring and employment', *Social Policy and Society*, vol 3, no 4, pp 391-9.

EC (European Commission) (1997) *Modernising and Improving Social Protection*, Luxembourg: OOPEC.

Employers for Work–Life Balance (2006) *Business Case: The Business Benefits*, www.employersforwork-lifebalance.org.uk/business/benefits.htm [accessed November 2006].

Employers Forum for Disability (2006) www.employers-forum.co.uk/www/csr/index.htm [accessed November 2006].

Esping-Andersen, G. (1990) *The Three Worlds of Welfare Capitalism*, Cambridge: Polity.

Esping-Andersen, G. (1999) *The Social Foundations of Post-Industrial Economies*, Oxford: Oxford University Press.

Gamble, A. (1988) *The Free Economy and the Strong State*, Basingstoke: Macmillan.

Giddens, A. (ed) (2001) *The Global Third Way Debate*, Cambridge: Polity.

Gittins, D. (1993) *The Family in Question: Changing Households and Familiar Ideologies* (2nd edn), Basingstoke: Macmillan.

Gray, A. (2004) *Unsocial Europe: Social Protection or Flexploitation*, London: Pluto.

Grover, C. (2005) 'Living wages and the "making work pay" strategy', *Critical Social Policy*, vol 25, no 1, pp 5-27.

Halsey, A. (1993) 'Changes in the family', *Children and Society*, vol 7, no 2, pp 125-36.

Hantrais, L, (2000) *Social Policy in the European Union*, Basingstoke: Macmillan.

Hills, J., Le Grand, J. and Piachaud, D. (eds) (2002) *Understanding Social Exclusion*, Oxford: Oxford University Press.

HM Revenue and Customs (2006) *Child Tax Credit and Working Tax Credit Take-Up Rates 2003-04*, London: HMRC.

Home Office (1998) *Supporting Families*, London: The Stationery Office.

Huston, A. (2004) 'Childcare for low-income families: problems and promises', in A. Crouter and A. Booth (eds) *Work–Family Challenges for Low-Income Parents and their Children*, Mahwah, NJ: Lawrence Erlbaum Associates, pp 139-64.

Hyman, J., Scholarios, D. and Baldry, C. (2005) 'Getting on or getting by? Employee flexibility and coping strategies for home and work', *Work, Employment and Society*, vol 19, no 4, pp 705-25.

King, D. (1999) *In the Name of Liberalism: Illiberal Social Policy in the United States and Britain*, Oxford: Oxford University Press.

Labour Party (2005) *Britain Forward not Back: The Labour Party Manifesto 2005*, London: The Labour Party.

Lane, K. and Wheatley, J. (2005) *Money With Your Name On It? CAB Clients' Experiences of Tax Credits*, London: Citizens' Advice Bureau.

Levitas, R. (1996) 'The concept of social exclusion and the new Durkheimian hegemony', *Critical Social Policy*, vol 16, no 2, pp 5-20.

Lewis, J. (2006) 'Work/family reconciliation, equal opportunities and social policies: the interpretation of policy trajectories at the EU level and the meaning of gender equality', *Journal of European Public Policy*, vol 13, no 3, pp 420-37.

Mishra, R. (1984) *The Welfare State in Crisis*, Hemel Hempstead: Harvester Wheatsheaf.

Morgan, D. (1975) *Social Theory and the Family*, London: Routledge and Kegan Paul.

Moss, P. (2000) 'Uncertain start: a critical look at some of New Labour's "early years" policies', in H. Dean, R. Sykes and R. Woods (eds) *Social Policy Review 12*, Newcastle: Social Policy Association, pp 68-88.

Moss, P. (2004) 'Learning with other countries', in Daycare Trust (ed) *Learning with Other Countries: International Models of Early Education and Care*, London: Daycare Trust, pp 3-7.

National Evaluation of Sure Start (2005) *Implementing Local Sure Start Programmes: An In-Depth Study*, London: Sure Start Unit, DFES.

Pascall, G. (1997) *Social Policy: A New Feminist Analysis*, London: Routledge.

Pateman, C. (1989) *The Disorder of Women*, Cambridge: Polity.

Scharpf, F. and Schmidt, V. (eds) (2000) *Welfare and Work in the Open Economy, Vols I and II*, Oxford: Oxford University Press.

Titmuss, R. (1958) *Essays on the Welfare State*, London: Allen & Unwin.

Williams, F. (1989) *Social Policy: A Critical Introduction*, Cambridge: Polity.

Williams, F. (2001) 'In and beyond New Labour: towards a new political ethics of care', *Critical Social Policy*, vol 21, no 4, pp 467-93.

Yeates, N. (2001) *Globalization and Social Policy*, London: Sage Publications.

SEVEN

The role of confidence and identity in civic participation: exploring ethnic group differences

Nahid Ahmad

Introduction

This chapter is based on findings from national research commissioned by the Commission for Racial Equality (CRE), which aimed to explore differences between ethnic groups in terms of levels of non-political civic participation, and the motivations and barriers to civic participation (Ahmad and Pinnock, 2007). The research included 77 participants from various ethnic groups taking part in focus groups across the UK, and 10 semi-structured interviews with representatives of various public institutions (for example, faith institutions, Local Strategic Partnerships, and the Race Equality Council). Ethnic group differences in civic participation will be explored here in terms of differential levels of confidence; some minority ethnic groups may be less likely to utilise civic participation opportunities due to lowered confidence on two levels: (i) an individual level and (ii) a community level. This argument is contrary to current British political discourse, which draws on an 'integration' agenda. Inherent within this discourse is the assumption that a more harmonious society will result from individuals from different ethnic groups having closer contact with one another. While on the surface this assumption does not appear to be harmful to British civic life, a deeper unpacking may reveal more. Within an integration agenda, policy drives and both local and national initiatives flourish in order to integrate those within minority ethnic groups into the broader 'British' society. Media attention turns its lens on the geographical locations of minority ethnic groups, constructing ethnic group-based 'ghettos', 'gangs' and 'no-go areas' (for example, Gibson, 2005; Jun, 2005; Leapman, 2006; Elgin, 2007). Punitive methods of policy making evolve, where, for example, the lack of English language skills in some groups is addressed with punishment tactics. Thus, the integration agenda brings with it moralistic connotations, where an ethnic group presence or indeed 'identity' is viewed negatively, and the onus to integrate is placed firmly within the minority groups, rather than the indigenous majority. This chapter will argue that identity plays a central role in the dynamics of civic participation among minority ethnic groups.

Arguably, that some minority ethnic groups show lower levels of civic participation cannot be denied. A series of citizenship surveys (in 2001, 2003 and 2005) carried out by government departments provides testimony to this. The 2005 survey (DCLG, 2006) reported lower rates for minority ethnic groups with regard to general active participation, comprising (i) social participation, (ii) formal volunteering, (iii) informal volunteering, (iv) employer-supported learning, (v) neighbourhood activities and (vi) engagement in social networks. This difference was largely due to lower participation in South Asian and Chinese ethnic groups, where 30% of South Asians and 31% of Chinese were engaged in informal activities, compared to 37% overall. Similarly, 20% of South Asians and 17% of Chinese were engaged in formal volunteering, compared to 29% overall. In other ethnic groups no marked differences were reported. For example, engagement rates in the white, black and mixed race groups were very similar for formal activities, and indeed in informal activities the mixed race group showed the highest rates of engagement.

Interestingly, where our research (Ahmad and Pinnock, 2007) showed some ethnic group differences, highest participation rates were among some minority ethnic groups, with the Indian ethnic group, followed closely by the Pakistani ethnic group, showing the highest participation rates for informal volunteering and engagement in social networks. In terms of religious identification, Muslims followed by Christians showed the lowest levels of formal volunteering. However, particularly noteworthy here is that the minority Muslim group were much more likely (68%) to indicate that they enjoyed civic participation than were their Christian counterparts (45%). Similarly, minority ethnic groups were more likely to feel it important to take part in community activities (72%), compared to white/white British participants (57%). Although this may in part explain why our sample showed higher rates of participation for some minority ethnic groups, it also highlights the vast potential in these groups for civic participation.

Self-confidence

Differences in civic participation rates across ethnic groups may, at least in part, be explained by issues related to self-confidence, self-esteem and identity. Some members of minority ethnic groups may be less likely to utilise civic participation opportunities due to lowered confidence, rather than due to a lack of interest, valuing or enjoyment of civic participation. Confidence may refer to personal self-confidence in pursuing social/ civic activities in the wider community, but may also include a collectivist 'community confidence', which is similar to personal self-confidence but is enacted between members of minority ethnic groups.

Psychological perspectives have traditionally explored self-confidence as a dispositional variable, amenable to the empirical research assumptions of variable control, manipulation and prediction. The related concept of self-esteem has also been explored from a similar perspective, but as directly linked to social identity, which refers to one's identification with a group (Hogg and Vaughan, 2005).

The relationship between civic participation and confidence has on the whole been previously researched in terms of civic participation having an enhancing effect on confidence (for example, Astin and Sax, 1998; Lopez, 2003; Limber and Kaufman, 2004). This research has explored the confidence-enhancing properties of civic participation for those with minority voices, namely young people and children. In this chapter, the focus is on those minority voices that are based on ethnic identity. It will be argued that in addition to civic participation promoting self-confidence for those with minority voices, self-confidence is also vital in enabling people with minority voices (minority ethnic groups) to utilise civic participation opportunities.

The role of self-confidence has been directly linked to the production of civic participation by Scheufele and Shah (2000), who conceptualise self-confidence (as well as 'opinion leadership') as a component of 'personality strength'. They conclude on the basis of structural equation modelling with survey data, that there is a relatively strong direct impact of personality strength on all dimensions of social capital (which civic participation is reliant upon). The dimensions of social capital as defined by the authors are: (i) social trust, (ii) life satisfaction and (iii) social engagement. The importance of this relationship may be heightened by making comparisons with the weaker relationship between informational variables and civic engagement, and by noting that the authors support the postulation that the impact of personality strength on social capital is beyond that of socioeconomic status. Thus, it appears that the confidence that someone has is more likely to motivate them to take part in civic activities than is having the available knowledge and information about civic participation opportunities.

Our research findings (Ahmad and Pinnock, 2007) also highlighted the role of self-confidence, which may be lowered by a 'minority' status, impacting on the degree to which minority ethnic individuals may engage in mainstream civic participation:

> 'Sometimes I won't go to a place, as a black person if I know I'm gonna be the only black person, or minority ethnic in the room.'
> (Black focus group participant)

We also found that self-confidence issues may interact with civic participation behaviour particularly for those with English language difficulties, and those 'minorities' within minority ethnic groups, such as women and children:

> 'The women and children are at home, they need to get out too and be confident in mixing with people, I know that my missus would be afraid to join and speak like we have done today, she hasn't done it before.' (Bangladeshi focus group participant)

Therefore self-confidence is an important contributor to civic participation, where to take part in such activities requires a degree of confidence in one's ability both to seek out and participate in such opportunities, and to influence others and contribute to societal outcomes. Higher levels of self-confidence will thus invariably be linked to higher life satisfaction, as is implied by Scheufele and Shah's (2000) three-dimensional model of social capital. Thus, as individuals feel confident to explore opportunities of civic participation, they will be more likely to seek out and participate in such activities, which will in turn lead to further affirmed feelings of confidence, and thus further participation. It can be argued that without the confidence in one's ability to behave in such ways, no amount of motivating factors, enjoyment of, or belief in the virtues of civic participation will lead to increased engagement.

Self-esteem has also been approached in previous research as an outcome of civic participation activities rather than as a predictor. Looking specifically at volunteerism, Omoto and Snyder (1995) explored the motivations for this 'helping behaviour' by focusing on those already participating in this activity. They found 'esteem enhancement' to be one of five scales of motivation for AIDS volunteers (values, understanding, personal development and community concern). 'Esteem enhancement' broadly refers to people being motivated to volunteer by feeling good about themselves. The authors identified other aspects of esteem enhancement as feeling needed, feeling less lonely, increasing life stability, and as a coping mechanism for other life stresses. Bearing in mind the close link between self-esteem and social identity (Hogg and Vaughan, 2005), it follows that feelings of identification with a group (and self-esteem) may both serve to act as a motivation for engagement in civic participation and be created by engagement in civic participation.

Community confidence

Our findings (Ahmad and Pinnock, 2007) also illustrated how minority status may impact on self-confidence such that civic participation opportunities may not be taken up if there is limited representation of minority ethnic groups. Thus, group identification may have a direct role to play in conscious decision-making processes regarding whether or not to participate in civic activities. The concept of 'community confidence' will be introduced here, which is said to be located within a given group and constructed between people in the group rather than something that is an internal state, as much of the current understanding of personal self-confidence suggests. This concept is particularly relevant to civic participation behaviour among marginalised groups. Individuals within minority ethnic groups, for example, may have a shared sense of reticence in seeking out mainstream opportunities for civic participation, and may thus seek to utilise alternative opportunities within the 'safe space' of their own ethnic groups. Our findings (Ahmad and Pinnock, 2007) showed that socially excluded groups may question the legitimacy of their participation in civic activities:

'A lot of people feel intimidated when they go to these meetings because they feel that maybe these are not the places for them to be, or they feel that they've no right to contradict their community because people think they shouldn't belong here.' (Interviewee: youth organisation)

In addition we identified that definitions of 'community' were often different within minority ethnic groups, representing ethnicity rather than geographical location (Ahmad and Pinnock, 2007). Classic social psychological research on group dynamics (for example, Sherif and

Sherif, 1953; Sherif et al, 1961; Sherif, 1962, 1966) demonstrates that members of an 'in-group' are drawn closer together in the presence of an 'out-group'. Thus, a greater degree of group identification may result from feelings of alienation from the host society, with group identification being used as a defence mechanism by some members of minority ethnic groups in order to preserve them from threat (for example, Johal, 2001). The sharing of confidence and identity between different individuals may be symbolised through language and social actions. Identity as a social action can be understood as the self needing to manifest itself through his/her actions (Hermans and Dupont, 2002). Thus, civic participation can be construed as a collection of such 'actions', which function to construct 'identity', which is defined by group membership (Tajfel, 1978).

There is a vast research literature on identity and ethnicity, mainly focused on young people and second-generation minority ethnic groups (for example, Rex and Josephides, 1987; Hall, 1995; Baumann, 1996; Jacobsen, 1998; Alexander, 2000; Hussain and Bagguley, 2005). This literature commonly explores the 'cultural clash' (Alexander, 2000) faced by those, particularly from a South Asian background, who struggle to align their ethnic/cultural identities with their 'British' identity.

Group identification based on ethnicity may be one explanation for the tendency for sections of some minority ethnic groups to be concentrated in certain areas. Philips and Ratcliffe (2007) identified the importance of South Asian attachment to predominantly South Asian areas, even for those who do not live in them. They found that this attachment was irrespective of social class and age, and was bound up in access to cultural amenities, places of worship and support networks.

Research has reported that there is little interaction between ethnic groups, with under 50% of white Britons mixing with people from different ethnic groups (Ipsos MORI, 2007). The current political climate, coupled with extensive media attention, has negatively constructed minority ethnic groups as choosing to live in segregated 'ghettos' (for example, Gibson, 2005; Jun, 2005; Leapman, 2006; Elgin, 2007). As Peach (1996) notes, 'ghetto' is an emotive term. The degree to which minority ethnic concentration in some areas is through 'choice' can also be debated. Phillips and Ratcliffe (2007) challenge the 'myth of Asian self-segregation', demonstrating the complexities of the geography of minority ethnic groups. Combining an analysis of Census and interview data, they find little support for the theory that British Asians are forming ghettos in Northern England. Their findings show that while some mono-ethnic settled communities have developed over time, by comparison there are far more locations where a diversity of ethnic groups are represented. Phillips and Ratcliffe's findings also highlight how choice of location may be restricted by legitimate fears of racism and discriminatory guidance from estate agents and vendors when seeking to buy a property.

Similarly, Johal (2001) postulates that minority ethnic groups form their own groups, which represent a 'safe space', in order to protect themselves from racism. Although Johal writes in the context of sport participation, his observations can equally be applied to civic participation. Johal deconstructs the commonly held perception that South Asians feel more 'comfortable' playing football in their 'own' company, by suggesting that it is more the case that they are forced to create their own mono-ethnic teams as a means of protecting themselves from racism while still enjoying participation in the sport. Applying this argument to civic participation, I suggest that mono-ethnic civic participation is a result of minority ethnic groups preserving themselves from perceived/actual threat, rather than as a result of the desire to form insular communities based on ethnicity. (See Ahmad and Pinnock [in preparation] for discussion of racism and civic participation.)

Uslaner and Conley (2003) suggest that mono-ethnic communities are counterproductive to civic participation, arguing that social ties to an ethnic community may lead people to withdraw from civic engagement in the larger community. Our findings (Ahmad and Pinnock, 2007) showed some evidence of the civic participation of individuals from minority ethnic groups being contained within those ethnic groups:

'We don't get involved with volunteering or taking part in things across the board, across the whole local community, so that is an issue because we've got lots and lots of volunteers for community-based activities but not outside the Sikh community.' (Interviewee: Sikh Temple Secretary)

However, some focus group participants in our research felt that establishing a strong ethnic group identity helped them to feel more confident in going outside of their 'own' community to participate in shared events. As one participant put it:

'By organising events or doing things within the community you get more recognition for it, you promote harmony, other organisations get to know about you also.' (Bangladeshi focus group participant)

Hence the role of ethnicity-based identity can be paramount to nurturing self-confidence. Rather than viewing mono-ethnic civic participation as a threat to integration, it can be argued that the strengthening of ethnic identities may help to overcome any lack of interaction between ethnic groups; support for setting up community groups based on ethnicity may serve to build confidence, which would thus enable those within the groups to branch out or 'build bridges' with those from other ethnic groups (Coutts et al, 2007). This supports research by SHM (2007) and Coutts et al (2007), which suggests that positive interaction or 'bonding' within groups can lead to better integration and less inequality. Findings from our research showed how barriers to civic participation were closely linked to lack of self-confidence, and this may in part explain why minority ethnic participation is often confined within mono-ethnic groups. The quote below shows how power differentials may impact on the degree to which there is an 'ethnicity gap' in civic participation, where in the face of deprivation the distance between ethnic groups is not as large as it is in more affluent areas:

> 'In more deprived communities I find that civic participation from often all ethnic groups is quite high. However, when working in slightly, in neighbourhoods where perhaps there is a little more money you often find that people who are empowered often take over and that makes, sort of (people) from minority ethnic groups feel intimidated.' (Youth organisation representative)

Interview respondents in our research reflected on barriers for minority ethnic groups, drawing on how 'comfortable', 'shy', 'intimidated' or 'confident' individuals from these groups may feel in participating in civic activities, where historical factors also have a role to play. The interview extracts below show some examples of this:

> 'I think ... that people who are comfortable in volunteering and are comfortable in speaking to people outside the community tend to get involved and those who particularly have no experience or training tend to shy away from such activities.' (Interviewee: Sikh Temple Secretary)

> 'In my opinion it's because they don't feel comfortable.... The Asians; Pakistani, Bangladeshi, Indian – they seem to be more open into the West and more active, history as well as culture and friendship play a part in this and has brought more closeness

to one another. The other Muslims from the Africa part (e.g. Moroccans) and Algerians they haven't had the experience, a bit sceptical and scared and do not have the confidence. All to do with background, education, trust and confidence of this community.' (Interviewee: Muslim Imam)

'Probably confidence within the host society, the longer people are here the greater the confidence you gain or the greater isolated you become.' (Interviewee: Senior Chaplain)

These findings support Putnam's (1995) perspective of civic participation and interpersonal trust as being mutually dependent. Where trust between ethnic groups is minimal so too will civic participation be. Our findings (Ahmad and Pinnock, 2007) also suggested that support from local councils for ethnicity-based community groups may be essential in garnering trust between those in minority ethnic groups and the host society. Such support would also go some way towards correcting the negative connotations implied by the integration agenda thus far, which has served to further alienate such communities.

Motivation and confidence

Group identification and community-oriented motivations may be heightened among those from minority ethnic groups due to their marginalised status in the UK, and this was supported to some extent by our findings (Ahmad and Pinnock, 2007). We found that while 57% of white/white British participants felt that it was important to take part in community activities, 72% of minority ethnic groups found this important. Qualitative data also showed that those from some minority ethnic groups appeared to value the spirit of 'community' more:

'The motivation to participate and get involved in community activities is the same for all Indians, our motivation is to help each other and do a good job.' (Indian focus group participant)

'It's all about me, me – being involved is about making your community successful, that is what is satisfying.' (Bangladeshi focus group participant)

In contrast to this, the white ethnic group were more likely to identify individualistic factors as their motivation for taking part in civic participation activities:

> 'I don't think people are strongly motivated by "the good of the community", I think probably 5% are motivated by this and the other 95% by "it does something for me". People get satisfaction.'
> (White focus group participant)

Within ethnic groups, our findings suggested that the black ethnic group gave the most importance to community-mindedness (87%), followed closely by the Indian group (83%). Slightly lower levels of importance were reported by the Pakistani (68%) and Bangladeshi (62%) groups, with the least importance identified by the white (57%) and Chinese (50%) ethnic groups. In comparison, differences were less prominent when analysed according to national identity, where both British and non-British respondents showed similar levels of those feeling that it is important to take part in community activities (67% and 73% respectively). Therefore it is likely that ethnicity and civic participation are intrinsically linked, where something unique to ethnicity invokes the valuing of civic participation, in a way that nationality does not. I propose that the difference here lies in identity, which particularly for minority ethnic groups, is stronger within ethnic groups than for the broader grouping of British nationality.

Considering that minority ethnic groups in our research (Ahmad and Pinnock, 2007) were more likely to value civic participation than the majority population, it was poignant to note that nearly half of the minority ethnic participants (44%) were either unsure or had no knowledge about community activities in their area. The gap in minority ethnic groups between attitude and behaviour pinpoints that barriers to civic participation in these groups need to be addressed. Addressing confidence issues may be the key to at least partially overcoming barriers. Our research found that gaining confidence was identified by participants as a personal motivating factor. Confidence may also however, be the bridge between other motivating factors and civic participation. The five key motivations for civic participation identified in our research were: (i) making friends, (ii) helping, (iii) being part of a community, (iv) interest and (v) personal development/satisfaction. All five of these involve confidence at various levels – one is only able to seek out and make friends, offer help, be part of a 'shared' community and show interest in this community if one has the confidence to approach others.

Similarly, personal development may directly impact on and involve improving one's confidence. Elsewhere, theorists have suggested that 'self-efficacy' is the important medium between intentions and behaviour – if an individual feels able to do something they are more likely to carry the behaviour through (for example, Bandura, 1977; DiClemente et al, 1985; Yates and Thain, 1985; Schwarzer, 1992; Calfras et al, 1997; Clark and Dodge, 1999).

Among our research participants (Ahmad and Pinnock, 2007) the value of 'community' held by many minority ethnic groups was often meshed with ethnic group identity, where definitions of 'community' often reflected ethnicity rather than geography. However, our findings also showed that although there was an interest in civic participation in mono-ethnic settings, this was contained within motivations for giving back to the wider community and sharing cultural differences. Related to both personal self-confidence and community confidence was pride in ethnic/cultural identities, which participants were eager to share with other ethnic groups. Confidence in themselves and in their ethnic identity were identified as an important basis for sharing cultural differences. Motivations to utilise civic participation opportunities were also related to, in some cases, a wish to challenge stereotypes, with the ultimate goal expressed by members of minority ethnic groups as wanting to establish greater understanding and harmony between people and cultures. These findings can be related to Day and Tappan's (1996) theorisation of moral identity. They suggest that two moral voices – justice and care – characterise moral identity. Use of the word 'voices' reflects the fact that moral identity is dialogical, and that people construct their moral identity on the basis of universal values shared in social contexts. Being motivated to 'give back' to the community may be likened to the moral voice of 'care', whereas challenging stereotypes, and to some extent the wishes to promote understanding/harmony among different groups, may be likened to the moral voice of 'justice'.

Understandings gained from a narrative approach lend themselves well to the study of civic participation behaviour among different groups, for civic participation is based on notions of 'communities', which are inherently social, and therefore embedded in language and storytelling shared within groups.

The narrative approach thus sheds light on how civic participation and the notion of 'community' are mutually dependent:

> Community is constructed in the very process in which two or more people construct a story, understandable for them both, about

what has happened. And whenever these shared stories become a part of the implicit horizon of understanding of a social group, they function as a guarantee of mutual solidarity. (Hermans and Dupont, 2002, p 240)

Religious identity

Interacting with ethnically based identity is religious identity, which is more than an 'ethnic resource' (Raj, 2000), having a role in civic participation that is independent of ethnicity. Rex and Josephides' (1987) notion of 'identity options' is applicable here, where it is postulated that people may utilise different identities based on their ethnicity, citizenship and religion. Thus, like ethnic identity, religious identity may too be utilised as motivation to take part in civic participation. Religion can be considered a platform for providing ideological, social and spiritual contexts within which identity can be constructed (King, 2003). Our findings (Ahmad and Pinnock, 2007) consistently showed that, for those who practised a religion, religion played a positive role in motivating them to engage in civic participation, regardless of their ethnicity. Particularly important are the civic spaces that religious institutions provide, such as places of worship and prayer groups, illustrated by the quote below:

'If people are practising a certain religion, then likelihood [is that] they will visit a place of worship which will/can provide a community hub.' (Interviewee: DCLG representative)

For those who practise a religion, a key influential factor is the framework of values that a given religion upholds, such as community-mindedness and concepts of 'love thy neighbour' and 'brotherhood', illustrated by the following quote:

'For us our motivation is religion. We are Christians and we are in fellowship with one another. We believe that religion and a place of worship is quite an important factor in creating an environment that ensures participation.' (Chinese focus group participant)

A discussion of religious or 'moral' identity within the context of communities may offer an exploration of how religion acts as a motivation for civic participation. Moral identity is deeply entwined with community, which is where civic participation is grounded. Indeed, taking part in civic activities is essential in constructing moral identity. Wallace (2002) explores the paradoxical nature of moral identity, where in order to gain a sense of 'self', the individuality of a person is substituted for a group-based collectivist identity:

> Only when one forfeits the self can one discover genuine selfhood; the journey to the true self begins by first abandoning one's assumptions about selfhood. Unless one empties oneself and leaves behind the quest for self-certainty one cannot truly find oneself beyond the traditional notions of the subject that provide false security and comfort. (Wallace, 2002, p 93)

For Wallace, the importance of religion lies in its social aspects, where it is not merely a philosophical belief system but also a 'situated discourse'. Thus, engagement in civic participation can be viewed as a discursive resource that allows people to construct identities based on religion:

> Theology, then, becomes essentially an activity in rhetoric and persuasion, a highly imaginative exercise in the art of engaging conversation and communication with people and communities from all walks of life. It is no longer an in-house discipline only for the benefit of true believers but now a form of dialogical engagement with the wider culture that offers the biblical ideal of service to others as a paradigm for capturing the hearts and imaginations of persons committed to social change. (Wallace, 2002, pp 100-1)

Religious identity does not necessarily construct boundaries between groups, however; Ecklund (2005) found that utilisation of ethnically defined identities allowed for commonalities rather than differences to be drawn out. In this study it was found that second-generation Korean Americans proactively used their cultural resources of religion to draw out commonalities with other ethnic groups, focusing on a shared identity beyond religion and ethnicity. Therefore, religious and ethnic identities can be positively utilised by public policy to broaden civic participation, rather than to assume a threat from such identities.

Conclusion

This chapter used research findings from a national study on civic participation and ethnicity in order to build on previous understandings of confidence and civic participation. It has been suggested that the relationship between civic participation and confidence in minority ethnic groups is cyclical, where participation in civic activities both requires and facilitates self-confidence. The central role of confidence in minority ethnic civic participation has been argued, borrowing from narrative and discursive approaches to understanding community dynamics.

It is suggested that policy makers wishing to broaden civic participation among minority ethnic groups need to consider advancing beyond rhetoric. Active consultation with community members is required to make these minority voices heard and *understood*. Direct involvement from the government is required within the remit of identity and confidence, where difference is celebrated. Empowering local leaders and those already active within minority ethnic groups will serve to cascade impact among community members.

Making a difference in this area depends not only on surface-level attempts to improve information access to minority ethnic populations. While improving information access is important, this does not take into account the changing face of minority ethnic groups in the UK today. Generational differences need to be considered. Civic participation cannot be broadened by simply making notices and signposting available in alternative languages. The diversity in minority ethnic groups, and even within each minority ethnic group, needs to be recognised. While language issues may still prevail among older members of the community, second- and third-generation British-born minority ethnic groups are faced with another set of issues, which may centre around identity. In order to enhance confidence these diverse identities require not only acknowledgement, but celebration that serves to legitimise their existence. Only in recognising our differences can we begin to work towards a unified, more integrated and harmonious whole.

Acknowledgements

This chapter draws on the findings from research that was commissioned by the Commission for Racial Equality, and thus the author is grateful to Jonathan Bamber and his team for their assistance during the research. The author is also grateful to Dr Katherine Pinnock for her assistance with the research, and to Ahsan Shah for his suggestions about identity in South Asian communities.

References

Ahmad, N. and Pinnock, K. (2007) *Civic Participation: Potential Differences between Ethnic Groups*, London: Commission for Racial Equality, available at: http://83.137.212.42/sitearchive/cre/downloads/civic_participation_report.pdf [accessed 18 January 2008].

Ahmad, N. and Pinnock, K. (in preparation) 'Community cohesion? Poverty, ethnicity and civic participation in the UK', *Benefits: The Journal of Poverty and Social Justice*.

Alexander, C.E. (2000) *The Asian Gang: Ethnicity, Identity, Masculinity*, Oxford: Berg.

Astin, A.W. and Sax, L.J. (1998) 'How undergraduates are affected by service participation', *Journal of College Student Development*, vol 39, no 3, pp 251-63.

Bandura, A. (1977) 'Self-efficacy: toward a unifying theory of behavioural change', *Psychological Review*, vol 84, no 2, pp 191-215.

Baumann, G. (1996) *Contesting Culture: Discourses of Identity in Multi-Ethnic London*, Cambridge: Cambridge University Press.

Calfras, K.J., Sallis, J.F., Oldenburg, B. and French, M. (1997) 'Mediators of change in physical activity following an intervention in primary care: PACE', *Preventive Medicine: An International Journal Devoted to Practice and Theory*, vol 26, pp 297-304.

Clark, N.M. and Dodge, J.A. (1999) 'Exploring self-efficacy as a predictor of disease management', *Health Education and Behaviour*, vol 26, no 1, pp 72-89.

Coutts, A., Pinto, P.R., Cave, B. and Kawachi, I. (2007) *Social Capital Indicators in the UK*, London: Commission for Racial Equality.

Day, J.M. and Tappan, M. (1996) 'The narrative approach to moral development: from epistemic subject to dialogical selves', *Human Development*, vol 39, no 2, pp 67-82.

DCLG (Department for Communities and Local Government) (2006) *2005 Citizenship Survey – Active Communities Topic Report*, London: DCLG.

DiClemente, C.C., Prochaska, J.O. and Gilbertini, M. (1985) 'Self-efficacy and the stages of self-change of smoking', *Cognitive Therapy and Research*, vol 9, no 2, pp 181-200.

Ecklund, E.H. (2005) '"Us" and "them": the role of religion in mediating and challenging the "model minority" and other civic boundaries', *Ethnic and Racial Studies*, vol 28, no 1, pp 132-50.

Elgin, T. (2007) 'London: is it a British city?', *Telegraph.co.uk*, available at: http://my.telegraph.co.uk/tim/august_2007/london_through_the_eyes_of_a_tourist.htm [accessed 18 January 2008].

Gibson, S. (2005) 'Is Britain sleepwalking towards segregation?', *London Housing magazine*, 1 December, available at: www.londonhousing.gov. uk/doc.asp?doc=16096&cat=2093 [accessed 18 January 2008].

Hall, K. (1995) '"There's a time to act English, and a time to act Indian": the politics of identity among British Sikh teenagers', in S. Stephens (ed) *Children and the Politics of Culture*, Princeton, NJ: Princeton University Press.

Hermans, C.A.M. and Dupont, J. (2002) 'Social construction of moral identity in view of a concrete ethics', in C. A. M. Hermans, G. Immink, A. de Jong and J.Van der Lans (eds) *Social Constructionism and Theology*, Leiden: Brill Academic Publishers.

Hogg, M. A. and Vaughan, G. M. (2005) *Social Psychology* (4th edition), Essex: Pearson.

Home Office (2003) *2001 Home Office Citizenship Survey: People, Families and Communities*, Home Office Research Study 270, London: Home Office [cited as 'Citizenship Surveys' in text].

Home Office (2004) *2003 Home Office Citizenship Survey: People, Families and Communities*, Home Office Research Study 289, London: Home Office [cited as 'Citizenship Surveys' in text].

Hussain, Y. and Bagguley, P. (2005) 'Citizenship, ethnicity and identity: British Pakistanis after the 2001 "riots"', *Sociology*, vol 39, no 3, pp 407-25.

Ipsos MORI (2007) *Race Relations 2006: A Research Study*, A research report for the Commission for Racial Equality, available at: www.cre.gov.uk/downloads/racerelations2006final.pdf [accessed 27 June 2007].

Jacobson, J. (1998) *Islam in Transition: Religion and Identity among British Pakistani Youth*, London: Routledge.

Johal, S. (2001) 'Playing their own game: a South Asian football experience', in B. Carrington and I. McDonald (eds) *Race, Sport and British Society*, London: Routledge.

Jun, J. (2005) *UK: Asian Muslim Ghettos Keep Growing, Hindering Integration*, Radio Free Europe; Radio Liberty, available at: www. rferl.org/featuresarticle/2005/09/2c5422de-c656-4b0d-879b-b30370a07b07.html [accessed 18 January 2008].

King, P. E. (2003) 'Religion and identity: the role of ideological, social, and spiritual contexts', *Applied Developmental Science*, vol 7, no 3, pp 197-204.

Leapman, B. (2006) 'London's criminal families replaced by ethnic gangs', *Telegraph.co.uk*, available at: www.telegraph.co.uk/news/main.jhtml?xml=/news/2006/04/23/ngangs23.xml&sSheet=/news/2006/04/23/ixhome.html [accessed 18 January 2008].

Limber, S.P. and Kaufman, N.H. (2004) 'Civic participation by children and youth', in N.H. Kaufman and I. Rizzini (eds) *Globalization and Children: Exploring Potentials for Enhancing Opportunities in the Lives of Children and Youth*, New York: Springer.

Lopez, M. E. (2003) *Transforming Schools through Community Organizing: A Research Review*, Cambridge, MA: Harvard Family Research Project, available at: www.gse.harvard.edu/hfrp/content/projects/fine/resources/research/lopez.pdf [accessed 18 January 2008].

Omoto, A. M. and Snyder, M. (1995) 'Sustained helping without obligation: motivation, longevity of service, and perceived attitude change among AIDS volunteers', *Journal of Personality and Social Psychology*, vol 68, no 4, pp 671-86.

Peach, C. (1996) 'Does Britain have ghettos?', *Transactions of the Institute of British Geographers*, vol 21, no 1, pp 216-35.

Phillips, D. and Ratcliffe, P. (2007) *Asian Mobility in Leeds and Bradford*, available at: www.geog.leeds.ac.uk/projects/mobility/ [accessed 12 November 2007].

Putnam, R.D. (1995) 'Turning in, turning out: the strange disappearances of social capital in America', *PS: Political Science and Politics*, vol 28, no 4, pp 664-83.

Raj, D.S. (2000) '"Who the hell do you think you are?" Promoting religious identity among young Hindus in Britain', *Ethnic and Racial Studies*, vol 23, no 3, pp 535-58.

Rex, J. and Josephides, S. (1987) 'Asian and Greek Cypriot associations and identity', in J. Rex, D. Joly and C. Wilpert (eds) *Immigrant Associations in Europe*, Aldershot: Gower.

Salford Health Matters (SHM) (2007) *Promoting Interaction Between People from Different Ethnic Backgrounds*, Research report for the Commission for Racial Equality (CRE), London: CRE.

Scheufele, D. A. and Shah, D. V. (2000) 'Personality strength and social capital; the role of dispositional and informational variables in the production of civic participation', *Communication Research*, vol 27, no 2, pp 107-31.

Schwarzer, R. (1992) 'Self efficacy in the adoption and maintenance of health behaviours: theoretical approaches and a new model', in R. Schwarzer (ed) *Self Efficacy: Thought Control of Action*, Washington, DC: Hemisphere.

Sherif, M. (ed) (1962) *Intergroup Relations and Leadership*, New York: Wiley.

Sherif, M. (1966) *In Common Predicament: Social Psychology of Intergroup Conflict and Cooperation*, Boston, MA: Houghton Mifflin.

Sherif, M. and Sherif, C.W. (1953) *Groups in Harmony and Tension: An Integration of Studies in Intergroup Behaviour*, New York: Harper & Row.

Sherif, M., Harvey, O.J., White, B.J., Hood, W. and Sherif, C. (1961) *Intergroup Conflict and Cooperation: The Robbers' Cave Experiment*, Norman, OK: University of Oklahoma Institute of Intergroup Relations.

Tajfel, H. (1978) 'Intergroup behaviour: II. Group perspectives', in H. Tajfel and C. Fraser (eds) *Introducing Social Psychology*, Harmondsworth: Penguin.

Uslaner, E.M. and Conley, R.S. (2003) 'Civic engagement and particularized trust: the ties that bind people to their ethnic communities', *American Politics Research*, vol 31, no 4, pp 331-60.

Wallace, M.I. (2002) 'Losing the self, finding the self: postmodern theology and social constructionism', in C.A.M. Hermans, G. Immink, A. de Jong and J. Van der Lans (eds) *Social Constructionism and Theology*, Leiden: Brill Academic Publishers.

Yates, A.J. and Thain, J. (1985) 'Self-efficacy as a predictor of relapse following voluntary cessation of smoking', *Addictive Behaviours*, vol 10, pp 291-8.

EIGHT

The problem of riches: is philanthropy a solution or part of the problem?

Beth Breeze

Introduction

This chapter is a response to the call for a research agenda focusing on the 'problem of riches' (Orton and Rowlingson, 2007a). It suggests that the topic of philanthropy fits within this agenda yet is currently under-researched in the social sciences. Original research into the distinctive features of contemporary UK philanthropists is presented, based on secondary analysis of the governing documents, annual reports and other documentary evidence relating to the philanthropic acts of 150 of the most significant major UK donors in 2006. Drawing on the literature, it then discusses ways in which philanthropy can both solve and contribute to the problem of riches. Both the data and literature review are used to assess the extent to which significant charitable gifts made by wealthy people can tackle the 'problem of riches' such as inequality, the promotion of happiness and the tension between private affluence and public squalor. The chapter concludes that philanthropy is often perceived to be part of the problem of riches, but has the potential to be a viable solution.

Definitions and the relevance of philanthropy

In this chapter 'philanthropy' refers to significant monetary gifts made by rich individuals for the public benefit; it does not include volunteering, corporate philanthropy or small donations made by 'ordinary' givers. No precise line is drawn beyond which 'charitable donations' become 'philanthropic acts' because there is no agreement on what this figure would entail, not least because a 'significant' gift depends on the size of the charity; while £10,000 could transform the fortunes of a local voluntary group it would be a drop in the ocean for a major international organisation. However, the sampling method used in this research requires that 'significant philanthropists' fulfil at least one of three criteria in the year 2006: that their personal or family foundation be among the 100 largest such organisations in existence, they are named in *The Sunday Times* Rich List Giving Index or they are described as philanthropists on multiple occasions in major print news stories.

While only a limited number of people are in a position to be significant philanthropists, their acts touch the daily life of every person in our society. Historically, philanthropists have built many of the municipal facilities that the public regularly use, including schools, hospitals, libraries, town halls, churches, parks, art galleries, museums and theatres. Contemporary philanthropy continues to privately fund a vast and diverse array of activities that promote the public benefit in areas ranging from the arts, to social welfare to educational provision. There is a common perception that all public services are organised and paid for by tax-funded arms of the state but in reality many of the facilities and services encountered on a daily basis owe their existence to philanthropic action.

As a leading American commentator observes:

> Philanthropic gifts have filled the world with knowledge, art, healing, and enduring cultural institutions dedicated to the betterment of society. Every day, all over the world, philanthropy touches the lives of countless people, bringing them education, improved health, intellectual and spiritual elevation, and relief from misfortune. Moreover, philanthropy's full potential for improving the human condition no doubt extends beyond any contribution that has yet been realised. (Damon, 2006, p 1)

Thus, philanthropy is pervasive in our society yet is little understood and, arguably, its full potential remains untapped.

The neglect of philanthropy in UK academia

The topic of philanthropy is curiously absent from the discipline of social policy and related social sciences. It receives no mention in the basic textbooks, has no meaningful existence in the journals and is not a primary area of inquiry of any leading academics in the UK.

The limited theoretical and empirical literature that exists is largely produced by historians (Rodgers, 1949; Jordan, 1959; Owen, 1965; Rosenthal, 1972; Prochaska, 1988, 1990; Daunton, 1996; Ross, 1996; Cunningham and Innes, 1998; Adam, 2004) and people working outside academia (Lloyd, 2004; Handy, 2006). For exception, see Halfpenny (1999) and Wright (2002).

To the extent that social policy has shown any interest in the philanthropic sector, it is as a potential deliverer of public services. While a lively debate is under way on the merits of contracting out state-run activities to non-profit organisations, this is irrelevant to the vast majority of philanthropic activity, which is not involved in delivering services and is funded by the donations of private individuals rather than grants and contracts from central or local government.

This academic neglect is difficult to square with the reality of the scale and impact of philanthropy in the UK:

- Over 180,000[1] registered charities and around 500,000[2] small voluntary and community organisations exist in Britain, delivering public benefit in a huge range of activities.
- The annual voluntary income of charities in 2005/06 was £10.9 billion (Harrison et al, 2007, p 7), which accounts for around 1% of GDP.
- While some big, household name charities have income from government contracts and some can charge fees, many rely on philanthropy as the main source of income (Reichardt et al, 2007, p 34).
- Most of the population make donations each month. Depending on how the question is framed, research finds between 52% and 70% of the population are donors. This percentage reached its highest level in response to the 2004 Asian tsunami when 80% of the population claimed to have made a contribution (Pharoah et al, 2006, p 38). The most recent survey finding states that 52.7% of the adult population gave at least once in the previous month (NCVO/CAF, 2007).
- The 30 most philanthropic individuals named in the 2007 *Sunday Times* Rich List Giving Index gave a combined total of £1.2 billion (Beresford, 2007).
- Since the year 2000, tax breaks have been available for charitable donations of every size made by UK taxpayers. In 2005/06 the public purse subsidised giving with around £1.41 billion in tax breaks.[3]

What is the 'problem of riches'?

The 'problem of riches' includes both the problems associated with being rich as well as the problems created for the rest of society by the existence of a rich minority.

According to Orton and Rowlingson (2007a, p 62), there are four potential arguments underlying the 'problem of riches'. First, the existence of a gap between rich and poor is known to have negative social consequences. More egalitarian societies enjoy better health, less stress, depression and anti-social aggression and higher life expectancy (Layard, 2003, 2005).

Second, as Galbraith (1977, p 195) first noted, the existence of private opulence alongside public squalor makes societies more vulnerable to a breakdown in social order. More recent warnings have suggested there may be riots in the streets if the divide between rich and poor keeps growing.[4]

Third, the concepts of wealth and poverty are interdependent, and possibly even causally related, therefore measures to tackle inequality ought to take place among the wealthy as well as among the poor. This aspect of the 'problem of riches' is not confined to Marxist analyses of the exploitative nature of capitalism but is shared by those who have observed the cycle of advantage that benefits those born into educated, property-owning families and prevents the UK being a genuinely meritocratic society (Rowlingson et al, 1999).

Fourth, the process by which some people become rich is said to contribute to inequality. Wealth is increasingly concentrated in fewer hands, leaving a smaller percentage for the entire non-rich population to share. The percentage of total personal wealth held by the richest 1% of the UK population grew from 17% in 1991 to 24% in 2002, while the share of total personal wealth owned by the bottom 50% of the population fell from 8% to 6% over the same time period (Dorling et al, 2007, p 4).

The 'problem' of the new super-rich

The problem of riches is said to be becoming more acute as a new tier of the super-rich is developing. The number of UK-based billionaires tripled between 2004 and 2007.[5] In 1997, the combined wealth of Britain's 1,000 richest people was £99 billion, a decade later in 2007 it was £360 billion (Beresford, 2007). Even after adjusting for inflation, these figures demonstrate that the richest are getting richer at an astonishing rate.

A report from the Joseph Rowntree Foundation (Dorling et al, 2007) finds that inequality in Britain at the start of the 21st century is at its highest level for over 40 years. The widening gap between rich and poor is driven more by increasing wealth among already wealthy households than by decreasing income among the poor. This so-called Matthew effect ('to he who has, more shall be given') is largely fuelled by dramatic increases in UK property prices, but this trend is not confined to one society. For example, the US super-rich are described as 'financial foreigners' in their own country, having their own healthcare system, education and travel network of private jets (Frank, 2007).

Those who problematise the new super-rich tend to locate their case within a timescale spanning less than a century, or four decades in the case of Dorling et al. In the absence of data covering, for example, the Victorian era, the case is unproven that our current society is more polarised in terms of wealth than ever before but there is certainly a climate of concern about the distribution of economic resources in contemporary society.

Given the growing incidence of riches, and the problems this is alleged to create for both the wealthy and the wider society, it is notable that poverty, rather than riches, is generally perceived as the bigger social problem. This chapter therefore supports the proposal that social policy's traditional concern with the poor ought to be broadened out to encompass the wealthy because, quoting Tawney (cited in Orton and Rowlingson, 2007a, p 59), 'what thoughtful rich people call the problem of poverty, thoughtful poor people call with equal justice a problem of riches'.

The rest of this chapter presents original research into the characteristics of contemporary philanthropists and a discussion of the relationship between philanthropy and the problem of riches.

New research on the characteristics of contemporary UK philanthropy

This research is based on an analysis of all publicly available documentary evidence relating to the philanthropic acts of 150 major donors in the UK in 2006.

The sample was composed of all significant philanthropists operating in the UK in 2006, defined as all donors that could be identified in at least one of three ways. First, the donors that fund the 100 largest private and family trusts and foundations identified in *Charity Trends 2006* (Pharoah et al, 2006, pp 116-32); four of these names were excluded as their foundations were found to be operating without the presence or influence of the founding donor. Second, all 30 philanthropists identified in *The Sunday Times* Rich List Giving Index in 2006 (Beresford, 2006). Third, all 52 people described as 'philanthropists' on multiple occasions in major print news stories in 2006; these names were identified by searching all UK newspapers on the LexisNexis database. This sampling method generated 178 names, 22 of which appeared twice and three of which appeared in all three lists, that is, they funded one of the largest private foundations, they were named in *The Sunday Times* Rich List Giving Index and they appeared in media reports. Once duplications were removed, 150 names remained in the sample. This sampling method is likely to have missed those significant philanthropists who have not set up a private charitable foundation, give anonymously and avoid media coverage. However, in the absence of any other means of identifying the intended sample, this method was considered the only viable option for assembling the sample needed to achieve the research objectives.

Private charitable foundations are the 'giving vehicle' of choice for most major donors because they provide a legal, tax-effective framework from which to control the distribution of money (NPC, 2007). In addition to the 96 names identified as funding one of the largest UK foundations in 2006, 24 donors identified via the *The Sunday Times* Rich List Giving Index and/or the LexisNexis analysis have also established personal foundations, meaning that 87% of the 150 significant philanthropists give in this way. The 120 foundations run by the philanthropists in this sample represent a combined asset base of just under £9.4 billion and an annual grant giving of over £480 million. As charitable foundations are legal entities, they generate publicly available documentation, which forms the basis of much of this analysis, including their entry on the Charity Commission register, governing documents, annual reports and financial accounts. Information about the philanthropic acts of non-foundation donors was gathered from press reports, interviews and speeches. Biographical information on all donors was also gathered from these sources and supplemented with data from the website Know UK (www.know.co.uk).

One hundred and nine variables were collected for each philanthropist and entered into an SPSS database in order to manage and analyse the data. Variables included gender, age, location, source of wealth, social characteristics such as schools attended and religion, scale of philanthropy (assets and annual grants), intended beneficiaries ('objects' recorded in governing documents) and actual destination of the 10 largest donations.

Ideal types of contemporary UK philanthropists

Analysis of the database, using SPSS functionality, identified patterns of relationships within the data, which form the basis of eight 'ideal types' of philanthropists; this coding was cross-checked for objectivity with three colleagues.

The aim of identifying 'types' is to discern systemic patterns within the data in order to understand philanthropic behaviour in the aggregate. Previous attempts to categorise philanthropists have focused on donor motivations (most notably Prince and File, 1994), whereas the intention in this chapter is to create categories that reflect empirically observable donative behaviour.

While the typology may not always resonate with the individual donors concerned, the aim is to establish the empirical regularity of giving rather than to explain individual motives.

The ideal types are outlined in Table 8.1, along with the percentage of significant philanthropists in 2006 who fit each category and a description of their giving behaviour.

Commentary on the typology of philanthropists and the problem of riches

This typology demonstrates the extremely large variety that exists within the umbrella concept of 'philanthropy' and the inadequacy of the vocabulary that exists to describe donors and their distributional preferences. The common moniker of 'philanthropist', with all its connotations, must cover a diverse group of people from East End boys made good to Lords of the Realm, while the word 'philanthropy' describes acts as varied as support for highbrow arts, rural youth clubs and starvation relief overseas.

By naming eight 'ideal types' within the generic category of 'philanthropist' it becomes possible to highlight which types of donor might be more or less likely to play a role in addressing aspects of the problem of riches, such as inequality. While 'culture vultures' are unlikely to be in the front line of a war on poverty, 'kindred spirits' who have themselves experienced deprivation before becoming wealthy might be more receptive to appeals for redistributive or social justice philanthropy. Similarly, 'salvation seekers' inspired by religious teachings that instruct

Table 8.1: Ideal types of contemporary philanthropists in the UK

Ideal type	%	Giving behaviour
Salvation seekers	18	Give primarily to projects that benefit members of their own religion. Within this category some differences exist, for example Jewish donors tend to support organisations in Israel and the welfare of other Jewish people, through charities such as Jewish Care and Norwood, while Christian donors tend to fund evangelical and missionary activities.
Kindred spirits	16	Support projects that benefit 'people like me' such that donors share a similar class background, life experience or trade with their beneficiaries. For example, a donor who has recovered from drug addiction funds a rehabilitation centre for addicts, and an individual who made a fortune in finance after a poor childhood in London's East End funds youth clubs and other activities for boys and girls in deprived parts of London.
Global players	16	Predominantly fund projects abroad, usually humanitarian, human rights and environmental projects. For example, development projects in Africa and conservation schemes in the Amazon.
Big fish	1	Have a strong local dimension to their giving, with a preference for supporting projects where they live or have their business. For example, a Manchester-based donor gives to a range of causes from the Lowry art gallery to marriage counselling and local schools, the common factor behind these diverse causes being their geographic location within the Greater Manchester area.
Patriots and players	14	Give to establishment causes, especially those favoured by royalty. Their donations are peppered with gifts to the Prince's Trust, Duke of Edinburgh Awards and donations to historic royal palaces. They are also keen supporters of national institutions such as the British Museum and British Library.
Culture vultures	10	The major focus of their grants is the cultural sector, including visual arts, performing arts and museums. Typical recipients include national arts institutions such as the Royal Opera House in Covent Garden and support for young artists at the start of their careers.
Big brands	6	No pattern of giving is discernible beyond recipients being primarily well known or 'big brand' charities such as the NSPCC, Cancer Research UK and the Royal National Lifeboat Institution.
Secret operators	6	Provide the minimum legally required information and avoid media coverage, making it impossible to identify the nature of their giving. This group is likely to include those who see anonymity as a virtue, those who dislike bureaucratic procedures and those who do not accept the public nature of philanthropy and the consequent obligation to report on their giving.

followers to care for the poor may respond to appeals for help to tackle the conditions created by growing global inequality.

How is philanthropy part of the problem of riches?

A review of the literature identifies five arguments in support of the proposition that philanthropy is part of the problem of riches:

(1) Philanthropy is not necessarily pro-poor.
(2) Philanthropy involves donor benefit.
(3) Philanthropy supports elite culture.
(4) Philanthropy is driven by donors' interests rather than by objective need.
(5) Philanthropy is inherently controlling and paternalistic.

Philanthropy is not necessarily pro-poor

There has been no substantial study of the distributive impact of philanthropic spending in the UK,[6] but US studies have consistently found that any redistributive impact is minimal because people tend to be philanthropic towards those only slightly below themselves on the income ladder (Vickrey, 1962; Clotfelter, 1992; Reich, 2006) and philanthropy by the richest members of society amounts to little more than recycling of money within elites (Ostrower, 1995).

Among the leading studies in this area, Jencks provides an authoritative analysis of the available data and concludes, 'the prospective beneficiaries are seldom indigent and are often quite affluent' (Jencks, 1987, p 322). A major research project to identify 'who benefits from charity' in the US concluded that 'relatively few nonprofit institutions serve the poor as a primary clientele' (Clotfelter, 1992, p 22). Ostrander (1989, p 219) finds that 'by far the largest segment of philanthropy does not directly serve, advocate for, or organize the poor', as does Brilliant (2001, p 226) who states that 'American philanthropy is not centred on the needs of the poor'. A study of US foundation grants found that funding for projects that help the powerless are dwarfed by the massive philanthropic contributions in support of universities, the arts, hospitals and the like (Morgan et al, 1977).

More recently, a study of US giving in 2005 found that 31% of donations from individuals were given to charities that provide for the needs of the poorest, therefore less than one third of charitable giving was focused on the needs of the economically disadvantaged (Rooney et al, 2007).

Therefore, while a proportion of philanthropy is redistributive, numerous studies challenge the conventional wisdom that philanthropy per se tackles inequalities.

Philanthropy involves donor benefit

It is historically typical for philanthropy to advance the welfare of donors as well as the welfare of beneficiaries – whether in terms of saving their souls, enhancing their reputation or more tangible benefits such as privileged access to institutions (for example, Owen, 1965; Rosenthal, 1972; Daunton, 1996; Waddington, 1996).

A major study of the distributional impact of philanthropic spending by Wolpert, based on an analysis of giving data from 85 metropolitan areas in the US, found that 'little generosity spans social, cultural or class boundaries … virtually all donations support local institutions from which donors benefit directly or at least indirectly' (Wolpert, 1989, p 381).

The existence of donor benefit is crucial to this debate because it may exacerbate, rather than tackle, patterns of inequality as philanthropists use tax breaks to fund their own preferences (DiMaggio and Anheier, 1990, p 151; Reich, 2006).

Philanthropy supports elite culture

Studies of major donors in the US have concluded that a prime purpose of philanthropy is to support elite culture, fund elite institutions and create bonding social capital within the upper classes (Odendahl, 1990; Ostrower, 1995).

Since the earliest recorded giving, there has been an obvious link between philanthropy and the elite as it delineates members of that class, provides opportunities for networking between class members, and combines fundraising with elite social opportunities. For example, donors in Ancient Rome could demand character references for court cases and elections (Nightingale, 1973, p 103) and gifts to churches during the Middle Ages were rewarded with dedicated altars (chantries) and the right to burial in that place, meaning that philanthropy 'was a medieval form of advertising, of public relations, where one displayed oneself was of importance' (Rosenthal, 1972, pp 85, 125).

In Victorian Britain, philanthropy offered an opportunity for 'new money' to buy the status required to be integrated into the elite by exchanging money for social capital (Leeuwen, 1994, p 596). The historian Owen (1965, p 165) claims that 'those who wished to rise in the world of society had best exhibit a decent interest in good works'. Prochaska (1990, p 366) notes that this impetus applied to people of all classes because 'whatever one's station, contributions to philanthropic causes were a sign of that much sought after status, respectability'. As well as entry into elite society, philanthropy provided ongoing opportunities to meet and build relationships with the noble and the famous (Waddington, 1996, p 187).

The same appears to be true at the start of the 21st century, at least in the US where empirical work has been conducted on this topic. Ostrower's study of rich givers in New York finds that philanthropy is a scene of status competition within upper-class society. Philanthropists' preference for funding elite institutions, such as Ivy League universities and arts institutions, rather than pro-poor welfare services, is due to 'donors deriv[ing] personal prestige from association with institutions that are prestigious in the eyes of their peers' (Ostrower, 1995, p 90). Similarly, Odendahl's work, based on interviews with 100 millionaire philanthropists, finds that 'charitable giving by the wealthy supports primarily upper-class institutions' (Odendahl, 1989, p 416).

Philanthropy is driven by donors' interests rather than by objective need

The distribution of philanthropic assistance is dependent on a variety of demographic and socioeconomic characteristics of recipients. Donors are free to choose who they wish to support, and often restrict their largesse to people who live in a defined area, are members of the same faith or meet some other arbitrary criteria such as a specific surname.

Unlike public sector provision, philanthropy is therefore driven primarily by donors' interests rather than by objective needs. This reflects the 'hyperagency' of the rich, who are able to define both problems and solutions (Schervish, 2005). The supply-driven nature of philanthropy makes it susceptible to meeting capricious needs via unorthodox methods. American critics of philanthropy have complained that 'wealthy people are free to use billions of [tax-subsidised] dollars to support their eccentricities and their hobbies' (Peterson, 1970, p 12). In a similar vein, British observers have noted that 'people have left their money to feed sparrows in perpetuity ... to give sugar to the police horses in Bristol.... They have left trusts for giving sweets to children, rewarding particularly handsome spinsters and teaching the Irish good manners' (Nightingale, 1973, p 128).

The insufficiency of philanthropy as a funding source is apparent in the wide variability of provision for different types of need, different types of beneficiary and in different geographical areas (for a good case study, see Bryson et al, 2002, on the distribution of almshouses). No guarantees can ever be given that all objective needs will be met, due to the inherently voluntaristic nature of philanthropy.

Philanthropy is inherently controlling and paternalistic

Philanthropy is sometimes understood as a means for the rich to secure their own safety and elevated position in society by diminishing some of the worst consequences of economic modernisation without relinquishing substantial control (Lassig, 2004, p 210). In historical accounts, the twin shocks of the Industrial and French Revolutions are frequently cited as drivers behind the expansion of English philanthropy, which took on a new role of 'riot insurance' (Owen, 1965, p 97; Whitaker, 1974, p 53). However, the most crude social control theories are now considered rather reductionist and an oversimplification of the philanthropic motive (Leeuwen, 1994; Daunton, 1996; Ross, 1996).

The argument that philanthropy is inherently paternalistic continues to enjoy wide support. Not only does philanthropy provide privileges rather than rights, donors can also require recipients to adopt certain values, such as religious beliefs, as a prerequisite for getting help; 'rice-bowl Christians' seeking aid from Western missionaries are a prime example.

Philanthropic paternalism is generally understood as a key driver towards the creation of a tax-funded welfare state in which access to assistance is based on rights, not privilege (for an early version of this argument, see Gray, 1905).

Paternalism may also extend to a degree of ownership that philanthropists feel for 'their' beneficiaries. For example in the 19th century the Royal Humane Society paraded individuals who had been rescued at its annual meeting to enable donors to enjoy the 'thrill of satisfaction as they contemplated the living fruits of their benevolence' (Owen, 1965, p 61). Contemporary fundraising techniques that promise correspondence from children in overseas sponsorship schemes, may one day appear similarly anachronistic.

How can philanthropy be part of the solution to the problem of riches?

However, there are five counterarguments, also found in the literature, that suggest that philanthropy could be part of a viable solution to the problem of riches:

(1) Philanthropy is a vehicle for redistributing from rich to poor.
(2) Philanthropy decreases the social distance between rich and poor.
(3) Philanthropy can play a role in building social capital.
(4) Philanthropy is a strategy for living with excess wealth.
(5) Philanthropy enhances the happiness of rich donors.

Philanthropy is a vehicle for redistributing resources from rich to poor

The popular understanding of philanthropy as a means for the rich to meet the needs of the poor dates back to the origins of modern British philanthropy. One of the committee members who drafted the original charity law legislation in 1601, Sir Francis Moore MP, stated that 'poverty is the principle and essential circumstance' that brings the activity within the compass of that statute (cited in Gladstone, 1982, p 56). More recently the historians Cunningham and Innes (1998, p 2) concur that no one doubted the primary role of philanthropy to be 'the problem of poverty'.

The potential for philanthropic acts to correct asymmetries in the human condition and create a fairer distribution of resources is described by Payton (cited in Fink, 1990, p 157). In a similar vein, Gurin and Til (1990, p 8) paint a picture of a 'social safety net that compassionately responds to society's otherwise neglected needs' and Frumkin (2006a, p 109) confidently argues that redistribution is one of the oldest and least controversial functions of philanthropy.

One US study attempted to quantify the effect of need on giving and concluded that private philanthropic contributions are responsive to the demands of the poor to the extent that a 1% increase in the poverty rate is associated with a $19 rise in gifts recorded on itemised tax returns (Abrams and Schmitz, 1984, cited in Brown, 1997, p 176).

Philanthropy decreases the social distance between rich and poor

While economists have inevitably focused on the financial transactions involved in philanthropy, one consequence of the inattention of the social sciences to this topic is a lack of focus on the social relationship that exists between donors and recipients.

Some types of philanthropy help to break down the walls that develop between rich and poor communities because they involve mutually dependent relationships in which 'donors have needs to be fulfilled as well as resources to grant, and recipients have resources to give as well as needs to be met' (Ostrander and Schervish, 1990, p 92). According to this account of philanthropy,'[d]onors depend on recipients for the moral and normative and perhaps social meaning of their existence' (p 75).

A similar theme emerges in Komter's analysis of gift giving, where she discusses the givers' need for the existence of recipients, and concludes that '[o]ne might say that to give is to live, not only as an individual but also as a member of society' (Komter, 2005, p 73).

A distinctive feature of what has been termed the 'new philanthropy' involves a desire on the part of the donor for greater personal involvement with the beneficiaries of their largesse. An advocate of this trend states:'These givers are different, they want to be involved, to initiate, not just respond."High engagement" is the fashionable phrase' (Handy, 2006, p 3).

'New philanthropists' are often contrasted favourably with traditional or 'arm's-length' donors as the former choose to serve on the boards of charities and volunteer in the projects that they fund. This 'hands-on' approach, whether it is truly novel or not, creates the potential for personal relationships to develop between donors and beneficiaries. However, further research is needed to explore how the potential for philanthropic activity to decrease social distance is restricted by the enduring power differential between funder and funded.

Philanthropy can play a role in building social capital

Philanthropy can contribute to building social capital, which is an important prerequisite for healthy societies, functioning democracies and strong economies, as has been highlighted by a range of social and political scientists (for example Putnam, 1995, 2000; Edwards and Foley, 1998; Hall, 2002).

An American researcher of individual and institutionalised giving claims that:

> The very act of [charitable] giving can and should be understood as a core civil society activity, which contributes both to the formation of social capital and to the functioning of democracy.

Philanthropy involves a process that draws individuals out into the public sphere and invites them into new experiences and worlds. (Frumkin, 2006b, p 375)

However, as this conclusion is based on the American experience, yet again, further research is needed to explore the role of philanthropy and charitable giving in building social capital within the UK.

Philanthropy is a strategy for living with excess wealth

Philanthropy is also a solution to the problem of possessing excessive wealth as described by the world's first billionaire, John D. Rockefeller, who realised that 'The novelty of being able to purchase anything one wants soon passes, because what people most seek cannot be bought with money' (quoted in Fleishman, 2007, p 40).

It is now a commonplace assertion among people of wealth that philanthropy can help them to deal with their personal 'problems of riches'. Some describe philanthropy as 'a bid to escape the loneliness of economic independence' (Whitaker, 1974, p 50). One wealthy donor admits: 'giving was just a front for figuring out who I was' (quoted in Schervish, 2005, p 73). Another, quoted in the same place, describes his multimillion dollar inheritance as 'a surprisingly alien burden' and says that, in the absence of quotidian necessity to shape his life, he needs philanthropy to help him 'carve out every goddamn day' (p 64).

Such therapeutic uses of philanthropy are not unique to the 21st century. The founder of modern philanthropy, Scots-born US industrialist Andrew Carnegie (1891) wrote that, in charity, the rich might 'perhaps also find refuge from self-questioning' (cited in Krass, 2002, p 247).

Philanthropy enhances the happiness of rich donors

The legal definition of philanthropy may involve a redistribution of private wealth for the public benefit, but the research shows that one of the main drivers behind philanthropic activity is a desire for self-actualisation (Lloyd, 2004) and to bring meaning to a life of wealth (Schervish, 2005).

The pleasure of giving is encapsulated in two quotes from rich donors (both from Panas, 1984, p 165):

I love helping people and I find great satisfaction in the love which is returned to me. There is the glow. The excitement. I love giving. It's almost neurotic.

I walk over to my desk, take out my pen, and get ready to sign a cheque for an important program. It's a great thrill. It means that I've done something that is very important. There's great joy in my giving. It's thrilling. It's exhilarating. It's important to be a part of sharing. It is my love. It is my joy.

Both the appeal of philanthropy and its limitations as a vehicle for redistribution are evident in these quotes. Major donors are not necessarily seeking to close the gap between themselves and the less well off. Rather, they are motivated by a wish to make their life meaningful, to count for something, to be thought well of and for the sheer enjoyment they get out of giving.

Conclusion

The empirically based 'ideal types' of philanthropists presented in this chapter demonstrate that different styles of philanthropy are more or less conducive to tackling inequality, and the literature review echoes this conclusion by showing that philanthropic acts can be understood as both contributing to and solving the problem of riches. But developments in both wealth creation and philanthropy indicate a promising trend for those concerned about the distribution of riches within society.

Philanthropy may be derided for giving credit to people who put back what their ancestors should never have taken in the first place (Panas, 1984, p 49), but the assumption contained in that jibe, that rich people are inheritors rather than wealth creators, is no longer true. The editor of *The Sunday Times* Rich List has observed that, in 1989, 75% of the list had inherited their wealth and 25% were self-made but by 2005, this ratio had been reversed (Beresford, 2005).

The bulk of today's super-rich are thus people with their feet on the ground, often from modest backgrounds in which poverty was not an abstraction but something to be overcome. When the self-made rich become donors, they may be less likely to fund elite organisations and more willing to use philanthropy to tackle the negative consequences that riches have on society.

Apart from taxation, philanthropy is the only legal route by which resources pass from the rich to the poor in our society. A large and enduring majority of the population believe that the gap between high and low incomes is too large[7] yet far less than half (32%) consider it the government's job to redistribute income to the less well off (Orton and Rowlingson, 2007b). As Orton and Rowlingson note, attitudes towards wealth redistribution are complex and there is no public consensus about how this problem should be tackled. Given the lack of enthusiasm for higher taxation, policies to promote philanthropy may be the more palatable option. Furthermore, many rich donors acknowledge that the pleasure of choosing where to bestow gifts far exceeds the pain of having it compulsorily taken by the state.

It is time for social policy to put the problem of riches on the agenda and any new research programme must include the topic of philanthropy. The existing theoretical and empirical literature is sparse, primarily written by historians and economists and distorted by an overdependence on data from the US. The paucity of research into contemporary UK philanthropy makes it difficult to draw firm conclusions about the overall impact of philanthropy but this chapter argues that there exists a potential for philanthropy to tackle, rather than contribute to, the problem of riches.

Notes

[1] According to the Charity Commission website, www.charitycommission.gov.uk (accessed 3 November 2007).

[2] According to a cross-cutting review of the voluntary and community sector (HM Treasury, 2002).

[3] According to *Charity Trends* (Harrison et al, 2007, p 165). The £1.41 billion in charitable tax relief is comprised of £750 million paid directly to charities through the Gift Aid scheme, £180 million paid back to higher-rate taxpayers, £20 million to donors on payroll giving schemes and £460 million of Inheritance Tax reliefs.

[4] For example, Sir Ronald Cohen of private equity firm Apax, cited in 'From richer to poorer', *The Sunday Times*, 22 July 2007.

[5] As reported in *The Sunday Times* (2007, p 8), which names 68 UK-based billionaires in 2007.

[6] This gap will be addressed by a new research centre, launching in 2008, focusing on charitable giving and philanthropy, which includes 'charitable giving and social redistribution' as one of three main strands of work. The initiative is funded by the Economic and Social Research Council (ESRC), the Office of the Third Sector in the Cabinet Office, the Scottish Executive and the Carnegie UK Trust.

[7] This view was held by 73% of the population in 2004 according to Orton and Rowlingson (2007b).

References

Adam, T. (ed) (2004) *Philanthropy, Patronage and Civil Society: Experiences from Germany, Great Britain and North America*, Bloomington, IN: Indiana University Press.

Beresford, P. (2005) 'The rich list', *The Sunday Times*, 3 April.

Beresford, P. (2006) 'The rich list', *The Sunday Times*, 23 April.

Beresford, P. (2007) 'The rich list', *The Sunday Times*, 29 April.

Brilliant, E. (2001) 'Patterns and purposes of philanthropic giving', in C.T. Clotfelter and T. Ehrlich (eds) *Philanthropy and the Nonprofit Sector in a Changing America*, Bloomington and Indianapolis, IN: Indiana University Press.

Brown, E. (1997) 'Altruism towards groups: the charitable provision of private goods', *Nonprofit and Voluntary Sector Quarterly*, vol 26, no 2, pp 175-84.

Bryson, J.R., McGuiness, M. and Ford, R.G. (2002) 'Chasing a "loose and baggy monster": almshouses and the geography of charity', *AREA*, vol 34, no 1, pp 48-58.

Clotfelter, C.T. (ed) (1992) *Who Benefits from the Nonprofit Sector?*, Chicago, IL: Chicago University Press.

Cunningham, H. and Innes, J. (eds) (1998) *Charity, Philanthropy and Reform: From the 1690s to 1850*, Basingstoke: Macmillan.

Damon, W. (2006) 'Introduction: taking philanthropy seriously', in W. Damon and S. Verducci (eds) *Taking Philanthropy Seriously: Beyond Noble Intentions to Responsible Giving*, Bloomington and Indianapolis, IN: Indiana University Press.

Daunton, M. (ed) (1996) *Charity, Self-interest and Welfare in the English Past*, London: UCL Press.

DiMaggio, P.J. and Anheier, H.K. (1990) 'The sociology of nonprofit organisations', *Annual Review of Sociology*, vol 16, pp 137-59.

Dorling, D., Rigby, J., Wheeler, B., Ballas, D. and Thomas, B. (2007) *Poverty, Wealth and Place in Britain 1968 to 2005*, Bristol/York: The Policy Press/Joseph Rowntree Foundation.

Edwards, B. and Foley, M.W. (1998) 'Civil society and social capital beyond Putnam', *American Behavioural Scientist*, vol 42, no 1, pp 124-39.

Fink, J. (1990) 'Philanthropy and the community', in J.V. Til (ed) *Critical Issues in American Philanthropy*, San Francisco, CA: Jossey-Bass.

Fleishman, J. (2007) *The Foundation: A Great American Secret*, New York: Public Affairs.

Frank, R. (2007) *Richistan: A Journey through the 21st Century Wealth Boom and the Lives of the New Rich*, London: Piatkus Books.

Frumkin, P. (2006a) 'American foundations and overseas funding: new challenges in the era of globalization', in S. Hewa and D.H. Stapleton (eds) *Globalization, Philanthropy and Civil Society: Toward a New Political Culture in the Twenty-First Century*, New York and Boston, MA: Springer.

Frumkin, P. (2006b) *Strategic Giving: The Art and Science of Philanthropy*, Chicago, IL, and London: University of Chicago Press.

Galbraith, J.K. (1977) *The Affluent Society*, London: Hamish Hamilton.

Gladstone, F. (1982) *Charity, Law and Social Justice*, London: NCVO Bedford Square Press.

Gray, B.K. (1905) *A History of Philanthropy: From the Dissolution of the Monasteries to the Taking of the First Census*, London: Frank Cass.

Gurin, M.G. and Til, J.V. (1990) 'Philanthropy in its historical context', in J.V. Til (ed) *Critical Issues in American Philanthropy: Strengthening Theory and Practice*, San Francisco, CA: Jossey-Bass.

Halfpenny, P. (1999) 'Economic and sociological theories of individual charitable giving: complementary or contradictory?', *Voluntas*, vol 10, no 3, pp 197-216.

Hall, P.A. (2002) 'Great Britain: the role of government and the distribution of social capital', in R.D. Putnam (ed) *Democracies in Flux: The Evolution of Social Capital in Contemporary Society*, Oxford: Oxford University Press.

Handy, C. (2006) *The New Philanthropists*, London: William Heinemann.

Harrison, R., Goodey, L., Clegg, S., Bull, A. and Leadbetter, A. (2007) *Charity Trends 2007*, London: Caritas Data.

HM Treasury (2002) *The Role of the Voluntary and Community Sector in Service Delivery: A Cross Cutting Review*, London: HM Treasury.

Jencks, C. (1987) 'Who gives to what?', in W. Powell (ed) *The Nonprofit Sector: A Research Handbook*, New Haven, CT: Yale University Press.

Jordan, W. K. (1959) *Philanthropy in England 1480–1660: A Study of the Changing Pattern of English Social Aspirations*, London: George Allen & Unwin.

Komter, A. (2005) *Social Solidarity and the Gift*, Cambridge: Cambridge University Press.

Krass, P. (2002) *Carnegie*, Hobeken, NJ/London: John Wiley & Sons.

Lassig, S. (2004) 'Burgerlichkeit, patronage and communal liberalism in Germany 1871-1914', in T. Adam (ed) *Philanthropy, Patronage and Civil Society: Experiences from Germany, Great Britain and North America*, Bloomington, IN: Indiana University Press.

Layard, R. (2003) *Happiness: Has Social Science got a Clue?*, Lionel Robbins Memorial Lectures, London: London School of Economics and Political Science.

Layard, R. (2005) *Happiness: Lessons from a New Science*, London: Penguin.

Lloyd, T. (2004) *Why Rich People Give*, London: Association of Charitable Foundations.

Morgan, J., Dye, R. and Hybels, J. (1977) 'Results from two national surveys on philanthropic activity', *Commission on Private Philanthropy and Public Needs*, Washington, DC: Treasury Department, pp 157-323.

NCVO (National Council for Voluntary Organisations)/Charities Aid Foundation (CAF) (2007) *UK Giving 2005/06*, London: NCVO/CAF.

Nightingale, B. (1973) *Charities*, London: Allen Lane.

NPC (New Philanthropy Capital) (2007) *Philanthropy amongst Ultra High Net Worth Individuals and Family Offices in Europe*, London: NPC.

Odendahl, T. (1990) *Charity Begins at Home: Generosity and Self-Interest among the Philanthropic Elite*, New York: Basic Books.

Odendahl, T.J. (1989) 'Charitable giving patterns by elites in the United States', in V. Hodgkinson and R.W. Lyman (eds) *The Future of the Nonprofit Sector: Challenges, Changes and Policy Considerations*, San Francisco, CA: Jossey-Bass.

Orton, M. and Rowlingson, K. (2007a) 'A problem of riches: towards a new social policy research agenda on the distribution of economic resources', *Journal of Social Policy*, vol 36, no 1, pp 59-77.

Orton, M. and Rowlingson, K. (2007b) *Public Attitudes to Economic Inequality*, York: Joseph Rowntree Foundation.

Ostrander, S.A. (1989) 'The problem of poverty and why philanthropy neglects it', in V. Hodgkinson and R.W. Lyman (eds) *The Future of the Nonprofit Sector: Challenges, Changes and Policy Considerations*, San Francisco, CA: Jossey-Bass.

Ostrander, S.A. and Schervish, P.G. (1990) 'Giving and getting: philanthropy as a social relation', in J.V. Til (ed) *Critical Issues in American Philanthropy: Strengthening Theory and Practice*, San Francisco, CA: Jossey-Bass.

Ostrower, F. (1995) *Why the Wealthy Give: The Culture of Elite Philanthropy*, Princeton, NJ: Princeton University Press.

Owen, D. (1965) *English Philanthropy 1660–1960*, London: Oxford University Press.

Panas, J. (1984) *Mega Gifts: Who Gives Them, Who Gets Them?*, Chicago, IL: Bonus Books.

Peterson, P.G. (1970) *Foundations, Private Giving and Public Policy: Report and Recommendations of the Commission on Foundations and Private Philanthropy*, Chicago, IL: University of Chicago Press.

Pharoah, C., Walker, C., Godey, L. and Clegg, S. (2006) *Charity Trends 2006*, London: Caritas Data.

Prince, R. and File, K. (1994) *The Seven Faces of Philanthropy: A New Approach to Cultivating Major Donors*, San Francisco, CA: Jossey-Bass.

Prochaska, F. (1988) *The Voluntary Impulse: Philanthropy in Modern Britain*, London: Faber and Faber.

Prochaska, F. (1990) 'Philanthropy', in F.M.L. Thompson (ed) *The Cambridge Social History of Britain 1750–1950*, Cambridge: Cambridge University Press.

Putnam, R. (2000) *Bowling Alone: The Collapse and Revival of American Community*, New York: Simon and Schuster.

Putnam, R.D. (1995) 'Bowling alone: America's declining social capital', *Journal of Democracy*, vol 6, no 1, pp 65-78.

Reich, R. (2006) 'Philanthropy and its uneasy relation to Equality', in W. Damon and S. Verducci (eds) *Taking Philanthropy Seriously: Beyond Noble Intentions to Responsible Giving*, Indianapolis, IN: Indiana University Press.

Reichardt, O., Kane, D. and Wilding, K. (2007) *The UK Voluntary Sector Almanac: The State of the Sector 2007*, London: NCVO.

Rodgers, B. (1949) *Cloak of Charity: Studies in Eighteenth-Century Philanthropy*, London: Methuen & Co Ltd.

Rooney, P., Brown, M., Milner, B., Wei, X., Yushioka, T. and Fleischhacker, D. (2007) *Patterns of Household Charitable Giving by Income Group, 2005*, Indiana, IN: Center on Philanthropy at Indiana University.

Rosenthal, J.T. (1972) *The Purchase of Paradise: Gift Giving and the Aristocracy 1307–1485*, London: Routledge & Kegan Paul.

Ross, E. (1996) '"Human communion" or a free lunch: school dinners in Victorian and Edwardian London', in J. B. Schneewind (ed) *Giving: Western Ideas of Philanthropy*, Bloomington and Indianapolis, IN: Indiana University Press.

Rowlingson, K., Whyley, C. and Warren, T. (1999) *Wealth in Britain: A Lifecycle Perspective*, London: Policy Studies Institute.

Schervish, P.G. (2005) 'Major donors, major motives: the people and purpose behind major gifts', *New Directions for Philanthropic Fundraising*, vol 47, pp 59-87.

Van Leeuwen, M.H.D. (1994) 'Logic of charity: poor relief in preindustrial Europe', *Journal of Interdisciplinary History*, vol 24, no 4, pp 589-613.

Vickrey, W. (1962) 'One economist's view of philanthropy', in F.G. Dickenson (ed) *Philanthropy and Public Policy*, New York: National Bureau of Economic Research.

Waddington, K. (1996) 'Grasping gratitude': charity and hospital finance in late Victorian England', in M. Daunton (ed) *Charity, Self-interest and Welfare in the English Past*, London: UCL Press.

Whitaker, B. (1974) *The Foundations*, London: Eyre Methuen.

Wolpert, J. (1989) 'Key indicators of generosity in communities', in V. Hodgkinson and R.W. Lyman (eds) *The Future of the Nonprofit Sector: Challenges, Changes and Policy Considerations*, San Francisco, CA: Jossey-Bass.

Wright, K. (2002) *Generosity versus Altruism: Philanthropy and Charity in the US and UK*, Civil Society Working Paper 17, London: London School of Economics and Political Science.

NINE

Policy from the pitch? Soccer and young refugee women in a shifting policy climate

Catherine Palmer

Introduction

Since the announcement in July 2005 that London had successfully won the bid to host the 2012 Olympic and Paralympic Games, its aspirational message of 'legacy' has brought a number of concerns for social policy into sharp relief. To be held in some of the country's most disadvantaged boroughs, much of the 2012 agenda is built around regenerating London's East End, ameliorating poverty and transforming the lives of children and young people in these areas. The capacity for the 2012 Games to leave a tangible, sustainable legacy for current and future generations remains open to debate, and is beyond the scope of this chapter. It does, however, highlight the growing intersections between sport and social policy. While sport engages with many current policy issues – crime, health, youth, unemployment, urban regeneration and social exclusion, to name but a few – it nonetheless remains an under-researched area in the field of social policy in the UK and elsewhere. It is this oversight that this chapter takes as its point of departure.

This methodological chapter explores some of the issues and challenges faced by a social researcher working in an Australian policy context. It is particularly concerned with the process and politics that underpinned an action research project conducted with a group of young Muslim, refugee women who play together in a 'New Arrivals' soccer team in Adelaide, South Australia. While the chapter is centrally concerned with sport, the issues it raises are of relevance to those engaged in policy research more broadly. In something of a departure from how social policy research is usually presented, the chapter focuses not on the findings of the research, but on the *processes* that underpin the research. The chapter begins with an overview of the soccer programme and its underlying preventative health agenda and concludes by considering the key issues of research transfer and the governance of knowledge. The social policy implications that arise from the research, particularly the need to translate research findings into meaningful, 'measurable' social policy, are addressed by reflecting on the dilemmas encountered when trying to translate research findings into policy practice. As is argued in the following pages, the task of social policy research is to do more than present research findings and their implications for policy; it is also to provide analysis of and reflection on the pragmatic realities that often underpin our empirical studies.

Setting

Before addressing the dynamics of this research process and their implications for policy and practice, some preliminary background is necessary. All of the young women who play in the New Arrivals soccer team are recently arrived refugees (rather than asylum seekers) who have resettled on humanitarian grounds in a public housing estate known as the Parks. Taking its name from the five suburbs in Adelaide's North-West that comprise the estate, the Parks was constructed by the South Australian Housing Trust between 1945 and 1964 as part of an overall economic development strategy that sought to provide low-cost rental housing for workers and their families that was close to the manufacturing and automotive factories in the area at the time.

As is the case in the UK and elsewhere, public housing estates in Australia have become 'problem places' that are home to 'problem people' (Arthurson and Jacobs, 2004). Economic changes, coupled with shifts in family structures and progressively tighter restrictions governing access to public housing, have 'resulted in tenants who increasingly experience problems of unemployment, low-income and poverty and, in some instances, increasing incidences of crime and violence' (Palmer et al, 2004, p 412). This shift over the past two decades from public housing for families and working tenants to public housing as welfare housing has meant that estates like the Parks now feature among some of the most disadvantaged urban areas in Australia.

As well as providing homes for those marginalised through poverty, unemployment or mental health issues, a significant proportion of public housing in the Parks is given over to accommodating newly arrived refugees, asylum seekers and other displaced persons. Many of the residents, including the young women in the New Arrivals soccer team, come from Somalia and Ethiopia, and more recently from countries such as Afghanistan, the Congo, Liberia and Sudan.[1] As is reported in the wider literature on refugees and asylum seekers, refugees in the Parks also experience racial harassment and violence, vulnerability and fear for their safety (Sales, 2002; Beirens et al, 2007). The broader political discourse of 'queue-jumpers', 'illegals' and indeed 'the war on terror' does not help to promote congenial relationships in the Parks, where incidences of violence and conflict are already quite high.

Such stark social realities have drawn recognition from community development workers and others that there is a need to provide 'diversionary activities' for disenfranchised local residents as a way of diverting them from drugs, crime and other anti-social behaviours (Crabbe, 2000; Morris et al, 2003). For many years, young men have been seen as a vulnerable population group, and have been given opportunities to abseil, bushwalk and rock climb and to experience the adrenaline of risk in ways that do not involve substance abuse or violence between themselves or against the women of their communities.[2] Providing opportunities for refugees and asylum seekers to take part in such activities remains a more difficult challenge. As Beirens et al (2007, p 224) point out:

> research in relation to youth work provision for young refugees is limited (Norton and Cohen, 2002), however the few studies that have been conducted, such as by Rutter (2003) and Macaskill (2002), identified significant gaps in relation to out-of-school provision and youth work.

Research suggests that women and girls from culturally and linguistically diverse backgrounds are less likely to take part in sport than their male counterparts (Cortis et al, 2007), which has led one commentator to conclude that 'the combination of gender and ethnicity has a much greater effect on general participation in some groups than others' (Carroll, 1993, p 59). In spite of this, the young women from the Parks have recognised that they have been left out of this recreational framework, and are now seeking the same opportunities for sport and recreation that are afforded to the menfolk of their communities. It is in this context that the soccer team at the centre of this chapter came to fruition.

Origins of the New Arrivals soccer programme

In 2003, a group of young Muslim, refugee women from the Parks agitated for their community health service to provide opportunities for them to take part in sport. They approached the youth worker from the health service who had been working most closely with them on resettlement issues (language, employment, education) and argued, quite convincingly, that there was a need to provide culturally safe sporting opportunities for women from the Somali and Ethiopian communities now living in the Parks. Soccer was chosen, as it was a sport that many of the girls had expressed a desire to play. They had seen their brothers, cousins and other male relatives playing soccer, both in their country of origin and on resettlement in Australia, and, in a moment reminiscent of *Bend It Like Beckham*, these young women wanted a similar opportunity to take part in team sport.

Following this request, the local health service allocated a community development worker to work closely with the local Somali community (in the first instance) to develop a programme whereby young women could train for and compete in a soccer carnival that is held as part of Refugee Week in Adelaide in each year. The first year of the programme (2003) involved roughly 16 young women from the Parks area, mainly of Somali background, who were aged between 12 and 20 years old. The numbers have grown significantly, and in 2006 there were about 40 young women from various backgrounds who competed at the Refugee Week carnival.

Developing a culturally appropriate soccer programme did, however, raise a number of issues. As is documented elsewhere (Hargreaves, 2000, 2007; Walseth and Fasting, 2003; Strandbrau, 2005; Dagkas and Benn, 2006), the embodied politics of identity that surround Muslim women's participation in sport and physical activity is by no means straightforward. As Hargreaves (2007, p 74) notes, 'the bodies of Muslim women in sport are experienced and mediated through different ideological interpretations of Islam [and] within the particular political arrangements of specific countries'. While there is great heterogeneity and fluidity among Muslim women vis-à-vis their adherence to and interpretation of Islam, their experience of sport and physical activity nonetheless involves a number of decisions and statements about their bodies and selves that are both personal and political at one and the same time.

Those involved with the New Arrivals soccer programme were mindful of the ideological positions and cultural factors that needed to be taken into account when developing the soccer programme and promoting it to the players and their parents. As has been noted elsewhere (Taylor and Toohey, 2002; Taylor, 2003), many Muslim women experience considerable difficulties accessing recreational programmes that meet their religious requirements. Those involved with the New Arrivals soccer programme operated from the premise that it was not so much the sporting activities themselves that were limiting, but the way in which they were organised that frequently precluded Muslim women from taking part. As such, their soccer programme included a female-only training environment and flexible uniform arrangements to accommodate those players who wore the *hijab* or, in some cases, the *khimar* or the *niqab*.

Importantly, a preventative health agenda underpinned the soccer programme. Research suggests that newly arrived families often have limited awareness of mainstream health services and many experience barriers to using them, such as a lack of interpreters and materials in their own languages, or a lack of information about their eligibility to access services (Allotey, 1998; Woodhead, 2002; Murray and Skull, 2005; Correa-Velez and Gifford, 2007). Accordingly, 'health work' often takes place within community sectors. For the young Somali women in the Parks, sport served as a vehicle for the broader health education work that the community development and youth workers were already doing with these young women around sexual health.

The high incidences of unplanned pregnancies and sexually transmitted infections that young Somali women presented to the health service, coupled with the cultural expectation of large families, often commencing below the legal age of consent (17 years in South Australia), prompted a need to provide these women with information about contraception, sexually transmitted infections and other health behaviours that were often difficult for them to discuss with their parents or older siblings. As I note elsewhere (Palmer, 2005a), this health education work also had a ripple effect throughout the Somali community, with information about health services being provided to sisters, aunts, cousins and other female friends and relatives through the young women who were involved in the New Arrivals soccer programme.

Methodology

The data reported in this chapter are part of a broader study examining the barriers to participation in sport that many refugee women face on resettlement in South Australia. This wider project developed out of my initial involvement with the soccer team. In 2004 (the second year of the programme), I was approached by a worker at the community health service whom I knew socially – and who knew I had previously played soccer – to help with coaching the team.

As a social researcher with a long-standing interest in the social meanings of sport, I seized the opportunity to document the progress of these young women as they geared up for the Refugee Week soccer carnival, particularly how they negotiated some of the fine-grained identity politics that were becoming more apparent each time we trained. I conducted ad hoc interviews with the players and took detailed field notes during and after each training session and at the final carnival as well. The girls were aware that I was conducting a piece of research which involved them, and formal ethics approval was obtained from the Department of Human Services, the government department within which the health service was located. Following Goodkind and Deacon (2004, p 724), I was particularly concerned to understand the experience and needs of refugee women as articulated by the women themselves. While extensive research has documented some of the challenges that refugee women face as a result of their resettlement (Manderson et al, 1998; Markovic and Manderson, 2000; Sideris, 2003), the focus has primarily been on adults, and I was keen to explore some of the unique challenges faced by younger women, particularly the ways in which this group of women articulated their social identities as young Muslims now growing up in Australia's fifth largest capital city (see Palmer, 2005b; 2007; forthcoming).

At the end of 2004, this opportunistic research developed into a more systematic piece of action research. The South Australian Office for Recreation and Sport put out a call for research proposals under their 'Move It! Making Communities Active Programme Grant' scheme. Two of the target groups were young women and people from culturally and linguistically diverse backgrounds. In collaboration with the community health service and the South Australian Women's Soccer Association, I secured funding to conduct further research with these young women, as the soccer programme had expanded to include players from an increasingly diverse range of backgrounds. Players from Liberia, Sierre Leonne and Sudan, among other countries, were now involved with the New Arrivals soccer programme, and this brought with it a new set of research questions for critical investigation.

This further research took the shape of an action research project that utilised a number of research methods, including the analysis of secondary data sources, a photo-voice component, interviews with policy makers, local agencies and community development workers in the Parks and other areas, two reflective discussion groups with the soccer team, discussions with the players during training, my field notes of observations during training and competition, and interviews with the parents (three mothers, one father) of participating young women. These were conducted through an interpreter to facilitate discussion from Somali to English and vice versa. All of the interviews were digitally recorded and transcribed verbatim. Each of the interviews lasted approximately 40 minutes, with the exception of the discussion groups, which took about 90 minutes each time. The interview and focus group data were then thematically analysed with the assistance of the NVIVO software package.

Although the players involved in the research were Muslim and refugees, it is important to note that this chapter is more about the politics and the process of social policy research than it is about Muslim refugees. A considerable body of research has explored issues of social exclusion for refugees and asylum seekers (Burden and Hamm, 2000; Zetter et al, 2005; Beirens et al, 2007), and other research on refugee communities more broadly and Muslim women more particularly has examined the barriers to participation in sport and physical activity (Johnson, 2000; Walseth, 2006; Kay, 2007). It is thus not my intention here to duplicate this research or, indeed, to report on the findings of my own research as these are presented elsewhere (Palmer, 2005b; 2007; forthcoming). The concern, instead, is to highlight the politics and processes that underpin a research project that locates a refugee community in a shifting policy context.

Issues for policy and practice

To turn now to some of the issues for policy and practice, it is important to note that the research was also part-funded by the (then) South Australian Department of Human Services. At the time the New Arrivals soccer programme was developed, the health policy agenda in South Australia was one of preventative and primary healthcare, and the soccer programme was regarded as a timely 'upstream' health intervention that could provide social supports, improve the physical fitness of the players involved, and facilitate knowledge of and access to health services in the Parks area. By contrast, the health policy priorities for refugees and asylum seekers, particularly in the first year of settlement, focused instead on assessing psychological and physical health, and the Department of Human Services was keen to bring its refugee health services and programmes in line with its broader population health agenda. While it is a point that will be elaborated shortly, it is worth noting that by the time the research was completed 12 months later the health policy context had shifted to one where managing chronic disease and illness was now the government's strategic priority, rather than primary healthcare. Trying to manage the project in light of this shifting policy agenda brought with it a number of issues for research transfer and the governance of knowledge, and it is to these issues that this chapter now turns its attention.

The evaluation of the New Arrivals young women's soccer programme indicated that it had been a clear success (Palmer, 2005a), and the health service was keen for other agencies and departments to be made aware of the findings and, indeed, the project itself. The Department of Human Services is a large government department that includes population health, mental health, Indigenous health, family and community services and public housing in its portfolio, as well as health service delivery and management. Of central concern here, the department services the public and clinical health needs of a number of vulnerable communities who are disadvantaged by poverty, unemployment, precarious housing tenure and mental health issues, and we were keen to engage policy makers and local service providers from these sectors with the findings of our research in order to increase its transfer into practice. This process undoubtedly had its benefits; however, it also increased the complexity of the research task, and highlighted the issues of research transfer and the governance of knowledge that are of central concern to this chapter.

An integral part of the research design was to engage with policy makers and field practitioners from the beginning so as to encourage ownership of and involvement with the project. An advisory committee, comprised of policy makers and practitioners from the health, sport and recreation sectors, the South Australian Social Inclusion Unit and bilingual workers from the local Somali community, was established to provide input on research design, analysis, implementation and dissemination. When outlining the rationale of the project, its methodology and plans for dissemination, much care was taken to ensure that those members of the committee who were relatively unversed in research were made aware of the often circuitous route between data collection and its subsequent implementation in social policy.

As an applied social researcher, I was obviously keen that my results would be read and then used by policy makers and practitioners; however, I was also aware that this would present various dilemmas. It is at this point that the chapter explicitly engages with the political pragmatics of conducting social research with vulnerable communities and the challenges that this then poses for translating research findings into policy practice.

Policy makers are in a hurry, social researchers take their time ...

From the outset, the project needed to manage the competing tensions of including those 'at the top'; those members of the policy and practice community who were sufficiently important to be able to influence and implement policy as well as the community development workers, agency workers and the young refugee women to whom the project more rightfully belonged. I had hoped that the engagement of these stakeholders through the course of the research would establish what Elliot and Popay (2000) have described as a 'dialogical model' rather than a problem-solving model whereby we could establish a dialogue about the research and its implications for social policy rather than me being seen as a problem solver for particular policy dilemmas.

To do this, the project was designed as a piece of action research in which a research 'problem' was identified by the Somali community and then 'solved' collaboratively over the research cycle, in doing so, joining practitioners and researchers together in a research partnership (Wadsworth, 1997; Baum, 1998). Here, the research problem was threefold: (i) to establish ways in which young Muslim women could take part in sport, (ii) to explore how sport can be used as a vehicle to communicate health education messages and (iii) to identify how young women from newly arrived communities use sport to construct notions of self and identity.

As is common to other action research projects, working through these problems involved great self-reflexivity for the workers, the young women and myself alike. For the workers, this involved rethinking their professional practice, and some of the assumptions they had made about 'culture' and 'difference' (Palmer, 2005a). For the young women, this involved rethinking their identity in, at times, some quite profound ways. The players in the soccer team were repeatedly accommodating multiple cultural identities as young Muslim women growing up in Australia's fifth largest city, and this was at times highly confronting for themselves and their families (Palmer, forthcoming). For me, this served to reinforce the inequities of sport, particularly the barriers to participation for populations who are marginalised for a whole range of reasons, be that age, disability, sexuality, poverty, or, in this case, gender, religion and ethnicity. To return to the aspirational message of

London 2012 that this chapter began with, it is the rhetoric of sport as transformative, democratic and inclusive, where the only barriers to participation are simply an unwillingness to 'have a go', that the New Arrivals soccer programme served to expose.

While the project developed very much from the 'bottom up', and out of the expressed needs of the Somali community, this did not always sit well with the policy makers higher up the organisational hierarchy. In many ways, action research, particularly with young people or vulnerable communities, is quite incompatible with the short, politically dictated timelines that policy makers typically work to, and this presented a considerable challenge for the New Arrivals soccer programme.

The critical need to establish trust with these young women did not appear to be recognised or appreciated by the policy makers who expected their results to be delivered to constraining timelines. This was an ongoing tension that was not easily resolved. All of the young women in the soccer programme had experienced trauma and violence through their displacement and resettlement. They had endured rape, torture and persecution, the loss of family members and other loved ones, as well as periods of time spent in refugee camps prior to settling in Australia. Creating a space where these women could trust, and then seek out help for their own and others' health needs, could not be done overnight.

Building respectful relationships between myself, the community development workers, the young women and their families involved much informal interaction, in addition to the more formalised research strategies of interviews, ethnographic observation and photo-voice. Evenings were spent watching *Australian Idol*, and a camp by the beach and a video screening of *Bend It Like Beckham* were organised for these young women, as the adults involved all felt the need to earn our position of trust in order for this research partnership to work. For the policy makers, however, such informal interaction was seen as 'time-wasting', rather than conducting 'proper' research. As the community development worker dryly observed: 'policy makers are always in a hurry, you lot [social researchers] take your time'. The rather different timescales to which academics and policy makers often work further created an uneasy relationship between me as the researcher and the policy makers who became impatient at what they perceived to be the length of time it takes for qualitative research to produce useful data. The policy makers on the advisory group, in particular, were looking for immediate applications to their current policy dilemmas, and the project could not realistically deliver on this, given its particular methodological approach.

In hindsight, greater explanation of the nature of action research as a methodology and further clarification that the pathway between research and policy implementation is frequently circuitous may have allayed some of these concerns and better managed the expectations of the policy makers with regard to what social research involves. By contrast, the community development and health workers who were involved with the young women both through the soccer programme and the broader health education work welcomed the 'bottom-up' approach to the project as it reinforced their existing choice of strategy for engaging vulnerable and marginal population groups.

While the project adopted an explicitly qualitative methodology of interviews, ethnographic observation and photo-voice to enable the voices, experiences and perspectives of the young women to be heard and valued, this presented a temptation for policy makers to cherry-pick results to suit their own planning needs and agendas.

The project had deliberately engaged a number of methods within a qualitative research paradigm out of recognition that studies employing single methods can rarely explain the complex dynamics that may shape individuals' life circumstances and opportunities, in this case displacement, torture and resettlement, as well as religion, the politics of the body and identity. Thus, the range of data sources and collection techniques utilised in the project provided a rich foundation from which to explore our research questions as well as to triangulate findings and improve confidence in the conclusions reached. It also meant that data collection occurred along different timelines, with some parts necessarily concluding before others in order to feed into the iterative cycle of research we were engaged with.

Despite this, the policy makers were keen to include parts of the research findings into their own strategic planning and development processes, while other data still remained to be collected. My insistence that any presentation of this would provide an incomplete picture of the findings fell largely on deaf ears. While I was able to present preliminary data fairly soon after collection had stopped, it takes time to analyse qualitative data, and this was much to the frustration of the policy makers. However, the workers who sat on the advisory panel and who were engaged with these communities at the sharp end on a daily basis were not so driven by the policy items of the day and were more understanding of the time frames that researchers work to. This is a point to which I will return. However, it is worth noting that although qualitative research often occupies an ambiguous place as a source of evidence for policy (due, in part, to the perception that data are collected without the checks and balances of scientific rigour), in this case, my attempts to maintain rigour through multiple data sources and mixed methods of data collection were regarded by the policy makers as hindering the collection of the very evidence that could, in fact, inform their policy and practice.

A shifting policy agenda

While managing policy makers' expectations of the nature of applied research was one challenge in getting policy from the pitch, a far more pressing challenge emerged at the end of 2005 when the policy environment shifted under foot. This changed the nature, purpose and relevance of the New Arrivals soccer programme. Following a major review and restructure of the South Australian health system (the Menadue Generational Health Review), the policy priorities shifted from preventative healthcare to primary care, with a focus on managing chronic disease. For the community health service at the centre of this chapter, working with individuals to manage chronic conditions such as obesity, diabetes or cardiovascular illness became a significant new focus for the organisation.

This had profound implications for the New Arrivals soccer programme. The new focus of the South Australian health sector on chronic illness meant that those programmes and initiatives that encouraged and modelled healthy choices and behaviours in order to *prevent* the onset of chronic conditions became marginalised, as the health outcomes were regarded as being more difficult to measure. Indeed, the issue of translating research findings into meaningful, 'measurable' social policy became, for the workers from the community health service, a source of growing anxiety as their organisational environment shifted to one that was increasingly evidence based and that emphasised that particular kinds of 'evidence' be included in their evidence base.

While the research had adopted an explicit and deliberate qualitative methodology, and the evaluation of the programme revealed that it had made a difference to the physical and mental health of the young women involved, the community health service, now amalgamated into a larger, overarching primary healthcare service, was under increasing pressure from higher up in the Department of Human Services, now restructured as the Department of Health (with public housing and families and communities removed from its portfolio), to provide *quantitative* evidence that the programme had achieved particular health outcomes.

As the researcher, it was requested of me that more 'rigorous' methods of data collection be used. It was suggested that I may want to administer a survey to these young women, with no regard for issues of cross-cultural translation and equivalency of concepts, with no regard for the pragmatics of sampling and the need to negotiate with community gatekeepers. It was also suggested that I do a skinfold test to measure the young women's body mass index before and after their involvement in the soccer programme. Not withstanding the questionable capacity of such measures to provide quantifiable data, to suggest that I would prod and poke a group of young women who had experienced some of the most horrific invasions of their most intimate selves was nothing short of absurd.

But, it does raise important questions as to what constitutes evidence in this era of evidence-based policy making. Why do the words, voices, experiences and stories at the heart of qualitative research not count as legitimate forms of knowledge? Certainly, there is an epistemological debate here, but there is also a political one as well, and it is to the implications of this for social policy that this chapter now turns.

Implications for social policy

The tensions outlined in this chapter serve to highlight two concerns for those engaged in social policy: research transfer and the governance of knowledge. Implicit in this is also the very notion of 'evidence'. The scenario sketched above, of a request to alter the project's methodology once it had all been completed so that it could quantify the success of the project against revised political priorities, immediately alerts one to the mercurial nature of evidence in social policy, and, indeed, the biases inherent in the kinds of data that constitute evidence. As many commentators have pointed out, qualitative research has been overlooked as a legitimate source of evidence in this era of evidence-based and evidence-informed policy making. As Graham (2005, p 35) notes, '[qualitative] research provides a way of accessing the experiences and perspectives of those targeted by welfare interventions, yet it is routinely excluded from the evidence reviews undertaken to inform these interventions'.

Although 'users' perspectives are increasingly regarded as an essential part of the evidence base of policy' (Graham, 2005, p 22), there still remains an uneasy acceptance of the methods used to gain these perspectives, particularly the time it takes to gather such information through qualitative methods. As the chapter has made clear, this is exacerbated when working with hard-to-reach or vulnerable groups and communities. Given the policy shift in Australia, as in the UK, on placing greater emphasis on public engagement in policy development (Bishop and Davis, 2002; Graham, 2005, p 22), it is curious that a methodology that enables service providers to access lives, values and perspectives remains, in this case, a devalued source of knowledge about an effective intervention that is clearly situated in a broader policy agenda of preventative health.

In the UK, what counts in policy is, as Tony Blair famously uttered, 'what works'. The South Australian government of Mike Rann has modelled itself closely on the Blair government, embracing similar policy imperatives, so it is perhaps not surprising to see resonances of the debates in the UK policy literature about the nature, purpose and value of evidence-based policy making in the Australian policy context as well. In many ways, the value of research is judged against its impact on policy, which is often measured in quantifiable monetary terms. That the costs and benefits of the New Arrivals soccer programme were fine-grained, nuanced and not driven by economic rationalism highlights the uneasy relationship between research and policy that underpins this chapter. Indeed, the assumptive worlds of research and policy do not always align perfectly. For this project, the views of the policy makers were that the research–policy relationship should unfold in a lockstep manner. While this perception of how research moves into policy and practice can be simplistically reduced to 'a problem is identified and then research provides policy options' (Black, 2001 p 275), the pathways between research evidence and policy is rarely linear. It is at the point of research *transfer* that this becomes increasingly circuitous and complex (Lomas, 2000), and it is the messiness of the 'black box' of research transfer that this chapter has shed some light on.

Conclusion

This chapter has sought to explore some of the pathways between social research and social policy in an Australian policy context. By drawing on the practical realities of conducting a piece of action research with a young refugee women's soccer team, the chapter has raised several issues for social policy more broadly. The material presented here addresses something of a gap in social policy research, which tends to report on research findings and their implications for policy rather than on the pragmatic issues and complexities that underpin the research. By focusing on the process and politics of conducting research in a shifting policy context, the chapter has argued for a greater consideration of the research process in our presentation and reporting of social policy research.

The nature of evidence and the questions of researcher and methodological credibility that were raised throughout the project also underscored the governance of knowledge and the privileging of a particular professional and epistemological standpoint. The value that was placed on certain kinds of evidence and the devaluing of particular approaches to data collection posed considerable barriers to getting policy from the pitch, and this may serve as something of a cautionary tale for others engaged in social policy. While it is widely assumed and accepted that evidence can and should influence policy, this chapter has illustrated that while it should, it not always can.

Notes

[1] The South Australian Settlement and Multicultural Affairs Department reports that, at 31 March 2007 (in the 2006/07 financial year), there were 446 'humanitarian arrivals' from Afghanistan, 280 from Sudan, 178 from the Congo and 147 from Liberia.

[2] Much research has documented the positive impacts of recreation programmes for 'at-risk' youth (see Wilson and White, 2001, for a summary), however this has tended to focus on the experiences of men and has duly been critiqued because the experiences of female youth are largely absent from the empirical research.

References

Allotey, P. (1998) 'Travelling with "excess baggage": health problems of refugee women in Western Australia', *Women & Health*, vol 28, no 1, pp 63-81.

Arthurson, K. and Jacobs, K. (2004) 'A critique of the concept of social exclusion and its utility for Australian social housing policy', *Australian Journal of Social Issues*, Special Edition on Social Exclusion and Social Inclusion, vol 39, pp 25-40.

Baum, F. (1998) *The New Public Health: An Australian Perspective*, Oxford: Oxford University Press.

Beirens, H., Hughes, N., Hek, R. and Spicer, N. (2007) 'Preventing social exclusion of refugee and asylum seeking children: building new networks', *Social Policy and Society*, vol 6, no 2, pp 219-30.

Bishop, P. and Davis, G. (2002) 'Community consultation symposium: public participation in policy choices', *Australian Journal of Public Administration*, vol 61, no 1, pp 14-29.

Black, N. (2001) 'Evidence based policy: proceed with care', *British Medical Journal*, vol 323, pp 275-9.

Burden, T. and Hamm, T. (2000) 'Responding to socially excluded groups', in J. Percy-Smith (ed) *Policy Responses to Social Exclusion: Towards Inclusion*, Buckingham: Open University Press, pp 184-200.

Carroll, R. (1993) 'Factors influencing ethnic minority groups' participation in sport', *Physical Education Review*, vol 16, no 1, p 59.

Correa-Velez, I. and Gifford, S. M. (2007) 'The right to be counted: research the health and wellbeing of asylum seekers in Australia', *Critical Public Health*, vol 17, no 3, pp 273-81.

Cortis, N., Sawrikar, P. and Muir, K. (2007) *Participation in Sport and Recreation by Culturally and Linguistically Diverse Women*, Social Policy Research Centre Report 4/07, Sydney: University of New South Wales.

Crabbe, T. (2000) 'A sporting chance: using sport to tackle drug use and crime', *Drugs: Education Prevention & Policy*, vol 7, no 4, pp 381-91.

Dagkas, S. and Benn, T. (2006) 'Young Muslim women's experiences of Islam and physical education in Greece and Britain: a comparative study', *Sport, Education and Society*, vol 11, no 1, pp 21-38.

Elliot, H. and Popay, J. (2000) 'How are policy makers using evidence? Models of research utilisation and local NHS policy making', *Journal of Epidemiology and Community Health*, vol 54, pp 461-8.

Goodkind, J. and Deacon, Z. (2004) 'Methodological issues in conducting research with refugee women: principles for recognising and re-centering the multiply marginalised', *Journal of Community Psychology*, vol 32, no 6, pp 721-39.

Graham, H. (2005) 'Qualitative research and the evidence base of policy: insights from studies of teenage mothers in the UK', *Journal of Social Policy*, vol 35, no 1, pp 21-37.

Hargreaves, J. (2000) 'The Muslim sports heroic', in *Heroines of Sport: The Politics of Difference and Identity*, London: Routledge.

Hargreaves, J. (2007) 'Sport, exercise and the female Muslim body: negotiating Islam, politics and male power', in J. Hargreaves and P. Vertinsky (eds) *Physical Culture, Power and the Body*, London: Routledge.

Johnson, M. (2000) 'Perceptions of barriers to healthy physical activity among Asian communities', *Sport, Education and Society*, vol 5, no 1, pp 51-70.

Kay, T. (2007) 'Daughters of Islam: family influences on Muslim young women's participation in sport', *International Review for the Sociology of Sport*, vol 41, nos 3-4, pp 357-75.

Lomas, J. (2000) 'Connecting research and policy', *Canadian Journal of Policy Research*, vol 1, pp 140-4.

Macaskill, S. (2002) *Starting Again: Young Asylum Seekers' Views on Life in Glasgow*, Glasgow: Save the Children.

Manderson, L., Kelaher, M., Markovic, M. and McManus, K. (1998) 'A woman without a man is a woman at risk: women at risk in Australian humanitarian programmes', *Journal of Refugee Studies*, vol 11, no 3, pp 267-83.

Markovic, M. and Manderson, L. (2000) 'Nowhere is as at home: adjustment strategies of recent immigrant women from the former Yugoslav Republics in southeast Queensland', *Journal of Sociology*, vol 36, no 3, pp 315-28.

Morris, L., Sallybanks, J. and Willis, K. (2003) *Sport, Physical Activity and Antisocial Behaviour in Youth*, Trends & Issues in Criminal Justice No. 249, Canberra: Australian Institute of Criminology.

Murray, S. and Skull, S. (2005) 'Hurdles to health: immigrant and refugee health care in Australia', *Australian Health Review*, vol 29, no 1, pp 25-9.

Norton, R. and Cohen, B. (2002) *Out of Exile: Developing Youth Work with Young Refugees*, Leicester: Youth Work Press.

Palmer, C. (2005a) *Evaluation of the New Arrivals Young Women's Soccer Programme*, Adelaide: Adelaide Central Community Health Service.

Palmer, C. (2005b) 'A world of fine difference: sport and newly arrived young refugee women in Adelaide, South Australia', Paper presented to Department of Gender Studies, University of Otago, Dunedin, New Zealand, September.

Palmer, C. (2007) '"A good Muslim girl": identity, tradition and progress in "the game the world plays"', Paper presented at the 4th World Congress of the International Sociology of Sport Association – Sport in a Global World: Past, Present and Future, 31 July-5 August.

Palmer, C. (forthcoming) 'Soccer and the politics of identity for young refugee women in South Australia', *Soccer and Society*.

Palmer, C., Ziersch, A., Arthurson, K. and Baum, F. (2004) 'Challenging the stigma of public housing: preliminary findings from a qualitative study in South Australia', *Urban Policy & Research*, vol 22, no 4, pp 411-26.

Rutter, J. (2003) *Working with Refugee Children*, York: Joseph Rowntree Foundation.

Sales, R. (2002) 'The deserving and the undeserving? Refugees, asylum seekers and welfare in Britain', *Critical Social Policy*, vol 22, no 3, pp 456-78.

Sideris, T. (2003) 'War, gender and culture: Mozambican women refugees', *Social Science and Medicine*, vol 56, pp 713-24.

Strandbrau, A. (2005) 'Identity, embodied culture and physical exercise: stories from Muslim girls in Oslo with immigrant backgrounds', *Young*, vol 13, no 1, pp 27-45.

Taylor, K. (2003) 'Issues of cultural diversity in women's sport', *Journal of the International Council for Health, Physical Education, Recreation, Sport and Dance*, vol 39, pp 27-33.

Taylor, T. and Toohey, K. (2002) 'Behind the veil: exploring the recreation needs of Muslim women', *Leisure*, vol 26, pp 85-105.

Wadsworth, Y. (1997) *Do It Yourself Social Research*, Melbourne: Victorian Council of Social Research.

Walseth, K. (2006) 'Young Muslim women and sport: the impact of identity work', *Leisure Studies*, vol 25, no 1, pp 75-94.

Walseth, K. and Fasting, K. (2003) 'Islam's view on physical activity and sport', *International Review for the Sociology of Sport*, vol 38, no 1, pp 45-60.

Wilson, B. and White, P. (2001) 'Tolerance rules: identity, resistance and negotiation in an inner city recreation/drop-in centre: an ethnographic study', *Journal of Sport and Social Issues*, vol 25, pp 73-103.

Woodhead, D. (2002) *The Health and Well-Being of Asylum Seekers and Refugees*, London: King's Fund.

Zetter, R., Griffiths, D., Signoa, N. and Mauser, M. (2005) 'Social capital or social exclusion? The impact of asylum seeker dispersal on UK refugee community organisations', *Community Development Journal*, vol 49, no 2, pp 169-81.

TEN

Social citizenship in post-liberal Britain and post-corporatist Germany: curtailed, fragmented, streamlined, but still on the agenda

Ingo Bode

Current institutional change in both liberal and 'conservative' welfare states is a major challenge to the social sciences. Major strands of academic thought have long argued that modernity chimes with the successive emancipation of the individual. In the Anglo-Saxon world, the ground-breaking work of T.H. Marshall (1965), shedding light on the subsequent proliferation of economic, political and social rights along with modernisation, had popularised the idea of *social citizenship*, viewed by many as a key reference for public policies in advanced nation states (Dwyer, 2004, pp 51-76). While the concept was awarded less paradigmatic value elsewhere, it pervaded other welfare regimes as well, including those classified by the comparative literature as 'corporatist' (or 'conservative').

This reading of modernisation is now fraught with serious doubts, however. While social citizenship was always a rationale informing policy agendas rather than empirical reality, the recent transformation of Western welfare regimes suggests that there is no future for the concept as we have known it. Both liberal and conservative welfare regimes have witnessed the spread of market values (Gilbert, 2002, pp 99-135) and a (more or less) radical transformation of basic benefit schemes, through workfare policies, for example (Handler, 2003; Ellison, 2005, pp 77-99). This appears to undercut the post-war promise of guaranteeing each citizen both a protection against material hardship and a right to self-determination in basic areas of human existence. Therefore, as a policy model, social citizenship would appear to be outdated.

At closer inspection, however, things are more complicated than this. While major welfare programmes have been subject to retrenchment, social rights have in some fields of welfare provision continued to be a strong normative reference, or have seen a comeback. Moreover, the cult of the individual, emblematic of late modern society, has strengthened the position of citizens in their encounter with public bureaucracies, at least at ideological level. With an eye on these inconsistencies, this chapter examines institutional change in two major Western European countries – Britain and Germany – commonly deemed to belong to different 'families of welfare'. It starts by reviewing some theoretical reflections on social citizenship and its prospects. It then undertakes a comparative assessment of developments relevant to social citizenship by drawing on the wider literature and a rough review of public debate. After providing a brief sketch of the (now) traditional 'social citizenship settlement' of the post-war era, understood here as enduring until the 1980s, it looks at institutional change in three fields: unemployment protection, retirement provision and healthcare entitlements. It will be argued that, in both countries, entitlements once derived from the idea of social citizenship have been curtailed in many fields but do persist in others, with this producing ever more fragmented landscapes. Approaches to social citizenship, it is contended, now appear streamlined across the two welfare regimes, embracing both a marketisation of citizenship and a selective (re-)emphasis of universalism. Post-liberalism in Britain, embodied by the New Labour era, and post-corporatism in Germany, epitomised by a frozen policy agenda following the recent overhaul of major welfare programmes, represent a hybrid configuration exposing the new settlement to an uncertain future.

Social citizenship: conceptions and visions

Regarding social citizenship, the seminal reference is T. H. Marshall and his book on 'citizenship and social class' (Marshall, 1965). While many have taken issue with his work – criticising it for being too Anglo-Saxon, gender-blind or ignorant about the role of civic participation (see, for example, Mead, 1997; Crouch et al, 2001; Turner, 2001; Lister, 2003) – Marshall's approach to citizenship is widely consonant with the building of the post-war welfare settlement throughout Western Europe (see Rees, 1996). Marshall understood citizenship 'as a status bestowed upon those who are full members of a community' and 'are equal with respect to the rights and duties with which that status is endowed' (Marshall, 1965, p 18). He set out how civil, political and social citizenship emerged as a coherent normative framework, first for smaller sections of the population and then for larger parts of the population, with the three types of citizenship being mutually reinforcing.

Marshall was not very clear about the extent to which social citizenship required fiscal redistribution, minimum welfare provision and collective responsibility. Moreover, writers drawing on his work have sometimes extended the concept beyond what he seemed to imply (Powell, 2002). Leaving these nuances aside, Marshall's concept can be used as a means both to assess the character of entitlements a welfare state grants to its citizens and to grasp changes in the conceptual settings relevant to these entitlements. For this undertaking, a particular interpretation of Marshall's model, suggested by Esping-Andersen (1990) in his seminal book on the foundations of (types of) Western welfare regimes, proves helpful. Drawing on the concept of 'decommodification', Esping-Andersen applied Marshall's approach to the regulation of waged labour. Decommodification, he posited, was achieved to the extent that citizens could 'freely, and without potential loss of job, income or general welfare, opt out of work' (Esping-Andersen, 1990, p 23). The idea of social citizenship in the sense of Marshall is encapsulated in this approach, although not being fully congruent with it (Powell, 2002, p 236).

As an ideal-type, social citizenship addresses a configuration in which individuals belonging to a national community enjoy a number of inalienable rights to social welfare provision in cash and/or in kind. It stands for a set of institutionalised ties between members of a (political) collectivity that are grounded in common rights and duties, with the former being a prerequisite to the fulfilment of the latter. Indeed, according to the classical mainstream interpretation of the concept, individuals can be full and equal members of a (political) community only if basic needs relevant to physical and social reproduction are met. Drawing on this definition, welfare regimes endorse social citizenship to the extent they bestow individuals with entitlements covering such needs irrespective of their economic status, and – since these entitlements are fundamental to be(com)ing a member of the community – regardless of the citizens' propensity to comply with rules set by political majorities.

Social citizenship, then, includes a legally guaranteed access to facilities and commodities that a given society deems indispensable for ensuring social and political participation – that is, welfare provision arguably *beyond* the poverty line. However, the very forms through which this is organised can and do vary. State-provided healthcare services, flat-rate pensions or means-tested income support – all prototypical institutional expressions of social citizenship – are by no means the only conceivable avenues to this end. Rather, entitlements to basic social welfare (and healthcare) provision are often ensured by institutions that, normatively, are *not* built on the concept of social citizenship. This particularly applies to those welfare regimes that the comparative social policy literature classifies as 'corporatist' (see below).

While perfect decommodification remained fiction in all real-types of Western welfare states, the relative latitude ordinary (breadwinning) citizens were enjoying when moving through the labour market was, at least implicitly, felt as a social right in the post-war settlement. Throughout this period, this materialised, inter alia, in unemployment benefits sheltering the social position of jobseekers over a longer period so as to safeguard their status as 'worker-citizen' (Turner, 2001). Further entitlements related to decommodified welfare included unconditional income support, basic pensions, and access to social and healthcare services free of charge. True, at that time, some of these entitlements were conditional on previous labour market participation. Yet waged labour was the norm for the bulk of (male) adults, and social legislation introduced credits benefiting those temporarily out of work. Women's social rights often were *derived* entitlements, causing hardship for those unable, or unwilling, to rely on the achievements of a breadwinning husband. Yet leaving this (significant) bias aside, conditionality of social protection was limited when compared to both early industrialism and the recent 'workfare era'.

Over the last two decades, the normative foundations of both the classical concept of social citizenship and major post-war institutions relying on it have been challenged (see Johansson and Hvinden, 2007). Emphasis has been placed on individual duty, self-responsibility, free choice and self-government – notions all of which do not appear consonant with the collectivistic momentum of the classical approach. Furthermore, critics have tackled the (seemingly) unconditional character of many welfare state rights, assumed to entail passivity, social exclusion and a declining work ethic. Others have argued that citizenship requires democratic participation in the provision of social welfare, widely neglected in the post-war settlement.

Such critics, and related controversy, are encapsulated in a trilogy distinguishing republican, socioliberal and libertarian alternatives to the classical model. Republican citizenship implies 'welfare democracy' (Fitzpatrick, 2002), extending to opportunities of direct involvement in the very process of welfare provision – which is a dimension this chapter will not further engage with. Socioliberal citizenship models link social rights to duties expected to be met by citizens claiming collective social support, with these duties sometimes embracing the active care for others in the community (for example through volunteer work). The libertarian model, likewise appealing to such duties, puts the accent on individual choice and self-responsibility, as opposed to the status of a passive welfare recipient. This model is consistent with the emergence of 'welfare consumerism' (Baldock, 2003) and 'welfare markets' (Bode, 2008). For the advocates of this model, the main challenge is empowering welfare recipients to operate as 'citizen-consumers' (Clarke et al, 2007) who, being aware of their individual needs and preferences, make conscious choices between welfare providers and agree personalised contracts with them. This libertarian reading is crucial for current developments around social citizenship, and the remainder of this chapter will pay particular attention to it.

Real worlds of social citizenship

This section inspects core characteristics of the British and German welfare state with an eye on the role of social citizenship past and present. It sketches recent institutional change in the three fields mentioned at the outset: unemployment protection, retirement provision and healthcare entitlements.

Britain: basic social citizenship and its fate

In some ways, social citizenship is a British concept – not only because of the intellectual heritage of Marshall, but also in the light of the UK post-war welfare settlement. The Beveridgean approach to social welfare provision was predicated on the idea that welfare services and benefits should be granted universally. It is clear that this universalism was to be set at ground level only. Hence one is dealing here with *basic* social citizenship. The very idea of state-guaranteed rights, irrespective of the social and economic status of a given person, has common roots with the (inherited) democratic socialist ideal of promoting material equality within society. Yet it has extended beyond this ideological community throughout the post-war era, which saw the implementation of flat-rate basic pensions, universal entitlements to medical as well as (some) social services, and to (means-tested) income support. Britain also experienced the proliferation of 'implicit' entitlements to (enhanced) social citizenship, epitomised by contributory schemes providing earnings-related benefits and helping workers maintain an achieved social status.

True, there has always been debate about the appropriateness of a social-rights-based approach to welfare provision in Britian. Especially in more recent times, many have stressed the necessity of balancing rights *and duties*, thus laying the grounds for 'remoralised social citizenship' (Kemshall, 2002, p 111). This has gone alongside an emphasis placed on equality of opportunity (rather than welfare outcomes) and on social inclusion through mere labour market participation. In this particular sense, basic social citizenship no longer appears as an uncontested core reference of the British social model. Nevertheless, recent social policies have not moved in one sole direction, as can be seen when inspecting the three particular fields of welfare provision mentioned earlier.

The British system of *unemployment benefits* always made income replacement benefits for the jobless conditional on their willingness to take paid employment. However, it was the welfare reforms of the late 1980s and 1990s that brought a new quality to this conditionality (Lister, 2002; Clasen, 2007). As unemployment benefits were dramatically reduced, joblessness lasting more than a couple of months became difficult to manage by those without savings and unwilling to accept an occupation suggested by the job centre. Payments are almost flat-rate and no longer calculated on previous earnings; those with insufficient contribution records are left with a small means-tested 'income-based Jobseeker's Allowance'. It should be noted that low(er) unemployment benefits do not necessarily lead into poverty as income problems may partially be alleviated by family benefits, including children's additions to Income Support and the means-tested Child Tax Credit.

In addition, 'workfare' policies urge large sections of the unemployed to accept any job available or to participate in the 'New Deal' programmes providing placements, training and voluntary work, with the latter being regarded as a moral duty of those excluded from waged labour. British activation policies – intended to make new forms of assistance with jobsearch available so as to overcome barriers to employment – first targeted the young unemployed and were more recently extended to groups deemed to live at a distance from the ordinary labour market, notably lone parents and disabled or otherwise incapacitated benefit recipients. This pressure can result in employment with a poor salary although one should mention that workfare goes alongside various measures to 'make work pay' (the introduction of a national minimum wage; the creation of means-tested Family Credit for low-income working families; a new Working Tax Credit; and various payments designed to facilitate work-focused activities). The fact remains that, compared to the past, the British unemployment protection scheme provides a much lower level of decommodification – the risk of drifting down into the group of the working poor is high, and individual professional projects are hardly respected.

By the same token, public (or publicly regulated) employment services – the Jobcentre Plus agencies – have been reorganised according to a mainstream business model, in order to deal with jobseekers as 'customers' with a *right* to receive appropriate services corresponding to their personal needs (Rosenthal and Peccei, 2006). It is questionable to what extent this right has actually been respected as the overall benefit system eventually undermines a service focus placed on individual job preferences. Conceptually, however, the reorganisation of job services implies a changing relationship between a publicly governed institution and the individual citizen, with the latter being understood as an actor having (more) comprehensive claims against the state.

What about those at the end of their working career? *Pension provision* has been an important issue over the last decade in Britain (Hill, 2007, pp 23-39). By tradition, the British pension system, based on universalistic basic provision and (added) means-tested guarantees, exhibits an anti-poverty, rather than a wage-replacement, orientation. While the post-war settlement saw the rise of a contributory second tier (the State Earnings Related Pension Scheme [SERPS], today the State Second Pension), a fully fledged social insurance scheme never came into existence. Rather, workers were given the option to 'contract out' of National Insurance and to enrol with corporate or – increasingly – personal pension plans. However, the universalistic ethos of the post-war settlement is reflected by a right to minimum retirement provision, amended stepwise since New Labour came to power. Today, for those who do not (fully) qualify for the State Second Pension and/or do not receive the full rate of the basic pension, a means-tested 'Pension Credit' steps in.

As this benefit barely protects against the risk of poverty, and since a rising number of claimants are expected to depend on this benefit in the future, the last few years have seen a growing demand for pension reform. An additional trigger has been problems in the corporate and private pension sector, covering ever fewer citizens, jeopardising accrued assets, and exposing pension entitlements to the vicissitudes of the financial market. Scepticism about personal saving plans has been widespread, due to saving plan bankruptcies, misselling practices and what has been referred to as personal plan cost disease. Given the devaluation of assets following the stock market crisis, many have seen 'vulnerability even among the better off' (Ward, 2004, p 52) and evidence for 'trust in *all* institutional ... provision [being] relatively low' (Taylor-Gooby, 2005, p 223, emphasis added).

As a reaction to all this, the government has taken steps to revamp the system. Relying on suggestions from the so-called Turner Commission, a reform enacted in 2006 instigated an automatic – state-subsidised and employer co-funded – enrolment of workers to (more solid and large-scale) corporate pension schemes. In addition, together with changes to contributory mechanisms (including a reduction in the number of minimum contribution years), public pensions are meant to become indexed to wages again (from 2012 onwards). It is interesting to see that the Conservatives were overall in favour of all this, a consensus symptomatic of how the public attitude on pensions has recently shifted – irrespective of the actually low *level* of the newly created entitlements. Altogether, the reform entails the relative expansion of publicly guaranteed pension entitlements and is indicative of a more universalistic 'pension philosophy'.

Having said this, there is (still) a strong emphasis placed on private pension provision. For many, decent retirement provision nowadays depends, and will depend in the future, on investments in personal saving schemes or defined contribution plans with diversified investment options. New Labour intensified efforts to make citizens 'pension consumers' and to change 'passive welfare subjects into active lifestyle managers' (Mann, 2006, p 80). It was keen to foster 'consumer education' and reliable advice services. More generally, it pushed 'asset-based welfare' policies, fostering the capacity of individuals to save on the capital market (Sodha and Lister, 2006). The citizen was seen here as a consumer with a right to be empowered in that precise role – and with a claim to individual capital building.

A further important area of citizenship-related welfare provision is *healthcare* as it embodies a cornerstone of social citizenship in the British configuration. In the post-war settlement, the primary-care-led and widely state-based National Health Service (NHS) exemplified a 'socialist' approach to welfare provision amid a highly market-liberal society. True, state-controlled healthcare went alongside rather restrictive funding. In principle, however, medical provision was not only seen as a universal right, but also as a field subject to 'consensus' management involving professionals, public sector agents and representatives of the local community. Up to the present, the NHS still operates through central funding via weighted capitation payments based on population health needs, with most resources stemming from general taxation.

User fees – mainly charges for pharmaceutical prescriptions and dental treatment – are of limited importance.

However, the country witnessed attempts to bring market governance into the public system (Allsop and Baggott, 2004). Ancillary services were largely contracted out to commercial suppliers, and, following the reforms of the 1990s, the economic coordination of the entire system became organised through 'internal competition' (between service providers). With quasi-independent (foundation) hospitals and the 'Independent Sector Treatment Centre Programme' offering day surgery and diagnostic procedures, profit-driven actors took centre stage – although they operated on behalf of public authorities and often in a local contract culture favourable to (long-term) gentlemen's agreements. Critics (see Pollock, 2005; Paton, 2006) have nevertheless bemoaned that internal markets may lead to poor quality for many and to new inequalities as the rationality of those working in the system no longer focuses on the patient's needs but on short-term outputs and micro-economic cost-effectiveness; only the better educated, it was argued, were able to counteract 'creaming strategies' of providers under market pressure.

Critics have also taken issue with the increase of private money flowing through the healthcare sector. At the beginning of the 2000s, indeed, £1 out of every £6 spent on medical services came from private sources; one out of ten Britons was enrolled with (additional) private insurance. Moreover, co-payments for pharmaceuticals, dental and ophthalmic services were on the rise (with exemptions for the most disadvantaged groups, however). Concerning user fees for drugs, the patients' dues (measured as prices adjusted for general inflation) went up by more than 300% between the 1970s and today. The NHS also saw a surge in private work and pay beds in public hospitals. However, while this implied a growing minority of citizens sidestepping queues and receiving exclusive medical services, it did not undermine universalism per se. What is more, New Labour doubled spending on the NHS between 1997 and 2005, and there is a pledge to raise investment further in the future, including for 'frontline' healthcare staff. While part of these investments may be eaten up by management costs related to the internal market, there is an overall tendency to buttress the collectivistic framework, to reduce rationing and to enhance services *for all*.

At the same time, however, the political elites emphasise 'self-care and self-regulation' (Kemshall, 2002, p 46) and put the onus on individuals or communities who are expected to adopt an active role in fostering 'healthy behaviour' for themselves and among peers or families.

Governments have also committed themselves to widening personal choice in healthcare provision; this may (further) strengthen the role of private providers. As with job services and retirement provision, the policy discourse stresses consumer rights to choice and exit (McDonald, 2006; Newman and Kuhlmann, 2007). While the patient's discretion in selecting NHS providers has hitherto remained limited, this strategy proves an ideological sea change amid a far and wide collectivistic system of healthcare provision.

Germany: corporatist social citizenship and its transformation

In Germany, the *notion* of social citizenship has always been a non-issue concerning both the institutional architecture of the welfare state and the public debate referring to it. While citizenship issues have recently raised some attention with respect to the integration of immigrants and minority ethnic groups, the concept of *social* citizenship is not part of what might be termed the official 'welfare culture' of this country. This holds true although suggestions to introduce an unconditional 'minimum income' have from time to time appeared in the public and academic sphere, including more recently when leading academics published a manifesto pleading for new steps in this direction (Grözinger et al, 2006). This has found but a limited echo, however. Rather, Germany has seen major social policies running *against* the very idea of a 'basic income', as will be illustrated below.

Overall, the German welfare state is (still) heavily infused with the Bismarckian legacy. This social policy tradition neatly links welfare (and healthcare) entitlements to the status of a salaried employee. Compared with Britain, these entitlements are altogether quite generous, in particular regarding unemployment benefits (over the first year) and public retirement provision (for current pensioners), whereas citizens falling outside these categories – inactive women, the self-employed, the long-term unemployed, disabled people – appear much worse off. Guaranteed flat-rate entitlements, emblematic of a universalistic welfare regime, are alien to this regime. While this is not the place to portray the entire German welfare system (for an overview, see Bleses and Seeleib-Kaiser, 2004; Clasen, 2005), a quick foray into its architecture shows that it does contain elements which de facto draw on the rationale of social citizenship. This *corporatist* social citizenship embraces minimum pensions, quasi-universal entitlements to medical and social services and a right to (means-tested) income support. Moreover, the broad coverage of social insurance involves significant *implicit* universal guarantees.

However, recent institutional change brought tremendous reorganisation, as becomes plain when inspecting the three fields looked at for the case of Britain above. Concerning *unemployment benefits*, the so-called Hartz reforms entailed a complete overhaul of a long-established – widely corporatist – protection scheme (see Seeleib-Kaiser and Fleckenstein, 2007). The old system had granted lifelong (if degressive) benefits to the large majority of those (male) citizens with some years of work experience, mostly beyond the poverty line. The Hartz reforms reduced income-related unemployment benefits to a maximum length of 12 months (18 months for those over the age of 55) and shifted long-term jobseekers onto a flat-rate allowance labelled 'Unemployment Benefit II' (roughly £260 per month for a single adult plus housing allowance). The former social assistance scheme was reserved to those unable to work more than three hours a day. The reforms also changed the definition of what was considered an acceptable occupation for those receiving 'Unemployment Benefit II'. These jobseekers must now accept any occupation available in surrounding areas, provided that the wage it provides does not fall below 70% of the local average salary (in a given industry). Different from previous regulations, formal skills or conditions of positions held prior to unemployment are considered irrelevant. Moreover, jobseekers can be compelled to take a so-called One-Euro-Job offered by public or non-profit employers on a fixed-term basis (six to nine months) and paid at one Euro (75p) per hour on top of Unemployment Benefit II. Like with Britain's New Deal, this activity is, to some extent at least, defined as a moral duty of those on income support.

Advocates of the reforms, including the social democrats, argued that the overhaul would prove beneficial to recipients of the (former) income support in that it offered the latter new gateways to job placement services. An improved treatment of jobseekers by the job service agencies was indeed a cornerstone of the Hartz reforms. Similarly to what happened to the job centre services in Britain, the German Labour Offices are now urged to deliver personally tailored services, with the unemployed being addressed as 'customers'. The new approach emphasises the right to individual service provision, rather than the status of a 'mass client' under administration of welfare bureaucracy. Somehow paradoxically, this goes alongside a substantial narrowing of the individual scope for self-determination concerning where to work, and under which conditions.

Regarding *pensions*, Germany has seen similar paradigmatic change (Schmähl, 2007). Until recently, the country's 'pension philosophy' was geared to pay-as-you-go and earnings-related retirement provision, often referred to as an emblematic expression of corporatist welfare. Wide-ranging defined benefit schemes, ensuring wage replacement rates heading 70% of gross average earnings, had been developed with the aim of guaranteeing workers the standard of living they enjoyed prior to retirement, rather than just avoiding poverty during old age. Social insurance coverage had successively been extended to further stages of the individual life course, including periods of education and family care, thus generating ever more 'implicit' entitlements to social citizenship. The system proved less generous for (the small number of) self-employed workers with modest incomes and, more importantly, for citizens with a longer career break or in temporary and part-time employment – although bad earning years had long been upgraded in the calculation formula. Importantly, while the breadwinner-based model embraced derived pension rights for married partners, numerous women with a limited employment record had to rely on (rather low) means-tested income support. Until the end of the 20th century, however, the number of citizens affected by this had markedly decreased.

Private and occupational retirement provision long played a marginal role, with less than a tenth of pension benefits stemming from this source at the turn of the millennium. Yet this is about to change. Pension reforms enacted between 2001 and 2005, endorsed by major factions of the political establishment, reduced the (future) standard wage replacement rate substantially. For those aged 40 or below at present, it will achieve little more than 55% of real wages at the age of retirement. This applies to the standard pensioner, that is, an employee with a full career and without work interruptions due to unemployment or care obligations – a condition which, however, cannot be taken for granted in contemporary Germany, given that unemployment among senior citizens is fairly high. A further element of the reforms was a cutback of work incapacity benefits. As a result, many claimants of the latter will be left with income below the poverty line, unless they benefit from additional private protection.

By the same token, reforms introduced funded pension plans under public regulation, creating a fully fledged welfare market in old-age provision (Bode, 2008, pp 37-40, 60-9). Holders of personal saving accounts receive direct flat-rate subsidies to complete their own contributions, with public support heading 30% of the capital saved over the first years. For those whose earnings exceed a certain threshold, generous tax breaks step in. Subsidies or tax exemptions are also awarded to workers enrolling with funded corporate schemes. Employers now are obliged to offer respective opportunities, with one of these being the so-called salary sacrifice option through which workers (and their employers) are exempt from social insurance charges otherwise due on the earnings (or sponsoring) converted into plan contributions. As to regulation, pension plans must protect the nominal value of the invested capital; (most) suppliers have to reinsure themselves against insolvency. Furthermore, the schemes must guarantee a minimum rate of interest (in 2008: 2.25%); however, there is an option to put money into investment funds that do not offer this guarantee but attract an increasing number of savers through high-return-on-investment promises. The overall development is paradoxical: while public regulation is infused with universalistic norms, not least as it deliberately attempts to empower low-income savers, the eventual level of pension provision is left to individual thrift and to the volatility of financial markets.

The political elite defended this reform, inter alia, by contending that it enabled citizens to find individually tailored solutions to their distinctive personal situation, given the advent of novel life course models and dispersed patterns of labour market participation. Women were viewed as being advantaged by options to build their own pension account in absence of a (comfortable) contribution record with social insurance. The emphasis was on the right to manage one's retirement provision independently and to capture personal opportunities as offered by the (financial) market. At the same time, minimum pensions were solidified by measures separating them from social assistance (income support) schemes in organisational terms. Following a long period of decline, take-up is now markedly rising (by more than 50% between 2003 and 2006). As a tendency, then, there are, as in Britain, universalistic pensions for the poor and a mixed (partially marketised) pension package for the rest of the working population.

German *healthcare insurance* is widely considered as a further core pillar of the Bismarckian welfare regime, even though it adopted a universalistic character over the post-war decades. Throughout the last century, funding became widely socialised whereas service supply was left to independent providers remunerated by a multi-payer system, (today) composed of approximately 250 non-profit sickness funds operating within a legal framework. Beyond payroll contributions, the sickness funds receive a small earmarked injection of levies on tobacco consumption. As for differences between the risk structures of their enrollees, a redistributive compensation scheme applies, which smoothes out up to 90% of the monetary impact of these differences. The overall funding regime conforms to the principle of social fairness

(*Solidarprinzip*), which always proved – and still proves – fundamental to the German healthcare system. However, this system is outstanding internationally in that private insurance companies are admitted to offer full coverage – yet only to citizens whose earnings exceed a certain ceiling (Thomson and Mossialos, 2006). This opting-out opportunity provides a minority (around 10%) of the German population with better, and often cheaper, access to medical care.

Furthermore, the system exhibits a particular version of the internal market (Bode, 2006). Sickness funds compete for enrollees, with contribution rates varying between 12% and 14% of the employees' salary. These rates partially depend on the risk structure of the enrollees of a given fund, with funds covering low-income households charging higher rates. The latest healthcare reform stipulates that contribution rates will be harmonised throughout the system; however, sickness funds can levy additional *flat-rate* contributions from their enrollees should they run into deficits. In addition, they have been given some leeway to grant discounts to enrollees participating in programmes providing special treatments – run for some years now (see Busse, 2004) – and to patients accepting a general practitioner (GP) as a permanent gatekeeper (usually, Germans can freely choose their GP). Sickness funds have also been authorised to award a bonus to those who do not get services reimbursed over a given period, like in the private insurance sector. In addition, whereas fee-for-service arrangements and block grants were long typical of the payment system, sickness funds may now enter into contracts with suppliers of drugs, medical devices, therapeutic aids and integrated care individually. There is, then, a propensity to differentiate the range and the properties of services available to the enrollees of the various sickness funds – a tendency consistent with the advent of a new 'consumer agenda' in the overall healthcare system (Newman and Kuhlmann, 2007).

Concerning those covered by social insurance, out-of-pocket payments have markedly risen over the last 20 years, although there are individual caps on these. In 2005, co-payments amounted to 13% of total expenses, up from 9.5% in 1995. Patients have to dispense up to £7 per medical prescription and per medical consultation (concerning the latter, once a quarter-year). Moreover, the daily 'hotel fee' for hospital treatment was augmented repeatedly; glasses, transport to outpatient treatment and over-the-counter pharmaceuticals were delisted. All this entails a rising burden on households with modest earnings. However, the latest healthcare reform also made enrolment with healthcare insurance mandatory, after the last few years had seen a rapidly growing number of uncovered (self-employed) citizens. Private insurers were compelled to accept any claimant within the confines of a basic service package. In this particular respect, a further step towards universalisation was taken.

Conclusion

This chapter has argued that the idea of social citizenship was, if incompletely, enshrined in both the liberal (British) and the corporatist (German) welfare regime during the post-war settlement. This operated in different ways, with Germany providing a number of quasi-universal benefits within a framework reserving the most generous outputs to highly skilled workers and Britain ensuring universal healthcare and a basic level of welfare provision, topped up with (modest) social insurance. As both regimes awarded guaranteed entitlements to a large majority of the (waged) population, accounts contending that in liberal welfare regimes, social rights address just the poor, whereas in corporatist regimes they are reserved to workers, warrant qualification.

More recently, however, these entitlements have been subject to *curtailment* in both countries. In particular, unemployment benefits have been reduced markedly, with an increasing risk of poverty among those outside of the (standard) workforce. In particular, decent guarantees for those long-term unemployed citizens with a reasonable employment record are no longer on offer. It is *basic* social citizenship that is called into question here. A similar development has taken place in retirement provision. True, public pensions always proved more generous in Germany than in Britain, yet, in both countries, defined benefit pensions were inherent to the 'ordinary' life course of (breadwinning) workers. Nowadays, in both nations, the achievement of a decent retirement income depends, or will depend, to a much greater extent than before, on a citizen's position in the labour market, on personal thrift and on developments in the financial industry.

In the same vein, institutional change in both countries is driven by a *new philosophy* associating citizenship with a personal right to tailored services, to accumulation of capital and to provider choice. The cult of the individual and the consumerist mentality entrenched in the mainstream economy sphere have spilled over to the field of social welfare and healthcare provision. Both cuts in classical social entitlements and the proliferation of welfare consumerism chime with the libertarian model of (social) citizenship as outlined in the first section of this chapter. This *transnational* movement towards marketisation implies that Germany, after downsizing its corporatist programmes markedly, is approaching the British model. Given this 'policy convergence' (Turner and Green, 2007), there is *streamlining* across welfare regime types, with the *marketisation of citizenship* as a key tendency.

The 'old' model is still on the agenda, however. Indeed, a *selective re-emphasis* on collectivistic welfare provision can be observed across both welfare regimes. Healthcare policies, although overall augmenting the financial burden left to the sick, have not erased the foundations of the social-citizenship rationale inherent in the post-war settlement. To some extent, this rationale has even been fortified, with universal coverage being completed in Germany and public investments in the universal healthcare sector having substantially grown in Britain. The same holds true for retirement provision. While Germany adopts a market approach here, its collectivistic tradition is mirrored by public regulation at a level unknown to the liberal world(s) of welfare. As regards Britain, the recent turn in its pension policies symbolises, if timidly, a revitalisation of the social-citizenship approach to pension provision. In this country, furthermore, workfare policies have recently been accompanied by massive statutory transfers to disadvantaged sections of the population and by enormous investments in public service provision, not least in favour of poor children.

From this perspective, Britain has moved into a *post-liberal* configuration. This holds true in a further sense as well. Indeed, the new configuration is post-liberal also in the sense that, somehow paradoxically, a state traditionally reluctant to interfere with private affairs is adopting an *interventionist role* in steering the behaviour of its citizens – a policy orientation less alien to the German tradition. It is noteworthy here that pressures on welfare beneficiaries go alongside a moral nexus being established between entitlements and duties (which is a key element of the social-liberal citizenship model) even though the respective discourse proves stronger than the policies actually implemented as, after all, there is still no relevant compensation for taking care of the community through volunteer work (as a means to meeting one's civic duties). The German configuration can be termed *post-corporatist* not only because it exhibits similar tendencies, but also in the light of the frozen status quo materialising subsequent to attempts to break with major social policy traditions (via the pension and the Hartz reforms). At present, the country sees an uneasy compromise between paradigmatic change and pragmatic conservatism, sustained by the 'grand coalition' government in office since 2005. Healthcare provision is emblematic in this respect, as, on the one hand, further initiatives towards deregulation have been taken, whereas, on the other hand, the long-standing trend towards general coverage has been completed within an overall untouched insurance regime. The outcome is 'neo-Bismarckian' regulation with more universalism and more marketisation at the same time (Hassenteufel and Palier, 2007).

Against this background, social citizenship is exposed to two movements of fragmentation. There is *conceptual fragmentation* in so far as universal rights are referred to in healthcare and, albeit more inconsistently, in retirement provision, while they are subject to a 'commodification of welfare' (Kemshall, 2002, p 25) when it comes to labour market participation and to supply-side regulations (provider selection). Marketisation is undeniable but there (still) is basic 'universalism' in the more reproductive spheres of the welfare regime(s) – an observation at odds with verdicts saying that *everything* is nowadays exposed to capitalistic domination (see, for example, Paton, 2006).

By the same token, both welfare regimes exhibit *procedural fragmentation* as the recourse to (quasi-)market governance (via regulated commercial provision; internal markets) tends to generate uneven outcomes in terms of coverage and quality, notwithstanding the new (discourse on) rights to 'consumer empowerment'. Indeed, (quasi-)market governance in healthcare provision, if fully applied, operates through 'creaming' (profitable cases), responsibility shifting and, regarding the situation of providers, capacity-building: windfall profits on the one hand versus performance-constraining sanctions on the other. This sits uncomfortably with the discourse of those who insinuate that (quasi-)market governance does not affect social citizenship (see, for example, Le Grand, 2003).

Overall, this twofold fragmentation generates a *hybrid configuration*, which leaves room for both a (selective) actualisation of the social citizenship agenda, at some point or in a given constellation, and further (embedded) marketisation yielding, again, both new opportunities and new constraints. *But why all these changes?* In so short a space, it is impossible to provide compelling explanations for the complex developments depicted thus far. Prominent accounts appear widely unconvincing. Take the narrative according to which *new risks* are proliferating in contemporary Western society, eroding the sociostructural underpinnings of the more collectivistic post-war settlement and entailing fundamentally new approaches to social welfare provision. True, there are changes in social stratification, yet basic cornerstones of the modern life course as established throughout the 20th century do persist both empirically and culturally for a large majority of the population. Especially, employment insecurity is a limited phenomenon (Fevre, 2007), with precarious work trajectories being confined to smaller sections of the workforce (unless part-time employment is classified as precarious in principle). Moreover, these have little to do with the aforementioned choice agenda as they mostly do *not* correspond to individual preferences. As regards new family models, widely seen as conducive to the emergence of new social risks, similar qualifications apply (Naumann, 2007). While the late modern life course, due to the increasing break-up rates of partnerships, may be more turbulent than in former times, the key empirical phenomenon deemed to embody a new risk, that is mothers engaging with salaried work and forced into complex care arrangements, is anything but new historically and cannot be understood as a trigger of the afore-sketched institutional change. Why should a phenomenon that, during the 1960s and 1970s, took shape alongside the *invigoration* of social citizenship be cause for its demise 20 or 30 years later?

Other sociocultural and economic explanations may be more compelling. Concerning welfare culture, it is obvious that new patterns of sense-making have pervaded the political establishment (especially the social democrats) over the last 10 years or so (Seeleib-Kaiser and Fleckstein, 2007). Yet where do these patterns originate? Two points can be made here. First, the tendency towards libertarian citizenship, materialising in both enhanced options to select protection schemes or welfare providers and pressures to ensure universal 'reproductive' welfare provision, is consonant with the prevailing ideology of the (well-educated) new middle classes, coming to dominate contemporary civil society at the same time as more collectivistic forces (especially trades unions) are losing ground. The value-set of this (growing) minority embraces both an appetite for greater individual choice and a universalistic emphasis on *basic* human rights.

Second, the political economy of the current settlement should not be left out of the picture either. Throughout the past decades, market-oriented welfare reform has been paralleled by shifts in the distribution of wealth across social groupings. Overall, the choice agenda has left sick or poorly educated citizens with a higher burden or with losses in well-being (regarding insurance-based income protection, for instance). Labour market policies have diminished the relative wage level of those with limited 'employability'. Pension reforms have laid the onus of coping with demographic change on workers, as capital owners and employers managed to have their levies reduced. All this has (further) boosted the share of capital income in the Gross Domestic Product (GDP). Many have seen this as inevitable, given the (alleged) pressures from globalisation. Regardless of whether this holds true or not, economic elites are left with greater societal power, which has contained the space for redistributive policies almost everywhere in the Western world. While this phenomenon may have complex reasons, it is widely compatible with the libertarian citizenship model and the worldview defended by its proponents. It is time to take these 'hard facts' more into account when the discussion turns to why 'old' ideas on social citizenship are no longer in good currency.

References

Allsop, J. and Baggott, R. (2004) 'The NHS in England: from modernization to marketization?', in N. Ellison, L. Bauld and M. Powell (eds) *Social Policy Review, 16: Analysis and Debate in Social Policy*, Bristol: The Policy Press, pp 29-44.

Baldock, J. (2003) 'On being a welfare consumer in a consuming society', *Social Policy and Society*, vol 2, no 1, pp 65-71.

Bleses, P. and Seeleib-Kaiser, M. (2004) *The Dual Transformation of the German Welfare State*, Basingstoke: Palgrave Macmillan.

Bode, I. (2006) 'Fair funding and competitive governance: the German model of health care organisation under debate', *Revue Française des Affaires Sociales* (English edition), vol 60, no 2-3, pp 191-216.

Bode, I. (2008) *The Culture of Welfare Markets: The International Recasting of Care and Pension Systems*, New York/London: Routledge.

Busse, R. (2004) 'Disease management programs in Germany's statutory health insurance system', *Health Affairs*, vol 23, no 3, pp 56-67.

Clasen, J. (2005) *Reforming European Welfare States: Germany and the United Kingdom Compared*, Oxford: Oxford University Press.

Clasen, J. (2007) *Distribution of Responsibility for Social Security and Labour Market Policy – Country Report: The United Kingdom*, AIAS Working Paper 07-50, Amsterdam: Amsterdam Institute for Advanced Labour Studies.

Clarke, J., Newman, J., Smith, N., Vidler, E. and Westmarland, L. (2007) *Creating Citizen-Consumers: Changing Publics and Changing Public Services*, London: Sage Publications.

Crouch, C., Eder, K. and Tambini, D. (eds) (2001) *Citizenship, Markets and the State*, Oxford: Oxford University Press.

Dwyer, P. (2004) *Understanding Social Citizenship: Themes and Perspectives for Policy and Practice*, Bristol: The Policy Press.

Ellison, N. (2005) *The Transformation of Welfare States*, London: Routledge.

Esping-Andersen, G. (1990) *Three Worlds of Welfare Capitalism*, Cambridge: Polity.

Fevre, R. (2007) 'Employment insecurity and social theory: the power of nightmares', *Work, Employment and Society*, vol 21, no 3, pp 517-35.

Fitzpatrick, T. (2002) 'In search of welfare democracy', *Social Policy and Society*, vol 1, no 1, pp 1-20.

Gilbert, N. (2002) *Transformation of the Welfare State: The Silent Surrender of Public Responsibility*, Oxford: Oxford University Press.

Grözinger, G., Maschke, M. and Offe, C. (2006) *Die Teilhabegesellschaft: Modell eines neuen Wohlfahrtsstaats*, Frankfurt/Main: Campus.

Handler, J. F. (2003) 'Social citizenship and workfare in the US and Western Europe: from status to contract', *Journal of European Social Policy*, vol 13, no 3, pp 229-43.

Hassenteufel, P. and Palier, B. (2007) 'Towards Neo-Bismarckian health care states? Comparing health insurance reforms in Bismarckian welfare systems', *Social Policy and Administration*, vol 41, no 6, pp 574–96.

Hill, M. (2007) *Pensions*, Bristol: The Policy Press.

Johansson, H. and Hvinden, B. (2007) 'Opening citizenship: why do we need a new understanding of social citizenship?', in H. Johansson, and B. Hvinden (eds) *Citizenship in Nordic Welfare States: Dynamics of Choice, Duties and Participation in a Changing Europe*, London/New York: Routledge, pp 3-17.

Kemshall, H. (2002) *Risk, Social Policy and Welfare*, Buckingham: Open University Press.

Kuhlmann, E. and Newman, J. (2007) 'Consumers enter the political stage? The modernization of health care in Britain and Germany', *European Journal of Social Policy*, vol 17, no 2, pp 99-111.

Le Grand, J. (2003) *Motivation, Agency, and Public Policy: Of Knights and Knaves, Pawns and Queens*, Oxford: Oxford University Press.

Lister, R. (2002) 'Towards a new welfare settlement?', in C. Hay (ed) *British Politics Today*, Cambridge: Polity, pp 127-57.

Lister, R. (2003) *Citizenship: Feminist Perspectives* (2nd edition), Basingstoke: Palgrave Macmillan.

McDonald, R. (2006) 'Creating a patient-led NHS: empowering "consumers" or shrinking the state?', in L. Bauld, K. Clarke and T. Maltby (eds) *Social Policy Review 18*, Bristol: The Policy Press, pp 33-48.

Mann, K. (2006) 'Three steps to heaven? Tensions in the management of welfare: retirement pensions and active consumers', *Journal of Social Policy*, vol 35, no 1, pp 77-96.

Marshall, T. H. (1965) 'Citizenship and social class' (first published 1950), in T.H. Marshall, *Class, Citizenship, and Social Development*, New York: Anchor Books.

Mead, L.M. (1997) *The New Paternalism*, Washington, DC: Brookings Institution Press.

Naumann, I. (2007) 'From the "women's question" to "new social risks": one hundred years of social policy discourse on the reconciliation of motherhood and work', Paper presented at the 5th ESPAnet Conference, Vienna, 20-22 September.

Newman, J. and Kuhlmann, E. (2007) 'Consumers enter the political stage? The modernization of health care in Britain and Germany', *Journal of European Social Policy*, vol 17, no 2, pp 99-111.

Paton, C. (2006) *New Labour's State of Health: Political Economy, Public Policy and the NHS*, Aldershot: Ashgate.

Pollock, A. (2005) *NHS plc: The Privatization of Our Health Care*, London: Verso.

Powell, M. (2002) 'The hidden history of social citizenship', *Citizenship Studies*, vol 6, no 3, pp 229-44.

Rees, A.M. (1996) 'T.H. Marshall and the progress of citizenship', in A.M. Rees and M. Bulmer (eds) *Citizenship Today: The Contemporary Relevance of T.H. Marshall*, London: UCL Press, pp 1-23.

Rosenthal, P. and Peccei, R. (2006) 'Consuming work: front-line workers and their customers in Jobcentre Plus', *International Journal of Public Sector Management*, vol 19, no 7, pp 659-72.

Schmähl, W. (2007) 'Dismantling an earnings-related social pension scheme: Germany's new pension policies', *Journal of Social Policy*, vol 36, no 2, pp 319-40.

Seeleib-Kaiser, M. and Fleckenstein, T. (2007) 'Discourse, learning and welfare state change: the case of German labour market reforms', *Social Policy and Administration*, vol 41, no 5, pp 427-48.

Sodha, S. and Lister, R. (2006) *The Saving Gateway: From Principles to Practice*, London: Institute for Public Policy Research.

Taylor-Gooby, P. (2005) 'Uncertainty, trust and pensions: the case of the current UK reforms', *Social Policy and Administration*, vol 39, no 3, pp 217-32.

Thomson, S. and Mossialos, E. (2006) 'Choice of public and private health insurance: learning from the experience of Germany and the Netherlands, *Journal of European Social Policy*, vol 16, no 4, pp 315-27.

Turner, B. S. (2001) 'The erosion of citizenship', *British Journal of Sociology*, vol 52, no 2, pp 189-209.

Turner, E. and Green, S. (2007) 'Understanding policy convergence in Britain and Germany', *German Politics*, vol 16, no 1, pp 1-21.

Ward, S. (2004) 'Are the UK's pension objectives attainable?', in G. Hughes and J. Stewart (eds) *Reforming Pensions in Europe: Evolution of Pension Financing and Sources of Retirement Income*, Cheltenham: Edward Elgar, pp 39-54.

Part Three
Engendering policy and politics

ELEVEN

Gender and New Labour: after the male breadwinner model?

Gillian Pascall

Introduction

New Labour's accession marked a shift in government assumptions about gender. Under earlier Labour governments, education and health legislation had given crucial citizenship rights to women and men equally (which women seized in order to participate fully as citizens) while the 1970s brought equal opportunities and sex discrimination legislation. These brought women into employment and public life, but the male breadwinner model of the family lingered through aspects of Thatcher and Major government policy until 1997 – women might join the labour market, become Members of Parliament (MPs) and ministers, but they should not expect government support in challenging gender relations at home, or through any national system of childcare. New Labour had new ideas about gender, with a more liberal attitude to varied family forms, a strong expectation that women's responsibilities lay in employment as well as parenting, that they should be expected to support themselves and their children and pay for their own pensions. New Labour has acknowledged the extent of change in families, and the need for women to sustain more independent employment and incomes. It developed a work–life balance agenda for economic reasons, to avoid social exclusion and support families, although rarely for gender equality (Lewis and Campbell, 2007a, 2007b).

How strongly has New Labour supported gender equality? If the male breadwinner model was an interrelated system of employment, care, time, income and power, how far in practice have women been enabled to support themselves and their children through equality in employment and working time, with social support for care and gender equality in care? How does gender equality in the UK measure against

Sweden, where gender equality has been a passion, and supports for dual-earner families have been long-standing? I argue that policy for women's *employment* has not been matched by policies in other areas. *Care* has been a second priority, with Sure Start, Childcare Tax Credits and rights for preschool children, but there is a long way to go before we could describe a 'universal service'. Gender inequality in *time* is crucial: on average, women are now only half of a one-and-a-half-breadwinner model. Policies for flexible working are aimed mainly at mothers, but policies for more equal time are nowhere on the agenda. And *income*? The tax credit system recognises lone mothers' needs to earn and to care for children, bringing rights as part-timers, rather than being treated either as mothers or as workers. But important change for lone mothers is balanced by potentially negative impact among partnered mothers. Women's incomes are still not equivalent to men's and few can earn themselves equality in income or pensions. New Labour has also been limited by its liberal, free-market stance. A commitment in principle to universal childcare services has not brought real public spending on the Scandinavian, or even Central European models. There are reasons to turn to social democracy, and unembarrassed public spending on childcare, as the underpinning for more complete equality of citizenship in the UK.

Models of gender in social policy

How far have New Labour governments moved from the gender assumptions of the 'male breadwinner model' towards gender equality? The UK was described as a male breadwinner model in Jane Lewis's path-breaking comparative account in 1992, with policies rooted in post-war ideas of gender difference, in contrast to a modified version in France, and a dual-earner model developing in Sweden (Lewis, 1992, 2001). Changes in families have been accompanied by quite radical changes in assumptions underpinning policy, with New Labour committed from 1997 to enhancing women's – especially mothers' – access to employment. At the millennium, women's lifetime earnings have been measured at half men's (Rake, 2000). But being the half in a one-and-a-half-earner partnership exposes women to great risks. The need for independent earning is growing, as decreasing marriage and increasing divorce mean that women are losing security through male breadwinners: the proportion of non-employed individuals who have a partner in work decreased continuously from 76% in 1974 to 40% in

1994 and has remained at that level (Berthoud and Blekesaune, 2006, p 21).

The characterisation of gender regimes based on the male breadwinner/dual-earner spectrum (Lewis, 1992) puts gender at the centre of comparative analysis and is a starting point here. Gender regimes are understood as systems of gender equality or inequality through which: paid work is connected to unpaid; state services and benefits are delivered to individuals or households; costs are allocated and time is shared between men and women in households and between households and employment. The decline of the male breadwinner model has implications for all these (Lewis, 2001). But changing gender assumptions in government and society have neither brought changing practice in all these domains, nor mean that gender equality has been prioritised. New Labour gender policies are analysed here in component parts of the male breadwinner/dual-earner system: paid work, care work, time, income and power, asking to what extent policies and practices can be seen as systems of gender equality or of traditional gender roles in each part.

We should also ask about the level and nature of policy intervention. The *Three Worlds of Welfare Capitalism* (Esping-Andersen, 1990) are relevant to gender, because social democratic countries have had gender equality as well as social equality at their heart (Ellingsaeter and Leira, 2006). Social democratic regimes have also underpinned gender equality with social policies, social spending and social commitment to parents and children. In the UK, commitment to free markets may be greater than commitment to gender equality.

Are there alternative scenarios for a more gender-equal future? The idea of making men's lives more like women's is central to Fraser's (1997) universal caregiver model: all employees would be assumed to have care responsibilities, while developing civil society would share care more widely. But gender equality needs more systematic support, beyond the capacity of civil society. The French working time model also has something to contribute to thinking about how to turn the one-and-a-half-earner model into a two × three-quarter one in which men and women have time to care as well as to earn. Government commitments to gender equality need underpinning with regulation of time and with social investment. Comparative data clearly show social democratic countries as the most gender equal: but they have still prioritised women's employment over men's care. In a model of universal citizenship, gender equality would go beyond paid employment – important as that has been – and attend to gender inequalities in care, time and power: men's and women's obligations to paid work and care as citizens would be underpinned by regulating working time and electoral systems and by social investment in citizenship rights.

Gender in employment

Increasing labour market participation has been a key government policy, for social inclusion, for economic growth, for responsibility, and as a basis for citizenship rights (Lister, 2002). Women have chosen paid employment too, seeking economic independence and autonomy. Increasing support for reconciling employment and family has benefited women and men. The emphasis on paid work as the only recognised work may be criticised for undervaluing unpaid care work, and for attending inadequately to the impact of care on women's independent access to earnings and pensions. We need to ask about the quality of women's work as well as the quantity. And we need to ask about gender equality. Governments everywhere hold to gender equality in principle, and pass legislation promoting it. But it often competes with other objectives, and may be little supported in practice. Have New Labour policies been underpinned by an ideology of gender equality, and how vigorously have they promoted gender equality in practice?

Women's increasing labour market participation pre-dates New Labour policies. Women have been making their own decisions for paid employment, in the absence of policies to support them. By 1997, lone mothers' labour market participation was lower than elsewhere, but employment among other mothers was high. Conservative ideological support for the family as a private domain, for a male breadwinner model and for family responsibility meant that mothers were making their own policies, bringing deep divisions between those with education, able to earn to pay for childcare, and lower earners who fitted employment around care responsibilities. New Labour brought a new ideological commitment to employment and some policies intended to sustain women's participation. These include the Childcare Strategy (discussed below under care), a New Deal for Lone Parents, Working Tax Credits and Child Tax Credits with a childcare component. Some measures to improve the quality of employment include strengthened employment protection for parents and for part-time workers. The national minimum wage aimed to lift low earnings, with particular relevance to women's low earnings, while the Women's Unit was established in central government to support women's causes, including employment and pay.

The Women's Unit has documented gender differences in lifetime earnings and shown that women's lifetime earnings are around half those of men, a practice aptly described as a one-and-a-half male breadwinner model, in which women's labour market participation does not bring equality in earnings or equal domestic partnerships (Lewis, 2001). The Women's Unit study showed great differences between mothers and other women, and between women with different levels of education (Rake, 2000). If a study published in 2000 could be seen as describing mainly the legacy inherited by New Labour, what has happened since? Have the many initiatives around work, especially women's work, brought better-quality, more continuous employment? Have conditions and rewards of part-time work improved?

The undervaluation of women's work is widespread, complex and dynamic (Grimshaw and Rubery, 2007). Even new women graduates receive lower rates of pay than their male counterparts, and the gap increases over time (Purcell and Elias, 2004); labour markets are segregated and job hierarchies within occupations gendered; men's power is built into the male working life model, favouring male jobs and working patterns. Long working hours make it difficult for women to return to full-time work after childbirth. Flexible patterns of work may favour women, but they may also be organised to favour employers, keeping workers on call, and unable to reconcile work and family responsibilities. Women have improved their educational resources, and now compete on more equal terms in some occupations. But as jobs feminise, their relative pay may decline. And increasing social and economic inequality may be associated with gender, reinforcing gender inequality among low-paid workers. Over time, the gender pay gap for full-time workers has decreased. But the UK has – compared with other European Union (EU) countries – a very high proportion of women in part-time work, many of whom are deeply disadvantaged, with very low pay and very short hours. Their pay gap has decreased scarcely at all (Grimshaw, 2007; Grimshaw and Rubery, 2007).

The gender pay gap has been closing over time, with a clear trend established since the 1980s. The ratio of women's pay to men's increased from 66% in 1984 to 73% in 2003. But New Labour's election in 1997 was 'not a catalyst for rapid improvements in women's pay; more damning, women's gains were far more substantial under the Conservatives during the 1987-95 period' (Grimshaw, 2007, p 135). The latter period of the Labour government has seen improvements again, with an increase to 77% in 2005. The national minimum wage has been a key strategy for lifting wages at the bottom, and New Labour's proud boast. But it was set very low and has failed to narrow the gap or lift women's incomes to a living wage. Grimshaw argues that New Labour has failed to examine labour market policies for their part in the gender pay gap (emphasising instead more individual and cultural factors such as girls' choices in education); it has allowed a two-tier workforce to develop before cooperating with trades unions in its third term to improve the position of low-paid part-time women workers; improving women's pay has conflicted with other policies, especially using a household means test for tax credit assessments, and the privatisation of public services; and governments have been wary of policies against widening wage differentials (Grimshaw, 2007, p 150).

Women's employment rates in the UK are compared with men's in Table 11.1, and with those in other European countries. The table represents those with a long-standing dual-earner tradition in the social democracies of Sweden and Denmark and countries of Central and Eastern Europe (Slovenia and Hungary), where women's full-time employment has had strong government support. France, described as a modified male breadwinner system (Lewis, 1992) because women could choose between employment and care, is included, as are countries that retain a strong male breadwinner tradition – Ireland and Malta. The percentage of women employed (at a very low threshold of one hour per week) is 65.9% in the UK – somewhat above the EU27 average – while the employment gap between men and women is 11.7% and somewhat below the EU27 average. But the UK is more unequal in this respect than the social democracies, with Swedish women's employment rates being only 4% behind men's.

Women's employment participation was already increasing, with little government support. It has been targeted by New Labour, in a clear ideological shift from the male breadwinner model, whose ideas were entrenched in government policies and assumptions in the post-war period and only a little modified by interim governments. Quality and equality in employment have both been targets, as governments have implemented policies to improve pay through the national minimum wage, conditions of part-time workers and a gender equality duty for public sector authorities. But these have not been enough to eliminate gender differences in the quality of jobs or pay, or other rewards from employment, in the context of widening social and economic inequalities.

Table 11.1: Female and male employment rates, as percentage of women and men aged 15 to 64, and difference between male and female rates, 2005

	Employment rate: female	Employment rate: male	Employment rate: male - female
Sweden	70.4	74.4	4.0
Denmark	71.9	79.8	7.9
Slovenia	61.3	70.4	9.1
Hungary	51.0	63.1	12.1
France	57.6	68.8	11.2
UK	65.9	77.6	11.7
Ireland	58.3	76.9	18.6
Malta	33.7	73.8	40.1
EU27	56.0	70.8	14.8

Note: Employment rates are calculated by dividing the number of women/men aged 15 to 64 in employment by the total female/male population of the same age group. The indicator is based on the EU Labour Force Survey. The survey covers the entire population living in private households and excludes those in collective households such as boarding houses, halls of residence and hospitals. The employed population consists of those persons who during the reference week did any work for pay or profit for at least one hour, or who were not working but had jobs from which they were temporarily absent.

Sources: Eurostat Structural Indicators, EUROPA website, and author's calculations

Gendered care

Childcare as public responsibility – rather than belonging privately to families – was a key change of principle under New Labour. By 2004, Gordon Brown was arguing that 'the early part of the twenty-first century should be marked by the introduction of pre-school provision for the under fives and childcare available to all' (Gordon Brown, Chancellor of the Exchequer, Comprehensive Spending Review). Commitment to social investment broke a long-established rule, bringing a Manifesto commitment to 'universal' childcare (Labour Party, 2005, p 76). Change in the means by which policy goals have been brought about has been incremental but there was a clear change of ideology (Lewis, 2007b).

First, Sure Start brought childcare together with other children's services to disadvantaged areas: these are to be more widely spread in new Children's Centres. Second, the childcare component of Child Tax Credit, assisting employed parents with formal childcare costs, currently includes employed families earning up to £59,000 per year. Third is public funding for preschool places for all three- and four-year-olds.

Are there problems with these strategies? Despite unprecedented commitment from HM Treasury to children and childcare, the system relies on the unreliable: private providers who do not necessarily respond to government incentives, and 17.7% of whom went out of business in the year to 2004 (HM Treasury and DTI, 2004, p 15). Scandinavian countries offer a more 'universal' model, with government provision, higher spending, well-trained staff, and low costs to parents. As in the UK, Scandinavian parents may not always have their expectations met, but there is a more comprehensive framework, with high-quality childcare as a social norm and social provision for children after parental leave and before school. This is underpinned by a passion for gender equality as well as for social equality (Ellingsaeter and Leira, 2006). Both these commitments could be said to be more half-hearted under New Labour governments.

International comparison of childcare arrangements is difficult, some countries having strong support for parental leave, while others have nursery provision for 0- to three-year-olds; preschool is key, but may be seen as education rather than childcare. The EU has begun the task of comparing: we can now cautiously assess how comprehensive the coverage is, how long the gaps are, how good the quality is and how much government is spending (Plantenga and Siegel, 2005). Table 11.2 shows the UK system as very partial, with limited coverage and long gaps between the end of 'effective leave' and preschool admission. For three- to five-year-olds, the UK's very short part-time hours compare unfavourably with other European countries. Even where preschool education is part-time elsewhere, opening hours may be longer: for example, Denmark's preschool system provides part-time education (three to six hours per day) but facilities are open from 7am to 5/6pm for leisure activities. Slovenia, with much lower per capita GDP than the UK, has preschool opening hours from 6am to 5pm (Plantenga and Siegel, 2005). New Labour plans to increase the scope of preschool places from the current 2.5-hour day to a 3-hour day by 2010, giving a 15-hour week in term time (with a long-term prospect of a 20-hour week) (HM Treasury and DTI, 2004). Meanwhile, the 2.5-hour day is too little acknowledged as a source of maternal pressure and gender inequality in the labour market.

There has been a real increase in spending and commitment to childcare. There are plans and promises to bring in out-of-school childcare places for 3- to 14-year-olds between 8am and 6pm on weekdays (HM Treasury and DTI, 2004, p 1). But these debates show how far the UK is from a universal system of childcare. Despite unprecedented concern with women's labour market participation, work–family reconciliation for parents, investment in children through quality services, social inclusion of parents and children, we still have a 2.5-hour day for preschool children, forcing parents (usually mothers) to patchwork care arrangements if they are to use the time for jobs.

We may also ask how much New Labour policies have enabled parents to care for their own children, and in particular about the gender implications of parental leave policies: do they aim to change the gender relations of care, bringing fathers into care, as employment policies have aimed to bring mothers into employment?

Leave systems have become an important aspect of New Labour's work–family balance agenda (Lewis, 2007a). Maternity leave with Statutory Maternity Pay has increased from 14 weeks to six months. Mothers can take an extra six months' unpaid leave, which will be paid leave from 2010. The level of maternity pay has nearly doubled, while Maternity Allowance has improved entitlements for mothers not entitled to the contributory Statutory Maternity Pay. These are important developments supporting mothers' care for children in the first year of life.

Policies to enable fathers' involvement in care have come slowly under New Labour, while support has been modest and encouragement non-existent. Adopting the 1996 European Parental Leave Directive brought fathers' entitlement to care time (three months but unpaid) after the birth of a child, as well as mothers'. But this minimalist approach (Lewis, 2007b), with entitlement to unpaid leave, was followed by further, somewhat reluctant, support for new fatherhood in April 2003, when two weeks' paid paternity leave was introduced, paid at the same level as Statutory Maternity Pay (now £108.85 per week). Under the 2006 Work and Families Act, mothers will be able to transfer their right to maternity leave – after the first six months – to fathers, who will then be entitled to take six months' 'additional paternity leave'.

While New Labour has developed leave entitlements, to enable reconciliation between work and family for mothers, there are limitations, particularly in comparison with Scandinavian countries, and particularly in relation to fathers. European data, drawing maternity leaves into parental leaves for comparative purposes, and allowing for

Table 11.2: Effective parental leave, paternity leave, childcare and preschool coverage

	Effective parental leave[a]	Paternity + parental leave reserved for fathers	Gap between end of effective leave and preschool admission	Estimated coverage (0-3 years) (not harmonised)[b]	Estimated coverage (from 3 to compulsory school age) (not harmonised)	Minimum qualification for preschool teacher
Sweden	119 weeks	2 weeks paid paternity + 2 months parental	30 weeks	63%	82%	University education
Denmark	36 weeks	14 days paid paternity + 2 months parental	118 weeks	68%	98%	3.5 years of higher vocational training
Hungary	114 weeks	5 days	38 weeks	6%	86%	Title of professional educator
France	48 weeks	2 weeks paid	42 weeks	31%	100%	
Ireland	11 weeks		105 weeks	41%	17%	3 years post-18 degree course
UK	25 weeks	2 weeks paid	131 weeks	10%	30%	Half of the staff to be appropriately qualified

Notes: [a] The length is weighted to reflect the level of payment.
[b] Non-harmonised data are used because they include the UK. When harmonised to take account of availability of leave, Sweden's coverage is 100% for 0- to 3-year-olds and 90% for three years to compulsory school age: Swedish parents take around 14 months' paid leave on average.

Sources: Plantenga and Siegel (2005) (drawing on Eurostat and national sources);
ILO examples of leave provisions for fathers (ILO Conditions of Work and Employment Programme website)

the level of payment, suggest that 'effective parental leave' in the UK is actually rather short (see Table 11.2). By this measure Sweden has 119 and Hungary 114 weeks of parental leave, while the UK has 25. This measure puts the UK among the lowest group of parental leave providers in Europe. The UK also has one of the longest gaps between the end of effective parental leave and pre-primary school admission age, with 131 weeks, compared with 38 weeks in Hungary and 30 in Sweden (Plantenga and Siegel, 2005, pp 10-11) (see Table 11.2).

Norway has been developing stronger entitlements to paid, non-transferable Daddy Leave to encourage fathers' care. Sweden borrowed this policy in 1995, increasing Norway's one month to two in 2002. Currently, Iceland has the most developed and effective policy, with a 3 × 3 system: three months for the mother, three for the father, and three for sharing between them. These policies have encouraged a rapid increase in fathers taking a share of parental leave, with three quarters taking their three-month quota. Scandinavian parents are subject to contradictory pressures too, to work long hours, and fathers still take only a small proportion of parental leaves in Nordic countries (Ellingsaeter and Leira, 2006; Lammi-Taskula, 2006; Nyberg, 2006). However modest in effect, these are important changes, bringing new assumptions about men as fathers, in households as well as among policy makers.

In the UK, policy ideas and future plans still entrench mothers' responsibility for care rather than fathers'. Fathers may lag behind mothers in taking responsibility for care, but most fathers see themselves as responsible (Fahey and Spéder, 2004), around 80% take some leave (Smeaton, 2006; Smeaton and Marsh, 2006; Dex and Ward, 2007) and – especially in full-time dual-earner households – spend time on childcare (O'Brien, 2005). In free-market countries, fathers may contribute more time to their children, in response to an absence of social support (Smith, 2004; Smith and Williams, 2007). In all these respects they are ahead of New Labour governments, which have emphasised women's and men's responsibility for work rather than men's responsibility for care.

In 10 years, New Labour has established a coherent work–family balance agenda giving employed mothers rights to parental leave during the first year, with support for childcare – including free part-time preschool places. There are important limitations, however: services are 'highly fragmented and unstable' (Lewis, 2007a, p 13). Problems of quality, trustworthiness, supply and affordability to parents still encourage discontinuous and part-time employment, especially among less-qualified mothers (Hansen et al, 2006). And fathers are nowhere in New Labour's frame of reference.

Gendered time

Women's increasing labour market participation has been encouraged and enabled by New Labour; but the male breadwinner model remains entrenched in unequal working lives. If the pay gap for full-time work were closed tomorrow, even – much more challenging – the pay gap for part-time work, we would not have gender equality, unless we could also bring more equal working time. Gender differences in working time are particularly marked for parents, with fathers likely to work long hours, while mothers are likely to work short part-time ones. Working-time preferences, on the other hand, are for more equal working time between men and women (Fagan, 2003).

Flexible working has been a key element of New Labour work–life balance policies. These began in 2003 with rights to request flexible working for parents of children under school age (under 18 where children are disabled) and were extended to carers of adults under the 2006 Work and Families legislation, with further extension to parents of older children currently promised. Policies have been developed cautiously, seeking agreement with business, persuading employers and employers' organisations that flexible working could be developed in their interests as well as parents' interests. Policies have aimed at gender neutrality rather than gender equality. As it is mothers more than fathers who currently make their lives flexible to meet children's needs, more women than men have requested flexible working, and most requests have been accepted. These rights have been used by around a quarter of parents with young children, and have been accepted by business organisations and by parents as enabling employment and reconciliation of work and families. The notion that employees have family responsibilities that employers should acknowledge has contributed to changing employment culture: mothers – and to a smaller extent fathers – have benefited from increasing rights and changing expectations (Lewis and Campbell, 2007a).

But regulating working time is another matter: there is no suggestion here of changing working culture, a move towards more rights, more family-friendly hours, or of gender equality as an ambition. New Labour has developed its time policies within a framework of individual choice. It has argued for freedom for companies and for employees to choose working hours. This model of individual choice ignores the joint responsibilities and decision making of parents: where parents have dependent children, fathers' choices impact on mothers' choices. Long working hours also prevent mothers from taking on more responsible jobs (Fox et al, 2006). New Labour inherited – and retains – an opt-out from the EU's Working Time Directive, giving individuals the right to opt out of the 48-hour week: the UK is the only member state not enforcing the Working Time Directive and the number of people working more than 48 hours has been increasing (Coates and Oettinger, 2007, p 127).

What routes are there to more equal working time? Three routes in other European countries could be characterised as Sweden making women's working lives as far as possible like men's, the Netherlands making men's working lives more like women's, while France offers a mid-point between men's and women's working lives. The Swedish route has been to support full-time employment – or nearly full-time employment – for women and men within a dual-earner model, through high public spending on childcare and parental leaves. The Netherlands has pursued a part-time route: the 'Polder model' developed to share employment through encouraging part-time work, while the social ideal of the 'Combination Scenario' aims to allow men and women equally to combine paid and unpaid work, which should be equally shared and equally valued (Plantenga, 2002, pp 53-4). Finally France has legislated for a maximum 35-hour week for everyone. As in the Netherlands, this started as a policy to share employment, at a time of high unemployment, but more equal sharing of paid and unpaid work in families was also an objective (Fagnani and Letablier, 2006).

Comparative data in Table 11.3 show that across the EU around one third of women's employment is part time, which is nearly five times the rate for men. The UK women's rate of 42.7% is well above the European average, but UK women are also disadvantaged by the extent to which they work short part-time hours for low pay. Part-time work is not a feature in Central and Eastern Europe, with only 5.8% of women in Hungary employed this way. The Netherlands, where part-time work has been encouraged, has 75.1% of women and 22.6% of men employed part time. The table also shows full-time male working hours in the UK at 44 per week, three hours above the EU average, and four hours above women's full-time hours. But UK men and women are also likely to work *very* long hours, with 18% working above 48 hours (Eurostat, 2007). These comparisons show the UK retaining gender inequality in working time, leading to unequal earnings and unequal pensions.

New Labour has made both ideological and practical changes in relations between work and family, through employment and work–family balance policies, which have enabled women's increasing labour market participation and attachment. It has recognised changing families

Table 11.3: Part-time work and full-time hours, 2005

	Part-time rate: female	Part-time rate: male	Part-time rate: female: male	Working hours: full-time male	Working hours: full-time female
Sweden	39.6	11.5	3.4:1	40	40
Denmark	33.0	12.7	2.1:1	40	38
Slovenia	11.1	7.2	1.5:1	42	41
Hungary	5.8	2.7	2.1:1	41	40
Netherlands	75.1	22.6	3.3:1	39	38
France	30.7	5.7	5.4:1	40	38
UK	42.7	10.4	4.1:1	44	40
Malta	21.1	4.5	4.7:1	42	39
EU25	32.4	7.4	4.4:1	41	39

Source: Eurostat (2007, table 3.2, p 46; table 3.4, p 50) and author's calculations

as creating a need to combine motherhood and employment, among lone parents and among couples. Policies that give parents the right to ask for flexible working time have been developed, and are clearly of use to mothers of young children, and some fathers of young children. These policies have had employment rather than gender equality at their heart: they pose some risks of entrenching the different working lives of men and women. Meanwhile they have ignored key gender differences in working time. Gender equality in access to security and earnings depends on more equal working time. While the gender pay gap for full-timers has reduced, gender inequality in working time – including career breaks and part-time work – has become a more serious factor in women's ability to support themselves. It has also become a more serious difference between women who can afford to pay for care they can trust, and those who cannot. But gender equality has not been the guiding commitment in these work–life balance policies. Reducing the working week would mainly limit men's working hours – but would enable mothers to sustain more continuous working lives. While embracing flexibility, New Labour has rejected regulation to limit the working week.

Gendered income

At the heart of the Beveridge system were assumptions that men would earn enough money through paid employment to support families, and women would be dependent on men's earnings and pension contributions. But the system devised in the 1940s was based on men's working lives. Women have joined the labour market, but women's working lives have been characterised by discontinuity, part-time employment and low pay. Women's lack of independent pensions has emerged as a continuing problem of the Beveridge framework in debates leading to the Pensions Act in 2007. Until 1997, lone mothers fell outside the male breadwinner assumptions, and were particularly likely to be on means-tested benefits. So tax credits for lone parents, including Childcare Tax Credits, on a basis that assumes and allows part-time work combined with care, represent a radical transformation of the male breadwinner model.

There are plenty of reasons for pensions to be on the social policy agenda: the ageing population and inadequate savings, whether through personal pensions (dating from the Thatcher years), company pensions or state pensions. While the question of how to produce enough savings to keep pensioners out of poverty is on the agenda, the gender dimensions have been too little debated (Bellamy and Rake, 2005). National Insurance pensions, occupational pensions, personal pensions or savings: everywhere men's contributions earn more entitlements than women's. As cohabiting partners and wives, women may be included in any of these arrangements, and the allocation of pension rights on divorce is now more likely to acknowledge unpaid work in women's contribution to marriage. But gender differences in working lives bring gender differences in entitlements to pensions, putting women at greater risk of poverty.

The core National Insurance pension entitlement in the UK is the Basic State Pension. But whereas nearly all men retire with the full state pension in their own right, a minority of women do so. Older women may have taken the Married Woman's Option to opt out of National Insurance, because they would be covered through their husbands, as indeed, some are: a wife may receive a pension at a percentage of her husband's rate and be entitled to inherit his pension rights. Others may lack entitlement because of low pay, below the lower earnings limit for contributions, and/or because care responsibilities have limited their labour market attachment and reduced entitlements. For all these reasons the full Basic State Pension was received by only 23% of women reaching 60 in September 2004, while on average those reaching 60 in 2005/06 have 70% of a full Basic State Pension (DWP, 2005, p 73). The Department for Work and Pensions (DWP) argues that the figures are changing rapidly because of women's increasing labour market participation, and the effects of Home Responsibilities Protection, introduced in 1978 to protect the basic pension rights of those caring for a child under 17 by reducing the number of years needed to qualify. The DWP has defended the contributory system, on the grounds that women in their early forties or younger are accruing pension rights equivalent to men and by 2025 over 80% of women reaching pension age will be entitled to a full Basic State Pension (DWP, 2005, pp 66-82). But this solution will not meet the needs of those retiring before 2025. There are problems at the heart of the National Insurance scheme, designed in the post-war era around men's working lives and secure families. Most women's working lives have been interrupted and low paid. Falling marriage rates and higher divorce rates, with now half of all marriages ending in divorce, mean that the Beveridgean model, which built women's dependency on men into the welfare state, is not a secure framework for women's pensions. The 2007 Pensions Act brings better recognition for those whose working lives are interrupted by care, with qualifying years for the basic pension reduced to 30, and a new system of credits in the National Insurance system. A universal citizens' pension would be a more radical solution to a system too much designed around men's lives: the cutting and pasting of the insurance system so far leaves 77% of women reaching 60 unable to claim a full Basic State Pension.

New Labour's response to pensioner poverty is to means test, to focus pension guarantees on the poorest pensioners. There is now a Pension Credit, paying around £40 per week to around 3.2 million households, with an income guarantee, currently £109 per week. In many ways this benefits women, whose life expectancy is greater than men's and who have a high risk of poverty in old age: they have been two thirds of the recipients of Minimum Income Guarantees. But the DWP estimates that between 22% and 36% of entitled pensioners do not claim.

If the means test – a classic liberal welfare state response to poverty – is the current solution for pensions, so New Labour has brought tax credits as a core strategy for encouraging work and reducing poverty. This has been extended since April 2003, with Child Tax Credits paid to 90% of families, and Working Tax Credits aimed at rather fewer. The new system splits the payment between carer and worker: now Child Tax Credit is paid to the main carer and addresses child poverty, while

Working Tax Credit offers the incentive to work (Bennett, 2005). The Child Tax Credits are now a major part of the government's anti-poverty strategy, and 'the biggest ever state boost to mothers' incomes' (Toynbee and Walker, 2005, p 71). The universal system of Child Benefit, paid on behalf of all children, remains. Hilary Land (2004, p 4) comments that we now have the closest thing to the Inland Revenue's claim of a 'single seamless system' of support for families with children that Britain has ever experienced.

There remain serious problems in accessing childcare. But for lone mothers, Working Tax Credit, incorporating an element for childcare, and Child Tax Credit, which they receive whether employed or not, bring real choice about balancing work and care: they can receive support if they work 16 hours, or more support if they work 30. This allows a shorter working week to be supplemented through tax credits, and may enable lone parents, who are mostly mothers, to lift themselves and their children out of poverty, and keep a foot in the labour market, while keeping time for care.

For mothers with partners, the tax credit system has more mixed implications. The Child Tax Credit brings material support for children and childcare. But there are concerns about joint taxation, with the tax credit system built on household means tests. Mothers will face high rates of marginal taxation/tax credit loss, bringing disincentives to employment (Bennett, 2005). Mothers in couples are also more likely to pay childcare costs; 80% of costs is the maximum proportion covered by credits. It is also targeted at smaller families, making childcare costs a significant barrier to work for mothers in larger families (Land, 2004).

The Beveridge system was designed in the post-war era around gender difference, with women expected to achieve social security through their husbands' employment. As families have destabilised, and women have joined the labour market, governments have changed the rules, to account – in some measure – for women's need for social security as individuals and as parents, with or without men. But the male model of working life still lurks beneath the surface: because of low pay, part-time employment and broken working lives, only a quarter of women reaching pension age now are entitled to a full Basic State Pension. This figure will not reach 80% until 2025, leaving many older women in poverty for the foreseeable future. New Labour has changed the rules in another key way, introducing means-tested tax credits as a solution to poverty for children, for workers, for childcare and for pensioners. This brings welcome resources to households with low incomes, many headed by women, but dependence on means tests brings well-established problems of penalties for work and limited take-up. New Labour assumes that women can now earn their own security as individuals – rejecting assumptions of male breadwinners – but unequal working lives put women at greater risk of poverty.

Gendered power

Gender systems are also systems of power: welfare states affect gender relations, women's autonomy as individuals, their ability to support themselves and their place in public politics. Equality legislation has brought women important rights, but inequalities in paid work, care, income and time bring unequal voice in households, civil society, local politics, state and European governments. In households the continuing gendered division of labour suggests that women's voices are weaker, and their lower incomes may give them less say in major decisions than men (Sung and Bennett, 2007). How far has New Labour come in engendering politics, to include the representation of women, to make gender equality issues salient in government, and to enable gender equality in households?

Women's representation increased dramatically upon the election of New Labour in 1997. Feminist action within the party ensured debates about representative politics, and brought all-women shortlists. Through these, Labour brought its representation of women on shortlists and elected MPs to 24% in 1997 (Annesley et al, 2007). A Women's Minister led responsibility for representing women's interests in government and Cabinet, and through a dedicated Women's Unit (now part of the Government Equalities Office) and continued support for the Equal Opportunities Commission (now part of the Equality and Human Rights Commission). Policy coalitions, including organisations such as the Women's Budget Group, have put feminist concerns on the agenda at the core of government. Devolution brought a new Scottish Parliament and Welsh Assembly, whose constitutions reflected feminist influences, and enabled selection and electoral systems to be used to foster women's representation. Gender equality in representation has been reached in the Welsh Assembly, which is now a world leader in this respect. At the level of government in Westminster, women have been represented as ministers, at around 30%, but not so well in core positions (Durose and Gains, 2007). These amount to considerable changes in the representation of women and the likelihood of gender equality being taken into account in New Labour government.

Internationally, women's low level of political representation is being targeted by quotas (Dahlerup, 2006). Accumulated evidence points to discriminatory processes as the key to women's continued underrepresentation, rather than women's choices or poorer qualification for election (Phillips, 1991). Therefore, solutions may be found through changing political processes. Proponents of the parity principle argue that representation is not democratic unless both men and women are equally represented. Proposals for gender quotas come in many forms, and are designed to ensure a minimum proportion of women are elected, or to give parity between men and women. A 'parity law' has been used in France to regulate the proportion of women candidates in local regional and European elections, although not in national parliamentary ones: it increased women's representation from 22% to 47.5% in the cities in March 2001 (Squires and Wickham-Jones, 2001).

Nordic countries are used to being at the top of gender leagues. The long, unbroken women's movement has worked to increase acceptability of stronger women's participation and the unacceptability of men's overrepresentation. Women's stronger position in employment, proportional representation, social democratic party dominance and party quotas – although not compulsory legal quotas – have increased women's representation in Parliament. This has been a gradual process built on consensual politics over decades. Sweden is still at the top of European countries, with 45% of women parliamentarians. But Nordic feminists are now surprised to find their position at the top of the international league taken by Rwanda, bringing about debates in Scandinavia about whether the consensual process has been too gradual (Dahlerup, 2006). New Parliaments in Scotland and Wales have also offered opportunities to build systems in which women can win seats in Europe too (albeit at a devolved rather than UK level) and have reached 50% in Wales, as we have seen. Quotas are rapidly growing as a means to avoid a 100-year wait for women to be fully represented, although they face barriers in some developed democracies, particularly those without proportional representation, with entrenched male MPs and party selection processes, and where the dominant ideology is based on liberal ideals emphasising equality of opportunity rather than equality of result.

Table 11.4 compares women's position in government, Parliaments and the civil service in the UK with other selected countries. The UK is around the EU average, and well below Sweden, which has 40% or more women in each category here. The UK political system has been highly resistant to the representation of women, and to the inclusion of a gender equality politics. Women have acted through the Labour

Table 11.4: Women in decision making

	% of women senior ministers in national government	% of women members of single/ lower house Parliaments	% of women among highest ranking civil servants	% of women among second highest ranking civil servants
Sweden	50	48	36	39
Slovenia	6	13	24	47
Hungary	14	10	11	19
France	13	13	21	32
UK	30	20	25	20
Ireland	21	12	13	10
Malta	15	9		
Average EU25	24	23		

Source: European Commission Database on Women and Men in Decision-Making (2006)

Party, which had been dominated by class inequality rather than gender inequality. They have made important gains in representing women and women's interests at all levels, from local government through central state institutions, civil society organisations, European and national Parliaments to the core institutions of the central state – especially the Treasury – where key decisions are more likely to be made. There has been a serious transformation of the business of government, but not serious enough, while women have to be content with around 30% of ministerial positions and 20% of MPs, and while agendas contradicting gender equality – such as the spread of free markets in public services – have been flourishing (Rummery et al, 2007).

Conclusion

This chapter has asked how far New Labour has shifted from the male breadwinner model of gender inequality? What have been the limits, and what might be priorities for a more radical assault on inequalities in work, care, income, time and power? Change there has been, in assumptions about mothers' place in the labour market, and the need for social support for work–family reconciliation. Policy for mothers' employment – including childcare – has been a key government priority. But policies for gender equality in care, time, income and power have been more muted. Neoliberal ideology has also reduced the impact of gender equality policies. Continuing social inequalities affect the degree to which women have access to quality jobs, childcare, control over time and security.

Social democratic regimes with high social spending are clearly the most successful for gender equality (Lewis, 1992). Where care work is supported by social spending, women are more likely to have full-time continuous employment, and be able to reconcile work with family responsibilities. Can governments afford gender equality if it means social spending? Academic social policy has for some time debated different welfare regimes and argued the superiority of the social democratic model: 'Far from being "horses for courses", the social democratic welfare regime turns out to be the best choice' whatever the goal (Goodin et al, 1999, p 260). Measuring child well-being in rich countries, on a wide range of measures, UNICEF (2007) shows the UK leaving more children in poverty than all the other countries covered, while Scandinavian countries are the highest achievers. An account of economic indicators concludes that: 'the best performing industrial economies at the beginning of the 21st century are those that have least in common with the neo-liberal model': the Scandinavian social democracies in particular (Panić, 2007, p 149). Perhaps the UK government cannot afford not to adopt a more social democratic stance and the gender equality that goes with it.

A universal citizenship model, in which both men and women have obligations to care and rights to support as carers, would increase gender equality and bring social and economic benefits to children and adults. Social support for childcare is a prerequisite: especially a more comprehensive provision for preschool children, beyond the 2.5-hour day. Policies towards involving men in care are needed: innovative parental leave policies (mainly Scandinavian) are about changing gender relations at home. Policies towards more equal time are necessary if women are to earn enough to ensure their own security. Women cannot be expected to keep themselves out of poverty in old age if they have unequal working lives. A universal citizenship model might go further than Scandinavian countries in enabling men's lives to be more like women's. We need policies around employment, but a wider agenda, and a more social democratic model, would shift us from the male breadwinner model in practice as well as in ideology.

References

Annesley, C., Gains, F. and Rummery, K. (eds) (2007) *Women and New Labour: Engendering Politics and Policy?*, Bristol: The Policy Press.

Bellamy, K. and Rake, K. (2005) *Money Money Money: Is it still a rich man's world?*, London: Fawcett Society.

Bennett, F. (2005) *Gender and Benefits*, Manchester: Equal Opportunities Commission.

Berthoud, R. and Blekesaune, M. (2006) *Persistent Employment Disadvantage, 1974 to 2003*, ISER Working Paper, Essex: ISER.

Coates, D. and Oettinger, S. (2007) 'Two steps forward, one step back: the gender dimensions of Treasury policy under New Labour', in C. Annesley, F. Gains and K. Rummery (eds) (2007) *Women and New Labour: Engendering Politics and Policy?*, Bristol: The Policy Press.

Dahlerup, D. (ed) (2006) *Women, Quotas and Politics*, London: Routledge.

Dex, S. and Ward, K. (2007) *Parental Care and Employment in Early Childhood*, Manchester: Equal Opportunities Commission.

Durose, C. and Gains, F. (2007) 'Engendering the machinery of governance', in C. Annesley, F. Gains and K. Rummery (eds) *Women and New Labour: Engendering Politics and Policy?*, Bristol: The Policy Press.

DWP (Department for Work and Pensions) (2005) *Women and Pensions: The Evidence*, London: DWP.

Ellingsaeter, A. and Leira, A. (eds) (2006) *Politicising Parenthood in Scandinavia*, Bristol: The Policy Press.

Esping-Andersen, G. (1990) *The Three Worlds of Welfare Capitalism*, Cambridge: Polity.

Eurostat (2007) *Living Conditions in Europe*, Luxembourg: Eurostat/European Commission.

Fagan, C. (2003) *Working-Time Preferences and Work–Life Balance in the EU: Some Policy Considerations for Enhancing the Quality of Life*, Luxembourg: Office of Official Publications of the European Communities.

Fagnani, J. and Letablier, M.T. (2006) 'The French 35-hour working law and the work–life balance of parents: friend or foe?', in D. Perrons, C. Fagan, L. McDowell, K. Ray and K. Ward (eds) *Gender Divisions and Working Time in the New Economy*, Cheltenham: Edward Elgar.

Fahey, T. and Spéder, S. (2004) *Fertility and Family Issues in an Enlarged Europe*, Luxembourg: Office for Official Publications of the European Communities.

Fox, E., Pascall, G. and Warren, T. (2006) *Innovative Social Policies for Gender Equality at Work*, Nottingham: University of Nottingham.

Fraser, N. (1997) *Justice Interruptus: Critical Reflections on the 'Postsocialist' Condition*, London and New York: Routledge.

Goodin, R. E., Headey, B., Muffels, R. and Dirven, H. J. (1999) *The Real Worlds of Welfare Capitalism*, Cambridge: Cambridge University Press.

Grimshaw, D. (2007) 'New Labour policy and the gender pay gap', in C. Annesley, F. Gains and K. Rummery (eds) *Women and New Labour: Engendering Politics and Policy?*, Bristol: The Policy Press.

Grimshaw, D. and Rubery, J. (2007) *Undervaluing Women's Work*, Manchester: Equal Opportunities Commission.

Hansen, K., Joshi, H. and Verropoulou, G. (2006) 'Childcare and mothers' employment: approaching the millennium', *National Institute Economic Review*, no 195, pp 84-102.

HM Treasury and DTI (Department of Trade and Industry) (2004) *Choice for Parents, the Best Start for Children: A Ten Year Strategy for Childcare*, London: The Stationery Office.

Labour Party, The (2005) *The Labour Party Manifesto 2005: Forward not Back*, London: The Labour Party.

Lammi-Taskula, J. (2006) 'Nordic men on parental leave: can the welfare state change gender relations?', in A. Ellingsaeter and A. Leira (eds) *Politicising Parenthood in Scandinavia*, Bristol: The Policy Press.

Land, H. (2004) *Women, Child Poverty and Childcare: Making the Link*, London: Daycare Trust.

Lewis, J. (1992) 'Gender and the development of welfare regimes', *Journal of European Social Policy*, vol 2, no 3, pp 159-73.

Lewis, J. (2001) 'The decline of the male breadwinner model: the implications for work and care', *Social Politics*, vol 8, no 2, pp 152-70.

Lewis, J. and Campbell, M. (2007a) 'UK work/family balance policies and gender equality, 1997-2005', *Social Politics*, vol 14, no 1, pp 4-30.

Lewis, J. and Campbell, M. (2007b) 'Work/family balance policies in the UK since 1997: a new departure?', *Journal of Social Policy*, vol 36, no 3, pp 365-82.

Lister, R. (2002) 'The dilemmas of pendulum politics: balancing paid work, care and citizenship', *Economy and Society*, vol 31, no 4, pp 520-32.

Nyberg, A. (2006) 'Economic crisis and the sustainability of the dual-earner, dual carer model', in D. Perrons, C. Fagan, L. McDowell, K. Ray and K. Ward (eds) *Gender Divisions and Working Time in the New Economy*, Cheltenham: Edward Elgar.

O'Brien, M. (2005) *Shared Caring: Bringing Fathers into the Frame*, Manchester: Equal Opportunities Commission.

Panić, M. (2007) 'Does Europe need neoliberal reforms?', *Cambridge Journal of Economics*, vol 31, no 1, pp 145-69.

Phillips, A. (1991) *Engendering Democracy*, Cambridge: Polity.

Plantenga, J. (2002) 'Combining work and care in the polder model: an assessment of the Dutch part-time strategy', *Critical Social Policy*, vol 22, no 1, pp 53-71.

Plantenga, J. and Siegel, M. (2005) *Position Paper 'Childcare in a Changing world'. Part 1: European Childcare Strategies, Part 2: Country Files, The Netherlands*, Groningen: Rijksuniversiteit.

Purcell K. and Elias P. (2004) *Higher Education and Gendered Career Development: Researching Graduate Careers Seven Years On*, Working Paper No 4, Bristol/Warwick: Employment Studies Research Unit, University of the West of England/Warwick Institute for Employment Research.

Rake, K. (2000) *Women's Incomes over the Lifetime*, London: The Stationery Office.

Rummery, K., Gains, F. and Annesley, C. (2007) 'New Labour: towards an engendered politics and policy?', in C. Annesley, F. Gains and K. Rummery (eds) *Women and New Labour: Engendering Politics and Policy?*, Bristol: The Policy Press.

Smeaton, D. (2006) *Dads and their Babies: A Household Analysis*, Manchester: Equal Opportunities Commission.

Smeaton, D. and Marsh, A. (2006) *Maternity and Paternity Rights and Benefits: Survey of Parents 2005*, London: DTI.

Smith, A. and Williams, D. (2007) 'Father–friendly legislation and paternal time across Europe', *Journal of Comparative Policy Analysis*, vol 9, no 2, pp 175-92.

Smith, A.J. (2004) *Who Cares? Fathers and the Time they Spend Looking After Children*, Sociology Working Papers, Oxford: Department of Sociology, University of Oxford.

Squires, J. and Wickham-Jones, M. (2001) *Women in Parliament: A Comparative Analysis*, Manchester: Equal Opportunities Commission.

Sung, S. and Bennett, F. (2007) 'Dealing with money in low- to moderate-income couples', in K. Clarke, T. Maltby and P. Kennett (eds) *Social Policy Review 19*, Bristol: The Policy Press, pp 151-74.

Toynbee, P. and Walker, D. (2005) *Better or Worse? Has Labour Delivered?*, London: Bloomsbury.

UNICEF (United Nations Children's Fund) (2007) *An Overview of Child Well-Being in Rich Countries 2005: Report Card No 7*, Florence: UNICEF Innocenti Research Centre.

Websites
European Commission Database on Women and Men in Decision-Making, www.db-decision.de/
Europa: Eurostat Structural Indicators, http://epp.eurostat.ec.europa.eu/portal/page?_pageid=1133,47800773,1133_47802558&_dad=portal&_schema=PORTAL
ILO: Conditions of Work and Employment Programme, www.ilo.org/public/english/protection/condtrav/family/reconcilwf/specialleave.htm

TWELVE

A review of engendering policy in the EU

Jill Rubery

Introduction

Equal pay for women and men was adopted as a core principle of the European Union (EU) when it was founded in 1957 by the Treaty of Rome, originally as the European Economic Community. The initial motivation for the inclusion of the clause was to protect against unfair competition in trade and the future significance of the inclusion of this principle was not anticipated or understood at the time. It was only in the 1970s that the EU began to develop a social policy programme and adopted gender equality as an explicit EU social objective, backed by new EU directives on both equal pay and equal treatment for women and men. In the 1990s, with the development of the European Employment Strategy (EES), there was a rediscovery of the potential importance of gender equality for all areas of EU policy, including economic and employment policy. Through the EES, the EU began to recognise that policies that take into account gender equality may have positive economic and employment outcomes as well as contributing to social justice and cohesion.

This recognition of the intertwining of gender issues with economic and social outcomes is associated with the development by the EU of gender mainstreaming as a policy approach. Gender mainstreaming involves the '(re)organisation, improvement, development and evaluation of policy processes, so that a gender equality perspective is incorporated in all policies at all levels and at all stages, by the actors normally involved in policy-making' (Council of Europe, 1998, p 13). The immediate reason for introducing gender mainstreaming within the EU's employment policy was to demonstrate a commitment to action following the 1995 Beijing World Conference on Women, at which all United Nations (UN) countries, including the EU, agreed to introduce gender mainstreaming into policy development and analysis. However, increasing awareness that taking the gender impact into account in policy design could help the EU achieve its overall economic and social goals undoubtedly sustained the interest of the EU in gender mainstreaming, particularly in the EES, beyond the initial post-Beijing enthusiasm. At the summit in Lisbon in 2000 that established the Lisbon strategy to develop Europe into a productive and socially inclusive society (expanded through the 2001 Gothenburg summit to include environmental sustainability), an employment rate target for 2010 of 70% was set for the EU's working-age population. A specific female employment rate target of 60% was added, thereby signifying the importance of female employment to the overall objective. This employment rate target for women has helped to keep issues with respect to female employment on the member states' policy agendas. This highlighting of the employment rate has had its downsides; by 2007, 10 years after the start of the EES, many member states are only focusing on this narrowly specified economic objective, raising the female employment rate, and the social justice element of gender equality has all but disappeared from view. However, it may still be premature to consider that all the steam has gone out of the EU's engendering of its policy programme. Even as visibility of gender issues within the EES has diminished, the EU has launched a number of initiatives to promote gender equality in a wider sense. These initiatives have drawn on and benefited from the experience of mainstreaming the EES. A new depth can be found in the analyses and objectives underpinning these new gender equality initiatives – including, for example, a new *Gender Equality Pact* (Council of the European Union, 2006), a new *Roadmap for Equality between Men and Women 2006–10* (CEC, 2006) and a communication on *Tackling the Pay Gap between Women and Men* (COM, 2007/424).

This review traces these developments, organised in three sections. In the first section the development of gender equality as a social objective of the EU is considered; the second examines the rise and fall of gender mainstreaming within the EES and the Growth and Jobs strategy; the third analyses recent gender equality initiatives within the EU and identifies some positive developments, both in defining the goal of a more gender equal society and in the analysis of the factors that act as barriers to equality within the economic and social systems in Europe. The review concludes with some reflections on the future for gender equality within the European project.

From an economic issue to a social objective and back again

Article 141 of the European Treaty, originally Article 119 of the 1957 Treaty of Rome, states that 'each Member State shall ensure that the principle of equal pay for male and female workers for equal work or work of equal value is applied'. This clause was motivated by economic reasoning, to protect the French against unfair competition in trade because they had already granted this right in national legislation (Venables and Joshi, 2007). This approach fitted with the initial orientation of the European Community as a free trade area without responsibility for citizens' social rights or employment conditions. The inclusion of the principle was done without understanding or anticipation of the potential of the clause to shape future legal and social policy development in the EU. Not only was gender equality to become a major field of European social policy but it was also in fact the equal pay directive that, through European Court of Justice test cases (especially Defrenne II), established a stronger and more direct role for European law than was envisaged when the Treaty was signed in 1957 (Caporaso and Cowles, 2001, p 22).

The EU's commitment to gender equality as a social objective started with the legislative measures of the mid-1970s, namely the passing of EU directives on equal pay for women and men and equal treatment for men and women as regards access to employment, vocational training and promotion, and working conditions. It continued with the launching, from 1981 onwards, of a series of action programmes for gender equality. During the 1980s and early 1990s further progress in promoting gender equality came from legal judgments that, for example, established the applicability of the concept of indirect discrimination within European law and determined that occupational pensions were a form of pay, with regard to the equal pay directive. There was also an extension of legislation to areas such as equal treatment in social security and pregnancy/maternity leave. The Southern European countries that became members of the EU during the 1980s were encouraged to take equal opportunities issues seriously, in part because of the legislative measures, but also because European structural funds supported specific programmes for women to improve their training and employability. The structural funds were an important resource for the new Southern member states.

However, up until the early 1990s there was little evidence of a return to any economic arguments for gender equality measures. The decision to create a single European market did see a return to concerns that countries that did not provide the high employment standards associated with the European Social Model would benefit unfairly from the reduction in trade restrictions. This argument was no longer linked to issues of gender inequality. There were still some concerns among trades unions, particularly in the Southern member states that the promotion of female employment through the growth of part-time work could undermine the employment rights associated with full-time work. Nevertheless, by and large, gender equality was considered a social justice not an economic issue. Nor at this time was much attention given to the more positive business case for gender equality; that is, the promotion of an active society and the utilisation of the full talents of the European labour supply.

In the early 1990s the EU did begin to pay attention to the potential problem of a falling employment rate in a context of extended transitions from school to work, declining ages of retirement and a growth in the projected size of the inactive older population. The need for more people in prime age to be in work to sustain the rising dependent population began to be identified as a policy priority (CEC, 1994). Moreover, the unfavourable development of the EU employment rate, compared with that of the US, highlighted a need for the EU to promote a more employment-intensive growth policy. However, initially almost no links were made between variations in the measured employment rate and the pattern of women's employment. It was not until the entry of Sweden and Finland into the EU, in the mid-1990s, that greater attention was paid to the characteristics of the Nordic models and their more equal and higher employment rates for men and women. Moreover, this expansion of the range of social and employment models encompassed within the EU also coincided with the preparations for the Beijing World Conference on Women and the strong international push for agreement on a new approach to gender equality – through gender mainstreaming.

Engendering the EES: the rise and fall of gender mainstreaming

From gender blindness to gender mainstreaming in four years

The first main step towards the establishment of the EES was the development of a White Paper by the then President of the European Commission, Jacques Delors, for the December 1993 summit, on *Growth,*

Competitiveness and Employment:The Challenges and Ways Forward into the 21st Century (CEC, 1994). This provided the basis for the inclusion of an employment chapter in the 1997 Amsterdam Treaty, which granted the EU competence in employment matters along with member states,[1] and thereby provided the basis for an EU-wide employment strategy – the EES – to be launched in the autumn of 1997. The White Paper was notable for its complete lack of a gender perspective, either in its policy approach or in its analysis of the employment issues facing the EU (Rubery and Maier, 1995), yet by the time the EES was actually launched, less than four years later, equal opportunities between women and men had been identified as one of the four pillars of the employment strategy.[2] Only another year later the EU member states voluntarily signed up to a commitment to gender mainstream all of the policy guidelines in each of the four pillars of the strategy.

To explain this shift in perspective over a short period of time, the following factors must be taken into account. First, and perhaps most importantly of all, the four-year period coincided with the preparation for and the actual holding of the Beijing World Conference on Women. The EU had played a major role in securing the agreed platform for action from the Beijing conference, and was thereby particularly bound by the commitment in the platform to promote gender mainstreaming. By 1996 the EU had adopted a communication committing itself to incorporate equal opportunities into all Community policies and actions (COM, 96/67) and that this should be done actively and openly at the planning stage of policy development. The EES was one of the first big new policy initiatives to be launched after this commitment that had major and undeniable relevance to gender equality issues. To include gender issues within the strategy to some extent suddenly became as normal as it had been to ignore them only four years previously.

The implementation of commitments made at Beijing may be the most important explanation but two other factors must also be mentioned. First, the Delors White Paper, despite failing to mention gender issues, did lead to an increased highlighting of the importance of women's employment, as a consequence of its promotion of a change in employment policy focus from the unemployment rate to the employment rate. Variations in aggregate employment rates among EU member states can to a large extent be explained by differences in the share of women in employment. Differences among EU countries in the employment rates of men are much smaller. Thus, poorly performing countries, according to the employment rate measure, tend to have low female employment rates (Rubery et al, 1998). The outcome was a new policy objective of raising the female employment rate. If the focus had been set instead on reducing the unemployment rate, the result could have been pressure for policies to reduce the number of women seeking or remaining in employment, in order to free up jobs for unemployed men. The second factor, which is more difficult to quantify, is the role played by particular individuals in promoting gender equality within the EES as it was designed. It is not a coincidence that the strong gender orientation of the EES coincided with the arrival of a Swedish director-general at DG Employment, Allan Larssen, whose vision was of an active but also socially equal societal model for Europe, with strong similarities to the characteristics of the Swedish model. This approach was reinforced by another strand of policy developed at the same time within DG Employment, also under the direction of Allan Larssen (Hermans, 2005), to regard social policy as a productive factor, including equal opportunities policy as one element of a productive social policy (Rubery et al, 1999).

Assessing the impact: the first five years of the EES

Despite this promising start, the achievements must be considered relatively modest, even during the first five years of the EES. The modesty of the achievement is clear in relation to the ambition of gender mainstreaming and the optimism associated with the declaration of equal opportunities as one of the four pillars. Measured by historical rates of progress towards gender equality, the impact of the EES in putting and keeping gender issues on the agenda is perhaps more significant. The setting of a specific female employment rate target for 2010 of 60%, alongside an overall employment rate target of 70%, for example, had the effect of expanding the scope of employment policy to include issues such as childcare and work–life balance, with specific targets for childcare, set at the 2002 Barcelona summit, of 33% coverage for children up to three years old and 90% for three- to six-year-olds.

The extent to which the member states have followed a twin-track approach to gender equality, that is promoting gender mainstreaming and gender-specific policies in the area of employment, has been monitored on an annual basis by the European Commission's Expert Group on Gender, Social Inclusion and Employment (EGGSIE). The current author has been coordinator of this network[3] through the 10 years of the EES. Evidence of positive impacts for gender equality during the first five years on the conception and practice of employment policy in EU member states can be summarised under six main headings (Rubery, 2005).

First of all – and perhaps most importantly – the commitment at EU level to gender mainstreaming was associated with the development or spread of mechanisms for gender mainstreaming at national level. The form through which gender mainstreaming was introduced, and the policy area affected, varied between the member states. With respect to the form, some member states focused on central, inter-ministerial committees, others appointed parity advisors to policy committees or made mainstreaming the responsibility of all ministries. Yet others focused on evaluation systems and gender mainstreaming tools. With respect to the policy area, the most common area where gender mainstreaming was applied was the employment service. In some member states the main policy bodies involved were at local or regional level (where engagement with the European structural funds was often stronger). In others, the focus was more on, for example, gender budgeting or gender impact assessment of new legislation. The diversity of form and practice makes it difficult to link these developments to the EES itself but there is little doubt that the commitment by the EU to gender mainstreaming helped to diffuse this concept to the national level. What is perhaps most surprising, as we review in more detail below, is that these impacts have rarely been referred to within the action plans prepared under the EES by member states, so that the extent of gender mainstreaming that has taken place has remained rather hidden from view.

The second main area of change was in the approach to active labour market policies. The very first years of the EES were primarily focused on meeting targets for dealing with the unemployed. Although there was no specific target for the female unemployed, some member states introduced gender targets or quotas into their activation policies and programmes, often as their main response to the gender equality and gender mainstreaming requirements. This impact was patchy for a number of reasons. First, not all member states paid attention to gender issues. Many limited eligibility for activation programmes to those claiming benefits, even in a context where access to benefits was highly unequal by gender, due to both problems for women in meeting minimum contribution requirements for benefits and because of the use of household means testing for access to long-term benefits. Women who are unemployed are more likely to live with an employed spouse than is the case for the male unemployed. The UK and Ireland were particularly notable for this exclusive focus on benefit recipients among whom women were grossly underrepresented, even compared with their representation among the unemployed on International Labour Organisation (ILO) definitions.

The third area where there was some clear recognition of gender issues was with respect to the setting of employment targets. In response to the EU-level 60% female employment rate target for 2010, a few member states set specific female employment rate targets or adopted the overall Lisbon female employment rate target. This development kept the gender equality issues on the agenda. However, few policy measures were attached to the setting of the targets.

The fourth area of development was in the tax treatment of spouses; the guidelines identified individualised taxation systems as beneficial for promoting female employment and some countries responded with full or partial reforms of household-based taxation systems. The Netherlands even came up with a tax system that marginally favoured households where the mother combined work and care, in contrast to more traditional systems where households with non-working spouses were treated most favourably (Plantenga, 2001). However, there was no uniform development in this area, with Germany notable for retaining its income-splitting system, and most of the reforms were at most partial.

The fifth area was that of childcare, where discussion of and initiatives to expand childcare became more common after the Lisbon summit in 2000 (Rubery et al, 2003, 2006). In some cases the focus on childcare was also associated with improvements to leave arrangements.

The sixth area of note was the inclusion of gender-specific policies and initiatives within the national action plans on employment. Member states could be criticised for only focusing on gender-specific policies and failing to implement the principle of mainstreaming; for example, new policies to develop women's information technology (IT) skills would be mentioned under the gender pillar but omitted from discussion of how to address IT skill shortages under the employability pillar (Rubery et al, 2001, 2003). However, with hindsight the detailed listing of gender-specific measures aimed at closing gender gaps certainly had the advantage of keeping the focus on the need for continuing specific measures and on the structures that led to gender inequalities in the first instance. It was only under the gender-specific measures that there tended to be any serious discussion of gender segregation or the measures to address the gender pay gap; for example, the issue of gender segregation and low pay was not mentioned in discussions of flexibility and part-time employment under the adaptability pillar.

This focus on the positive impacts may be misleading; the policy areas that remained untouched by gender mainstreaming were more numerous than those where positive effects could be identified. Even where positive effects were identified, they only applied to a minority of member states (Rubery et al, 2001, 2003, 2006; Rubery, 2005). Moreover, often initiatives were short-lived and faded out before any real concrete achievements could be pointed to. These changes in direction were often related to changes in government, but also to the fads and fashions in politics and to a lack of real understanding of gender issues among policy makers. Some member states had taken steps to promote awareness of gender issues among policy makers but both a lack of developed competences in these areas and a shortage of gender equality champions also accounted for reversals of progress (Rubery et al, 2003). A further problem is that the impact of the EU may be presumed to be greater in those member states where gender mainstreaming is the weakest. It is in this context that any recognition of the concept, however weak, may be attributed to the influence of the EU. In contrast, where gender mainstreaming was already rooted in the member state's political processes, any subsequent progress in gender mainstreaming might have occurred without prompting by the EU.

A major conceptual problem, in assessing the impact of the EU in promoting a more gender equal society, is the lack of any clearly defined vision as to what such a society would look like. The EU has effectively allowed member states to define their own vision of gender equality, thereby facilitating the presentation of their existing policies and practices in a positive light. A gender equal society might be regarded, say by Finland, as based on equal and full-time participation by men and women, but the Netherlands might regard a society based on one-and-a-half earners per family as the goal. Few member states have considered changes in male behaviour to be part of their goal of a more gender equal society.

A further issue to consider is whether there is a flaw in the whole approach of developing action plans for assessment and critique. Governments may present their policies with a positive spin and seek to avoid potential criticisms, by, for example, failing to cite policy evaluations unless these are wholly positive. There is a general lack of reference to independent and quantitative evaluations of policy impacts in the action plans (COM, 2002/416). The action plans must in practice be regarded as political documents, not scientific reports. Establishing whether or not policies are actually implemented is difficult: for example, quotas specified for female participation in active labour market policies are not necessarily fulfilled but this failure is certainly not actively reported in subsequent action plans (Rubery et al, 2003, 2006). Policy measures may be specified only in vague terms and promises. For example, 'additional' childcare places may not be realised or double counted between one plan and the next. This perspective on the EES suggests that evidence drawn from the national action plans alone may be deeply flawed. However, to the extent that changes in policy orientation can be independently verified, any significant development of new policy approaches might be considered quite an achievement, in a context where governments may have incentives to present current policies in a positive light.

From the 'European Employment Strategy' to 'Growth and Jobs': a return to a narrow 'economic' perspective

It is perhaps ironic that ever since the evaluation of the first five years of the EES identified equal opportunities between women and men as one of the few significant highlights (COM, 2002/416), the main thrust of the EU's employment programme has been to erode the visibility of the equal opportunities dimension. This occurred in a series of steps. The first decision after the five-year evaluation was to simplify and reduce the guidelines; the four pillars – on employability, entrepreneurship, adaptability and equal opportunities – disappeared and the number of guidelines was reduced from over 20 to 10. One of the 10 was explicitly concerned with equal opportunities for women and men but this immediately reduced the apparent concentration of effort from 25% of the programme to 10%. The European Commission sought to compensate, in part, by adding in new targets to significantly reduce gender gaps by 2010, but in practice these were only taken up by a minority of member states (Rubery et al, 2003). The overall verdict, after the first year of the new guidelines, was that the change had resulted in diminished visibility of gender issues, particularly outside the specific gender guideline, in contradiction to the commitment to gender mainstreaming. Serious though this change appeared at the time, it was as nothing compared to the final disappearance in 2005 of any specific guideline relating to gender. This occurred when a further change was introduced: the EES was converted into one of three chapters of the National Reform Programme (NRP) for Growth and Jobs (the renamed and relaunched Lisbon strategy), alongside chapters on macro- and micro-economic policy.

These latter changes followed the Kok review of the Lisbon strategy (CEC, 2003), initiated in part because of slow progress in meeting the Lisbon goals, particularly the various employment rate targets, although that for female employment of 60% is the most likely to be achieved by

2010.[4] The decision was to call for a simplification of the strategy and to focus on the priorities of growth and jobs. Effectively this sidelined the commitment to job quality and lifelong learning and narrowed the objectives to more jobs and growth. In addition to these problems the focus on gender equality effectively narrowed to a commitment to raising the female employment rate and the restating of the commitment to gender equality, without this general commitment being linked into the policy agenda. The Kok report in fact exemplified the continued poverty of understanding of gender issues at the heart of employment analysis, reminiscent in these respects of the period under Delors. For example, the Kok report (CEC, 2003) called for policies to ensure that, in a recession, those who become unemployed remain closely attached to the labour market, that is in effect for the unemployed to be prioritised over the inactive who wish to return to work, most of whom are women.

The main problems with the new NRP format, from a gender equality perspective, are: first, that the streamlining reduces the overall attention paid to employment; second, that the new guidelines no longer include a specific guideline on gender equality, although issues related to gender equality are mentioned under various of the guidelines, principally under the new guideline on the life course; third, that the commitment to gender mainstreaming is much less visible, with examples of what is meant by this principle no longer provided in the text, such that it can be more easily ignored by member states; and, fourth, perhaps most importantly, that member states are now allowed to select which guidelines and topics to focus on. The result of this latter provision is that the NRPs follow very different formats and do not necessarily focus on these guidelines under which gender issues are concentrated. Overall the most important difference, in comparison to the situation prior to the NRPs, is the lack of a specific requirement to report on gender-specific policies; the mainstreaming of employment policies has been weak throughout the process but the specific pillar and even the specific guideline in the interim period of 2003/04 did lead to a much more detailed account of policies related to gender. This account has shrunk in size and even disappeared in some cases under the NRP process.

There is still a separate annual Joint Employment Report (JER) produced by DG Employment. Although this has become shorter and less detailed, the critique of the reduced emphasis on gender issues in the NRPs is made strongly. For example, the JER for 2005/06 (CEC, 2007) criticised the failure to frame the reports within a 'lifecycle approach, including gender mainstreaming, with a view to facilitating employment and career transitions' (p 6), pointed to the fact that 'policies to support female employment and bring about gender equality are somewhat underdeveloped' (p 9) and that 'reconciliation of work and private life are often considered to be a women's issue' (p 10). The Commission has maintained a degree of emphasis on gender equality issues that is now missing in the member states' NRPs. The second-round NRPs were hardly better. According to the evaluation of the reports by the EU's expert group (EGGSIE), although in eight member states the visibility of gender issues increased, it declined in another six. The evidence for gender mainstreaming was also no better, with only seven member states providing evidence of anything more than very limited gender mainstreaming and only three member states recording any improvements in gender mainstreaming (Rubery et al, 2006).

However, the decline in visibility of gender issues in the NRPs is not necessarily indicative of a reduction in focus on gender equality issues within member states. Reports by the EU's expert group EGGSIE provided a more mixed picture of developments at member state level in both gender equality and gender mainstreaming, much of which is not reported in the NRPs. Thus, perhaps surprisingly, 17 out of 25 member states had made some positive changes to gender mainstreaming processes or infrastructure in the 2005/06 period. The positive developments were found primarily in member states with previously weak commitments to gender mainstreaming. Some notable examples include the following. The UK has introduced a new requirement on all public authorities to promote gender equality. In Portugal, representatives from gender equality bodies have been incorporated in the working groups preparing the national action plan on employment. In the Czech Republic, equal opportunities has been included as a factor in the development of a diverse range of new laws, including social services, health and minimum incomes. In Greece, the arrangements for gender equality and gender mainstreaming, both in employment policy and in organisational practices, have been strengthened. In Spain and Belgium, there are new laws to promote the coordination of gender mainstreaming.

These positive developments were counterbalanced by some backsliding. For example, in Ireland the National Development Plan that had put gender mainstreaming on the Irish map was coming to an end and the renewal of commitments to gender mainstreaming was uncertain. In Denmark the public employment service, which has been a best practice beacon of gender mainstreaming for many years, was being restructured and the gender equality coordinators were to be reduced from 28 to 8. In at least three member states reversals in progress on gender mainstreaming had already occurred, with experts for Hungary, Poland and Slovakia all reporting a diminution either in the status and/or the size of the resources devoted to gender mainstreaming activity.

Gender-specific policies were still developing: a number of member states were introducing new equality laws or developing new national plans or objectives for gender equality. Overall, although trends were mixed, the pattern of developments was more consistent with continuing political cycles in the extent of commitment to gender equality and gender mainstreaming issues than with a strong general decline in commitment to the gender equality goal. Initiatives along each of the twin tracks of gender-specific policies and gender mainstreaming still seem to be evident within EU member states. This suggests that the gender equality agenda is not fully dependent on prompting from the EU. There is still the question as to how long this might continue, particularly in member states coming recently to gender equality policies, if the impetus from the EU declines.

New gender equality policies

As the momentum behind the gender mainstreaming of the EES has waned, so the EU has been busy making new commitments to promoting gender equality. In this process it has linked itself to new and deeper analyses and understandings of the causes of gender inequality, with potentially profound implications for what might actually need to be done to achieve a significant difference to the current state of gender equality in the EU. The three initiatives that we consider here are the *Gender Equality Pact* (Council of the European Union, 2006) agreed at the 2006 spring summit, the new *Roadmap for Equality between Women and Men* (CEC, 2006),[5] also agreed in the spring of 2006, and, most recently, the communication on *Tackling the Pay Gap between Women and Men* (COM, 2007/424), agreed in the summer of 2007. Although, from the EU's perspective, all of these documents/agreements have a high profile and status, their actual likely impact on member states is far from clear. They are neither hard law – that is, directives that have to be transposed into national law – nor soft law – that is, requiring action plans from member states that are monitored and benchmarked according to agreed goals. Nevertheless, they should help to retain a gender perspective in EU policy, that is perhaps most effectively transmitted through the structural funds (for those in receipt of large amounts of structural funds) and through the *acquis communautaire*[6] for new member states. Beyond these effects, the impact is primarily through the use of these documents to frame EU action programmes and awareness-raising conferences and events. Nevertheless, the analysis presented in the documents, and agreed at EU level, may take on significance by helping to shape the terms of future debate.

Three elements of the analysis contained in at least one of these documents, and sometimes more than one, are worth identifying as signalling either a new departure or a return to more promising approaches to gender equality, compared to the recent development of the EES. Specifically, the documents return to the concept – evident in the overall approach to the EES at the start of the process – that social policy, and explicitly equal opportunities policy, can be a 'productive factor'. Two other elements represent more new departures. First, there is the beginning of an attempt to spell out what a more gender equal society would look like, in a way that could potentially challenge the weaker and more conservative approaches taken by some member states. This is signalled by an emphasis, for the first time, on the objective of economic independence for women and, further, by a greater emphasis on the need for men to change behaviour, for example to participate more in leave and flexible working associated with childcare. The second new departure is an explicit recognition – at least within the European Commission communication on tackling the pay gap (COM, 2007/424) – that labour market structures shape gender equality, such that changes may need to be made to the overall shape of the distribution of employment rewards to bring about greater equality (Box 12.1). This approach contrasts strongly with, for example, the approach taken within the UK's Women and Work Commission (2006) report. This report focused on issues of gender stereotypes and women's choices, together with some recognition of the problems of family burdens. It stopped short of defining equality with respect to opportunities for economic independence for women and did not address the problems posed by the overall high degree of wage inequality for reducing the gender pay gap in the UK (Grimshaw and Rubery, 2007).

Box 12.1: Developing the gender equality agenda: new EU initiatives

A: Equal opportunities as a productive factor

The three considerations giving rise to the *Gender Equality Pact* (Council of the European Union, 2006) are cited as:

> to contribute to fulfilling EU ambitions on gender equality as mentioned in the Treaty; close the gender gaps in employment and social protection, thus contributing to make full use of the productive potential of the European labour force; contribute to meeting the demographic challenges by promoting better work–life balance for women and men. (Annex II, p 2)

The European Commission communication on *Tackling the pay gap* (COM, 2007/424, p 9) states that: 'The promotion of equality is not only an ethical matter but creates a competitive advantage for companies by allowing their staff to make full use of their productive potential'.

The *Roadmap for Equality between Women and Men* (CEC, 2006, p 18) makes the more specific argument that: 'A balanced participation of women and men in economic decision-making can contribute to a more productive and innovative work environment and culture and better economic performance'.

B: Defining a more gender equal society

(i) Economic independence as a new definition of gender equality

The *Roadmap for Equality between Women and Men* (CEC, 2006, p 2) gives as its first priority: 'Achieving equal economic independence for women and men'.

The communication on *Tackling the pay gap* (COM, 2007/424, p 4) states: 'The pay gap has a major impact on the status of women in economic and social life throughout their working lives and beyond. It constitutes an obstacle to equal economic independence for women and men'. The *Gender Equality Pact* (Council of the European Union, 2006) does not explicitly mention economic independence but, by seeking to 'promote women's employment in all age brackets and reduce gender gaps in employment' (p 2), it makes an explicit commitment to reducing the differences in lifecourse biographies of women and men that underpin women's economic dependence.

(ii) Change in men's behaviour

The Roadmap for Equality between Women and Men (CEC, 2006, p 16) points out that:

> The fact that far more women than men make use of [flexible working arrangements] creates a gender imbalance which has a negative impact on women's position in the workplace and their economic independence.... Men should be encouraged to take up family responsibilities, in particular through incentives to take parental and paternity leaves and to share leave entitlements with women.

The Gender Equality Pact (Council of the European Union, 2006, Annex II, p 2) seeks to 'promote parental leave for both women and men'.

C: Role of labour market structures in generating gender inequalities

The Roadmap for Equality between Women and Men (CEC, 2006, p 10) attributes the persistence of the gender pay gap not only to direct discrimination but also to structural inequalities that include 'segregation in sectors, occupations and work patterns, access to education and training, biased evaluation and pay systems, and stereotypes'.

The communication on Tackling the pay gap goes further not only in pointing to the question of how the work done by every individual is valued and, in particular, of how different jobs are evaluated (COM, 2007/424, p 4) but also by identifying that there are 'societal differences in the evaluation of work in male and female dominated sectors or occupations' (COM, 2007/424, p 17), thereby identifying differences in labour market structures as a potential contributory cause.

In addition to these developments in the analysis, there are some notable developments in the proposed action by the EU that signal a continued evolution in the policy approach and, to some extent, a renewed vigour. Even with respect to the apparent decline of gender mainstreaming, the EU has recommitted itself to promoting gender mainstreaming and indeed to producing manuals to guide member states in how to approach gender mainstreaming.[7] *The Roadmap for Equality between Women and Men* (CEC, 2006) is also reinforcing the focus on change to men's pattern of behaviour by monitoring not only gender gaps based on headcount employment rates but also the patterns of employment and working hours of both men and women with children under age six and under age 12, including for the first time the part-time employment gap between women and men for all in employment. The share of women working part time due to lack of childcare facilities will also be monitored. Objections can rightly be raised that much of this focus on promoting women's employment as a means to economic independence could be interpreted primarily as a means of implementing the activation policy of the EU. It is not necessarily aiming to promote gender equality, nor is it adopting a definition of gender equality that takes adequate account of the right to care as well as the right to work. There is some force to these objections as clearly more needs to be said about appropriate structures for a dual-earning society, including rights for flexible working and on limiting pressures for long working hours. However, the notion of promoting economic independence is not incompatible with opportunities for more diverse life choices. These could still be provided but a focus on economic independence would require new policy initiatives to compensate and support whichever partner chooses to take on a higher share of the caring work.

The link between equal opportunities and other EU objectives, such as social cohesion, is also being strengthened. For example, there are commitments to monitor the share of women in poverty and gender equality in pension provision. The communication on *Tackling the pay gap* (COM, 2007/424, p 7) also suggests the possibility of new policies, such as the promotion of transparency at the workplace with respect to equal pay, and the possibility of looking at this via the provision for information and consultation[8] and announces plans to include equal pay as a factor in a 2008 guide for 'incorporating social criteria into public contract performance' (COM, 2007/424, p 10).

Conclusions

The engendering of the EES has delivered less than was expected of it at the high point of its development, when equal opportunities was designated one pillar among the four pillars of the policy and member states were committed to gender mainstreaming of all four policy pillars. There has been a rapid decline, indeed almost a disappearance, of gender mainstreaming from the employment strategy over the last two years, since the employment strategy was integrated with economic policy. This development suggests that the commitment to gender mainstreaming was highly fragile. Moreover, any attempt to revive gender mainstreaming may run counter to the trend of both simplifying and streamlining EU processes of providing member states with more flexibility in how they comply with the processes. Gender mainstreaming is not a simple concept and member states have demonstrated that, when given a choice, they do not choose to address this issue. A renaissance of gender mainstreaming is thus unlikely and instead new mechanisms may need to be found to pursue the gender equality agenda. That said, there is still evidence of a positive legacy from the experience. First, the EU is itself showing greater awareness of the causes of gender equality and is moving further in defining what a more gender equal society might look like, through its embrace of the objective of promoting economic independence for women and through a greater focus on the behaviour of men as well as women. The second legacy is found in the member states themselves, where there is still evidence of a momentum to develop both gender mainstreaming and gender equality measures. The extent of the momentum is difficult to measure, as it is highly variable and subject to reversals, in line with changes in the political climate. Nevertheless, gender equality is still on the agenda of European member states and is being kept there by the real demographic and social challenges that Europe has to face. A huge gap in understanding as to what may need to be done to address these challenges still remains. The EU is beginning to show some real progress in defining the issues; the development of these recent policy documents presents an opportunity to transpose this approach and to embed it into national policy analysis and approaches, particularly where gender awareness remains weak. Whether this opportunity will be taken up depends on actors at the national level, as well as on continuing efforts to promote gender equality by the EU.

Notes

[1] As Trubek and Mosher (2001) note, the issue of EU competence – that is, power to act – in this area was problematic as member states had always been reluctant to cede even limited competence to the Union for social policy and industrial relations. The Amsterdam Treaty forged a compromise as it provided for multi-level surveillance of common action plans on employment but did not require member states to adopt centrally determined regulation.

[2] The other three pillars were employability, entrepreneurship and adaptability.

[3] This expert network has a member for each member state; all are experts on equal opportunities and employment issues. They evaluate the member states' national action plans and a synthesis report is produced by the coordinators (see, for example, Rubery et al, 2003, 2006).

[4] In 2006 the EU27 overall employment rate was 64.3%, 5.7 percentage points below the 2010 target, while the EU27 employment rate for women was 57.1%, only 2.9 percentage points below the target. The rate of increase in the female employment rate has also been stronger than that for men for many years. The largest deficit is in the employment rate target for older workers (aged 55–64) of 50%; the EU27 rate in 2006 was only 43.5%.

[5] There are six objectives of the new *Roadmap* (CEC, 2006). These are: (i) achieving equal economic independence for women and men, (ii) enhancing reconciliation of work, private life and family life, (iii) promoting equal participation of women and men in decision making, (iv) eradicating gender-based violence and trafficking, (v) eliminating gender stereotypes and (vi) promoting gender equality outside the EU. These are wider objectives than the economic equality objectives with which the EES is concerned. Our discussion here still focuses on the economic equality issues.

[6] This is the term used for the accumulated body of European law that applicant member states need to implement in their national legislation. It extends beyond hard law directives to include, for example, recommendations and opinions. The continuing focus on equal opportunities may lead to more attention being paid to this part of the *acquis*.

[7] The current author has in fact been part of the team producing the first manual relating to gender mainstreaming of employment (Plantenga et al, 2007).

[8] This provision was apparently already foreseen in the 2002 directive on equal treatment but its repetition may increase the chances of enactment.

References

Caporaso, J. and Cowles, M. G. (2001) *Transforming Europe: Europeanization and Domestic Change*, Ithaca, NY: Cornell University Press.

CEC (Commission of the European Communities) (1994) *White Paper on Growth, Competitiveness and Employment: The Challenges and Ways Forward into the 21st Century*, Luxembourg: Office for Official Publications of the European Communities.

CEC (2003) *Jobs, Jobs, Jobs: Creating More Employment in Europe: Report of the Employment Taskforce chaired by Wim Kok*, Luxembourg: Office for Official Publications of the European Communities, available at: http://europa.eu.int/comm/employment_social/employment_strategy/pdf/etf_en.pdf [accessed 22 January 2008].

CEC (2006) *The Roadmap for Equality between Women and Men 2006-2010*, Luxembourg: Office for Official Publications of the European Communities, available at: http://ec.europa.eu/employment_social/publications/2006/ke7205596_en.pdf [accessed 22 January 2008].

CEC (2007) *Joint Employment Report (2005/06): More and Better Jobs: Delivering the Priorities of the European Employment Strategy*, Brussels: CEC.

COM (96/67) *Incorporating Equal Opportunities for Women and Men into all Community Policies and activities*, Communication from the European Commission, Brussels: European Commission, available at: http://ec.europa.eu/employment_social/equ_opp/com9667.htm [accessed 22 January 2008].

COM (2002/416) *Taking Stock of Five Years of the European Employment Strategy*, Communication from the European Commission, Brussels: European Commission, available at: http://europa.eu.int/comm/employment_social/employment_strategy/impact_en.htm [accessed 22 January 2008].

COM (2007/424) *Tackling the Pay Gap between Women and Men*, Communication from the European Commission, Brussels: European Commission, available at: http://ec.europa.eu/employment_social/news/2007/jul/genderpaygap_en.pdf [accessed 22 January 2008].

Council of Europe (1998) *Gender Mainstreaming: Conceptual Framework, Methodology and Presentation of Good Practices*, Final Report of Activities of the Group of Specialists on Mainstreaming, EG-S-MS (98) 2, Strasbourg: Council of Europe.

Council of the European Union (2006) 'ANNEX II European Pact for Gender Equality', in *Presidency Conclusions*, Brussels: European Council, 23/24 March 2006, available at: http://europa.eu/bulletin/en/200603/i1013.htm [accessed 22 January 2008].

Grimshaw, D. and Rubery, J. (2007) *Undervaluing Women's Work*, Working Paper Series No. 53, Manchester: Equal Opportunities Commission, available at: http://83.137.212.42/sitearchive/eoc/PDF/WP53_undervaluing_womens_work.pdf?page=20331 [accessed 22 January 2008].

Hermans, S. (2005) 'The Social Agenda of the European Union and the modernisation of the European Social Model', in *'Towards a modernisation of the European Social Model'*, *Collegium*, no 33, Winter, pp 5-26, College of Europe Bruges.

Plantenga, J. (2001) *Evaluation of the Netherlands' National Action Plan 2001: A Gender Equality Perspective*, European Expert Group on Gender and Employment Report to the Equal Opportunities Unit, DG Employment, available at: www.mbs.ac.uk/research/europeanemployment/projects/gendersocial/publications.aspx [accessed 22 January 2008].

Plantenga, J., Remery, C. and Rubery, J. (2007) *European Commission – A manual for gender mainstreaming of employment policies*, available at: http://ec.europa.eu/employment_social/gender_equality/docs/2007/manual_gend_mainstr_en.pdf [accessed 22 January 2008].

Rubery, J. (2005) 'Reflections on gender mainstreaming: an example of feminist economics in action?', *Feminist Economics*, vol 11, no 3, pp 1-26.

Rubery, J. and Maier, F. (1995) 'Equal opportunity for women and men and the employment policy of the EU – a critical review of the European Union's approach', *'Transfer', European Review of Labour and Research* (Quarterly of the ETUI), vol 1, no 4, pp 520-32.

Rubery, J., Grimshaw, D. and Figueiredo, H. (2001) *Gender Equality and the European Employment Strategy: An Evaluation of the National Action Plans for Employment 2001*, European Expert Group on Gender and Employment Report to the Equal Opportunities Unit, DG Employment, available at: www.mbs.ac.uk/research/europeanemployment/projects/gendersocial/publications.aspx [accessed 22 January 2008].

Rubery, J., Grimshaw, D., Smith, M. and Donnelly, R. (2006) *The National Reform Programme 2006 and the Eender Aspects of the European Employment Strategy*, The coordinators' synthesis report prepared for the Equality Unit, European Commission, available at: http://ec.europa.eu/employment_social/gender_equality/docs/2007/gender_ees_2006_en.pdf [accessed 22 January 2008].

Rubery, J., Humphries, J., Fagan, C., Grimshaw, D. and Smith, M. (1999) *Equal Opportunities Policy as a Productive Factor*, European Work and Employment Research Centre, UMIST, available at: http://ec.europa.eu/employment_social/employment_analysis/gender/equal_opps_as_prod_fact.pdf [accessed 22 January 2008].

Rubery, J., Smith, M., Fagan, C. and Grimshaw, D. (1998) *Women and European Employment*, London: Routledge.

Rubery, J., Smith, M., Figueiredo, H., Fagan, C. and Grimshaw, D. (2003) *Gender Mainstreaming and the European Employment Strategy and Social Inclusion Process*, European Expert Group on Gender and Employment Report to the Equal Opportunities Unit, DG Employment, available at: www.mbs.ac.uk/research/europeanemployment/projects/gendersocial/publications.aspx [accessed 22 January 2008].

Trubek, D. and Mosher, J. (2001) 'New governance, EU employment policy, and the European Social Model', Paper presented at the Conference on Reconfiguring Work and Welfare in the New Economy, European Union Center, University of Wisconsin-Madison, May, available at: www.jeanmonnetprogram.org/papers/01/011501.html [accessed 22 January 2008].

Venables, T. and Joshi, T. (2007) *50 Questions and Answers on Citizens and the Treaty of Rome*, Brussels: ECAS (European Citizen Action Service), available at: www.ecas-citizens.eu/index.php?option=com_alphacontent&section=20&cat=920&task=view&id=67&Itemid=113 [accessed 2 March 2008].

Women and Work Commission (2006) *Shaping a Fairer Future*, London: Women and Equality Unit/Department of Trade and Industry, available at: www.womenandequalityunit.gov.uk/publications/wwc_shaping_fairer_future06.pdf [accessed 22 January 2008].

THIRTEEN

Forming Australian families: gender ideologies and policy settings

JaneMaree Maher

Introduction

The relationship between family-friendly policy settings and the ways in which care and employment are managed within families is a complex one. In the Australian context, Gillian Whitehouse (2002), examining parental employment patterns, has argued that gender ideologies may be as important in shaping care/work decisions as the policy framework within which such decisions are made. Australia has experienced strong labour market growth in recent years and there has been dynamic rhetoric around sustainable economic growth and labour market shortages. This labour market need has thrown focus on the importance of women's paid labour. At the same time, there has been significant emphasis on the maintenance of the national fertility rate. In this chapter, I draw on some key findings of the *Families, Fertility and the Future* study from 2002/03 to examine the gendered ideologies of care and employment in Australia over the past five years. I argue that the ways in which respondents described their negotiation of work–life issues offers a ground to critically examine current family and industrial policy developments in Australia, focusing on care and employment. I argue that families are responding to the implicit, not explicit, messages about family and work, where gendered ideologies of care are being reinforced through the commodification and individualisation of caring labour. Despite an avowed commitment to women's paid work and rhetoric focused on 'working families', current family and industrial policy settings are reinforcing and potentially revitalising the male breadwinner family model in Australia. In conclusion, I argue that despite rhetoric around 'working families', Australian workplace and family policies continue to reveal a traditionally gendered approach to the reconciliation of work and care.

How do we work and care? Australian policies and practices

Faced with the dual imperatives of encouraging women's paid work and maintaining fertility over the past decade, the Australian Federal government has employed a number of policy strategies and discursive approaches to family and workplace initiatives. This nexus was identified by Probert (2002) as offering a potential opportunity for women to advance claims for gender equality in the workplace. In 2002, the Prime Minister identified the work–family issue as 'a barbecue stopper debate' for the nation. In that year, the national work–family debate centred on nationally funded paid maternity leave; currently Australian women have a legislated right to unpaid leave with some sector-based agreements for paid leave (O'Neill, 2004a). The Federal Sex Discrimination Commissioner led a vigorous, but ultimately unsuccessful, campaign for 14 paid weeks of maternity leave in 2002/03. Since that time, the focus of national work–family policies has been on direct benefit payments to assist families in managing work and care, supported by a great deal of national 'talk' around balancing work and family (see Heard, 2006, for a full analysis). The Australian National Budget of 2007 was widely hailed as an effective election year budget, but was also presented by the Federal Treasurer as a budget designed to get mothers back into the workplace. This labour market approach built on the Treasurer's renowned, or infamous, reproductive focus of 2004 and 2005 where he announced his budgets as designed to encourage women 'to have one for the mother, one for the father and one for nation' (AAP, 2006). This sustained public attention on how women, in particular, work and care, encouraged me to reconsider the key findings of the *Families, Fertility and the Future* study (2002–04) in light of these contemporary developments in family-friendly policy and employment discourse.

The *Families, Fertility and the Future* study

The *Families, Fertility and the Future* study was conducted at the height of public and policy discussion about the option of a nationally funded maternity leave scheme in 2002/03. The debate about maternity leave was framed by rhetoric around falling fertility rates, what might be done to maintain and increase the birthrate, and labour market need. Our research team interviewed 100 women and 14 men from across the State of Victoria investigating the factors that were significant to them in decisions about having and raising children. In the study findings, important gender differences appeared around work and family decisions and around patterns of care. These findings revealed significant ongoing strength in relatively traditional models of family and employment, despite the broader national discussion.

Women were keen to talk about issues of work and care and particularly reflected on the importance of workplace flexibility for balancing work and family, valuing them more than specific policies like maternity leave for the most part (Maher and Dever, 2004; Maher et al, 2004). By contrast, the response rate of men to the study was extremely low – only 14 across two metropolitan districts and two regional areas. The recruitment drive included local radio spots, notices in community newspapers and other contacts through schools and community groups. All recruitment material was extremely open and specifically non-gendered ('Do you have children? Are you thinking about children? Do you have a story about work and family?'). This issue clearly did not resonate with men in the community. While it is not possible to determine reasons for non-response, the sense engendered in the research team that family decisions were still understood as women's business was reinforced by a number of factors that emerged during the study. Ten of the men who responded were partners of women who initially volunteered to be interviewed. These men generally felt comfortable about family size, and work and family configuration – the sense of struggle around children, work and care that predominated in the women's accounts (whether they had children or not) was markedly absent in the men's stories (Singleton, 2005). Daniel said, 'I think that three [children] is enough ... it is a size that is comfortable, that is comfortable for us', but later revealed his wife's struggle around the third pregnancy and maintaining her employment. Rory was asked about leave and work and said: 'It was great ... that she didn't lose her job ... [it] was certainly a factor that made it an easier decision to have kids'. Later, his wife decided to completely leave the workforce; she 'decided being Mum at home was enough'.

Although this is a small sample and relatively homogeneous, these accounts do reflect broader aggregate data about, and research into, men's work–family experience in Australia, with the combination of employment and family seemingly significantly less problematic for men than for women. Australia has a sex-segregated workforce with higher ratios of part-time women workers, many of whom are clearly using part-time work as a mechanism to balance work and family (OECD, 2002). In a longitudinal study examining preferred hours of work from the Australian HILDA database, Reynolds and Aletraris (2006) found that women report a greater level of mismatches in actual and preferred hours of employment due to family issues. Craig's (2005) analysis of national time-use data reflects longer hours in employment for men with children than men without in Australia; she identifies much father care as being provided with mothers present (Craig, 2006). The employment rate of mothers increases in line with the age of the youngest child; fathers' employment is unaffected (Baxter et al, 2007). Whitehouse and Hosking (2005) identify a persistent paternal pay premium arising from this work pattern. Albion (2004) found that while women had a greater uptake of flexible work options, they expected reduced conditions – the small number of men who sought flexible work options did not accept pay loss as part of such negotiations. Our finding that men are generally less involved in the negotiation of work–family stresses is supported by this demographic data.

From the interview data, it became clear that not only did men labour less in the family sphere, but also the burden of managing the work–care nexus fell onto their female partners, as Rory's comment indicates:

'As the economic need for both of us to work happened by the time the last one came around, [childcare] certainly became an issue and I think she went back to work when the last one was three or four years old and it was very frustrating because the cost of childcare almost negated *her* wage. It was so expensive.' (Rory, 39 years, professional, 1 child; emphasis added)

As Singleton (2005) analysing data from this study notes, although men are active in discussions about having children, family-friendly policies, career issues and childcare are less significant for men than they are for women:

'We did talk about maternity leave because she was looking at changing jobs.' (Ron, 44 years, professional, 1 child)

'[For] the third [child] if she was going to continue with her career after that break ... she had done a lot of study so that she could go forward.' (Daniel, 41 years, professional, 3 children)

'She ... sacrificed her university postgraduate studies and her career development to be at home with Masie.' (Jack, 43 years, professional, 1 child)

While this assumption about where the care burden fell was expressed by the men, it was shared by the women who participated, and it shaped their conflicted accounts of work and care (Maher et al, 2004). Women's responses around maternity leave, around workplace flexibility and around career and children were focused on the effects on their caring responsibilities. The responses revealed little expectation of significant support from either men or the state for balancing these competing responsibilities. This is well illustrated by their gendered approach to parental leave. As Rory said, after describing his wife's maternity leave, '[paternity leave] wasn't on our agenda ... it wasn't something we decided to go with'. While maternity leave was important to the women, very few mentioned paternity leave as a mechanism for balancing work and care. This is reflective of the social and political reality in Australia – the Equal Opportunity for Women in the Workplace Agency (EOWA, 2006) finds the incidence of paid paternity leave to be very small and the uptake even less but women's lack of attention to this potential policy mechanism was one of the key indicators of how singularly they understood that the burden of care fell to them. Smithson and Stokoe (2005) have identified the default to a generic male breadwinner and female carer framework when gender-neutral language is used to describe care – this pattern was clearly identifiable in the responses here, where general discussions of work and care drew responses focused only on women's roles in negotiating the intersection.

Importantly, while most analyses of family-friendly policies and direct benefits like maternity leave are linked in academic and policy discourses to employer and national benefits such as labour market provision (O'Neill, 2004a), this understanding was not shared by the women or men in this study. Our respondents did not readily perceive any benefits for the employers or the nation in supporting family-friendly policies. Despite the national rhetoric focused on family, the production of children and the labour market throughout the period of the study, these workers did not locate family-friendly benefits as part of a reconciliation effect (OECD, 2002) designed to support workplaces by achieving labour market supply. When women were in a position where their work–family aspirations were supported by their workplace, they were more likely to describe their circumstances as lucky than to consider that their paid work contributed to useful employment outcomes and provided vital caring labour (for further discussion, see Maher, 2008).

Asking women and men in this study about policies that were important to balance work and care produced very limited reference to any policies other than those that might allow *women* to combine work and family. Women clearly accepted that their employment would necessarily be reshaped and often not positively by their decisions about family, embedding the necessity of career changes or breaks as part of their considerations of childbearing and rearing (for further discussion, see Maher et al, 2004). Although these women's assumptions had moved well beyond a work and motherhood split in their own lives – most indicated a quite significant degree of attachment to the workplace – they continued to see the burden of managing the intersection of work and care as primarily women's work. They articulated little expectation of significant partner commitment or state support for the bearing and rearing of children. The responsibility of care was simultaneously gendered and individualised. It is this gendered and individualised understanding of family-friendly benefits that is relevant for examining the developments in family and industrial policy that have occurred in Australia since 2004. In more recent policy shifts, the management of work and family has been consistently linked to direct payments designed to achieve reconciliation. In the following section, I examine these shifts in conjunction with changes to the industrial regime, arguing that the combination of commodified care and workplace deregulation have the potential to intensify the burden that the women in the *Families, Fertility and the Future* study were carrying around work and family.

The contemporary landscape for work and care

The push for paid maternity leave headed by the Federal Sex Discrimination Commissioner was unsuccessful (HREOC, 2002a, 2002b). The Commissioner initiated a follow-up project called *Striking the Balance* (2005), which recently released its final report (2007) entitled *It's About Time*, but the recommendation for maternity leave was only one of a suite focused on family support. A number of other State and Federal Government investigations of the employment–care nexus have occurred since 2004; the most prominent was the *Balancing Work and Family* report from the Federal Parliament's House Standing Committee on Family and Human Services (2006). This report was released in a storm of controversy, not least because the public servants were reported as working very family-unfriendly 12-hour days to complete the report.

The recommendations focused heavily on forms of tax relief for families and the augmentation of childcare rebates in line with recent policy shifts around family benefits. Payments such as the Maternity Allowance for the birth of children have been increased in recent years. In the 2007 Federal Budget, an administrative shift in the Child Care Tax rebate resulted in families receiving that benefit as a direct payment in this financial year rather than as a delayed tax deduction.

In our study, a very broad range of women was interviewed, and it was evident that this type of economic benefit was of much less significance to women than other forms of support like leave or workplace flexibility. When describing their decisions about children and about work, women paid some attention to policy initiatives offering time like maternity leave, but little attention to policies offering financial assistance such as the Baby Bonus, since renamed the Maternity Allowance, and Family Tax Benefits Part A and B (tax schemes designed to compensate families for women's lost wages). In talking of support for care, these payments were referred to only in passing and never identified as important in decisions around children or around work. Yet this form of financial assistance has been the primary mechanism of support in most recent Australian family policy initiatives focused on work and family.

Lewis (2001) has observed that many labour market strategies focused on work and family depend on the commodification of care – where money is offered as an adequate substitute for structural supports to integrate family and work. The shift in the Australian context away from discussions of leave (time) towards cash benefits provides a key illustration of this commodification of care. This trend has intersected with simultaneous and significant changes to the Australian industrial regime, which have been addressed to families using the rhetoric of flexibility, but in fact are delivering very different and often lesser outcomes for women workers.

In 2006, the Australian Federal Government introduced the Work Choices Act, which was designed to radically change the relations between employers and employees. The magnitude of this industrial change, and the ideological underpinning, are outside the scope of this analysis, but there are some specific aspects of 'family friendliness' that have been at the forefront of the way this change has been sold. In the Federal Government *Work and Family* paper (Andrews, 2006), released by the Minister for Employment and Workplace Relations, families are identified as key beneficiaries of these new workplace policies since flexible work is identified as key in assisting in the integration of work and family. From our study, this was clearly the case – flexible work was much more important than benefits in making families work. Yet, as Strazdins et al (2006) have noted, when examining earlier key industrial reforms that delivered increased flexibility, much depends on the type of flexible work that is made available. Their analysis of the shift of mothers out of the retail sector, for example, indicates that unregulated flexible hours may ultimately prove a barrier to maternal employment. Their study also revealed that these impacts were clearly gendered as fathers were not utilising family-friendly provisions. They observed:

> an industry shift in mothers' but not fathers' employment [which suggested] that either the task of juggling paid work and children's care remained very much women's work or that fathers could not access family-friendly conditions at work. (Strazdins et al, 2006, p 397)

Pocock (2005) argues that these outcomes would intensify under the 2006 Work Choices Act, since casualisation, deregulated hours and less guaranteed leave all make the management of family care responsibilities more difficult.

Early analyses of these industrial changes indicated a strong negative gendered effect. The majority of the new individualised agreements under the Work Choices Act did not contain family-friendly policies (ACTU, 2007; Peetz, 2007). Given that women are the primary users of such family-friendly policies to reconcile work and care, the loss of these provisions will have more impact on women than on men. Women are also disproportionately represented in the casualised workforce and in sectors where deregulation regarding wages is intense. The National Foundation for Australian Women found that deregulated agreements are not delivering wage growth in feminised sectors (NFAW, 2006), and that wage inequality was increasing. Initial figures (later withdrawn) released by the Office of the Employment Advocate revealed that women's real wages dropped 2% in the first nine months the legislation was in operation – a sharp reminder of women's differential industrial bargaining power (ACTU, 2007; Peetz, 2007). These intersecting trends represented significant disadvantage for all workers, especially the lowest paid, but they impact particularly on women balancing work and care. This new work–family regime was meant to offer flexibility to employers and the opportunity to bargain for increased wages for workers; this is the key mechanism to negotiate work–family balance. This promise intersects with the movement of care from structural supports within a broad social matrix to a commodified market item (as indicated by the

Federal policy focus on direct financial benefits). The ability to cover the cost of care, then, is central in this new landscape of work and care; but the deregulation of labour market conditions is not delivering increased wages to women managing work and care. Their capacity to pay for commodified care to support their employment is reduced rather than enhanced.

The pattern of family benefits and industrial change over the last five years in Australia has worked to entrench the view that the reconciliation of employment and care is an individual responsibility and that the value of care can be understood in solely monetary terms. This is effectively the framework the Federal Government is proposing through its combined labour market reforms and its financial benefits approach to care. But women already earn less than men and care more, and this gap is being increased under these new conditions (NFAW, 2006). The change in men's involvement in care is limited (Craig, 2006). State support for care, like funded childcare places, still lag substantially behind demand (Child Care Workforce Think Tank, 2003) and workplaces are delivering flexibility that may not support families (O'Neill, 2004b). In the Federal *Work and Family* paper (Andrews, 2006), much is made of enterprise agreements that contain family-friendly benefits but these agreements are being replaced by Australian Workplace Agreements, which supposedly offer increased wages in exchange for lesser conditions. These industrial changes, in conjunction with the reliance on the direct financial benefit for families, intensify the trade-off of structural supports for increased wages to manage work and family, but there is little evidence that women receive the increased wages.

Bacchi (2005, pp 57-8) has observed that dominant understandings of the 'problem' of women's inequality have been focused on workforce participation with emphasis on 'freeing' women to take up work rather than 'creating different lives for women'. Crompton (2001) suggests that increasing pressure to deregulate labour markets will put pressure on families; balancing these competing needs requires 'practical support' as moral exhortations and deregulated labour markets cannot deliver assistance (Crompton, 2001, p 287). The existing policy approach, which combines industrial changes and the financial benefit approach to family support in Australia, may well be diminishing women's existing opportunities rather than expanding women's opportunities to work and care. In the Australian context, the deregulation of the labour market is presented in terms of family friendliness despite considerable evidence that the forms of flexibility being delivered are not family friendly and that gendered burdens of care continue unchanged. Despite changes in the gendered patterns of employment, the gendered patterns of care are the same and the burdens of employment fall firmly on women at home as well as at work. This produces a commodified understanding of care, where women's wage inequality may pressure women into providing more care, thereby reinforcing and revitalising the traditional family models of the male breadwinner.

Lewis and Smithson's (2005) cross-national analysis of the ways in which the 'social context' influences how entitlements are imagined and expected is useful here. One of the most important features of the *Families, Fertility and the Future* findings was a reduced expectation that the responsibilities of combining work and family were the business of government or employers. Neysmith et al (2005, p 192) have cautioned that 'the expectations placed on women to be employed, and the insecurity of the types of jobs available to them, are important for understanding why women negotiate responsibilities and build communities in the ways that they do. The *Work Choices* legislation, in its invocation of the individual as the locus of workplace bargaining, structurally embedded the individual as the key actor in the labour market. This combination locates the burden of managing labour market participation within families and, due to the persistence of gendered models of care, specifically with women. It runs counter to the rhetoric of women's inclusion and engagement in the labour market, it runs directly against the impetus for women to combine childbearing and employment and, on early evaluations of the impact of industrial relations changes, seems likely to revitalise the male breadwinner model in families with dependent children. As in our study findings, families seem adept at interpreting the gendered separation of employment and care that is entrenched in the policy settings despite the national rhetoric of a more integrated matrix of work and family. Even while receiving cash benefits, women accepted that their decision to have children meant that they would have to find a way to form their working families around the demands of the labour market, rather than expecting or accessing any form of structural support that would allow them to negotiate family care in concert with those demands.

Conclusion

'Because ... Australian society says no, women should be able to do it all by themselves.' (Miranda, 39, professional, 3 children)

This comment from one of the participants in the *Families, Fertility and the Future* study evokes two important aspects of family-friendly policies in contemporary Australia. Miranda is acknowledging the withdrawal of structural social support from families but also articulating her recognition that the labour of childrearing and managing the work–family nexus is highly feminised. Lewis (2001, p 152) argues that in conjunction with the settlement between capital and labour represented in welfare states, 'mainstream social policy and sociology literature ... has begun to recognize there was a second key settlement between men and women', which resulted in the dominance and preservation of the male breadwinner model. Crompton and Lyonette (2005, p 604) reflect that 'both normative *and* structural constrains shape women's decisions'. Although recent policy benefits to families in Australia have been explicitly focused on building adult female participation in the labour market and maintaining fertility, the combination of direct financial benefits as the key support mechanism combined with labour market deregulation results in the ongoing intensification of the gendered care burden. Lewis and Giullari (2005, p 87) have observed that 'pressure for women to care is stronger than it is for men and is a part of gendered identity formation'; when wage increases are offered in the deregulated market as the mechanism to reconcile work and care, and gendered pay inequalities increase as a result of the deregulation, then women's capacity to negotiate the wages–care burden will be reduced, potentially resulting in an intensification of these already established gendered patterns of care.

In the years examined here, the term 'working families' became a catchphrase in these debates, especially for those opposing the latest wave of industrial relations reform. This term has resonance with voters apparently and underpins key campaigns against the workplace reforms being promoted by the Howard Liberal National Government. The resonance with pre-industrial family forms is also poignant as industrial conditions like the eight-hour day are eroded in Australia. This term seeks to expose the entrenched separate spheres model of work and family where the commodification of care and the intensification of work are disaggregated in policy settings and government responses. Whitehouse and Hosking (2005, p 4) have argued that 'work/family models are determined more by social attitudes and values than by policy frameworks': in the current Australian policy landscape, there is remarkable congruence between the social attitudes and the policy frameworks, since the commitment to women's paid work is revealed as rhetoric and support for care is reduced to financial payments that diminish the value and complexity of that contribution. Australian families are 'working families' since choices about work hours and conditions are being negotiated not simply between workers and employers but within family groupings. Yet there is evidence that the current model for family support and the industrial regime together make it likely that these negotiations could produce a revitalised male breadwinner model (see Broomhill and Sharp, 2004), where employment and care remain as separate spheres, where care is assessed solely in monetary terms and where women bear the burden of forming and maintaining family life around these constraints.

Note

At the end of November 2007, a new Labour Federal Government was elected; a key part of its platform was to roll back some aspects of these industrial changes, most particularly the pressure for individual workplace agreements.

References

AAP (2006) 'Women take up baby challenge', *Sydeney Morning Herald*, 2 June.

ACTU (2007) *One Year On: The Impact of the New IR Laws on Australian Working Families*, Melbourne: ACTU, available at: www.actu.asn.au/ Images/Dynamic/attachments/5183/One-Year-On-IRLaws-ACTU-270307-final-4a.pdf [accessed 23 January 2008].

Albion, M. (2004) 'A measure of attitudes towards flexible work options', *Australian Journal of Management*, vol 29, no 2, pp 275-94.

Andrews, K. (2006) *Work and Family: The Importance of Workplace Flexibility in Promoting Balance between Work and Family*, Canberra: Australian Parliament, www.workplace.gov.au/NR/rdonlyres/83731176-45FE-4D2E-B3DA-2B412A7D86F8/0/WorkandFamilyissuespaper.pdf [accessed 23 January 2008].

Bacchi, C. with Eveline, J., Binns, J., Mackenzie, C. and Harwood, S. (2005) 'Gender analysis and social change: testing the water', *Policy and Society*, vol 24, no 4, pp 45-68.

Baxter, J., Gray, M., Alexander, M., Strazdins, L. and Bittman, M. (2007) *Mothers and Fathers with Young Children: Paid Employment, Caring and Well-Being*, Social Policy Research Paper 30, Canberra: FACSIA.

Broomhill, R. and Sharp, R. (2004) 'The changing breadwinner model in Australia: a new gender order?', *Labour and Industry*, vol 15, no 2, pp 1-24.

Child Care Workforce Think Tank (2003) *Australian Government Report on the April 2003 Child Care Workforce Think Tank*, Canberra: FACS.

Craig, L. (2005) 'The money or the care: a comparison of couple and sole parent households' time allocation to work and children', *Australian Journal of Social Issues*, vol 40, no 4, pp 521-40.

Craig, L. (2006) 'Parental education, time in paid work and time with children: an Australian time-diary analysis', *British Journal of Sociology*, vol 57, no 4, pp 553–75.

Crompton, R. (2001) 'Gender restructuring, employment, and caring', *Social Politics*, vol 8, pp 266-91.

Crompton, R. and Lyonette, C. (2005) 'The new gender essentialism – domestic and "family" choices and their relation to attitudes', *British Journal of Sociology*, vol 56, no 4, pp 601-20.

EOWA (Equal Opportunity for Women in the Workplace Agency) (2006) *Paid Paternal Leave*, Canberra: Australian Government Publishing.

Goward, P. (2003) 'Australia's dirty big secret', *The Age*, 29 May.

Heard, G. (2006) 'Pronatalism under Howard', *People and Place*, vol 14, no 3, pp 12-25.

House Standing Committee on Family and Human Services (2006) *Final Report Inquiry into Balancing Work and Family*, Canberra: Australian Government Publishing, available at: www.aph.gov.au/house/committee/fhs/workandfamily/report.htm [accessed 23 January 2008].

HREOC (Human Rights Equal Opportunity Commission) (2002a) *Valuing Parenthood: Options for Paid Maternity Leave: Interim Paper*, Canberra: Australian Government Publishing, available at: www.humanrights.gov.au/sex_discrimination/paid_maternity/pml/index.html [accessed 6 March 2008].

HREOC (2002b) *A Time to Value: Proposal for a National Paid Maternity Leave Scheme*, Canberra: Australian Government Publishing, available at: www.humanrights.gov.au/sex_discrimination/paid_maternity/pml/index.html [accessed 6 March 2008].

HREOC (2005) *Striking the Balance: Women, Men, Work and Family*, Canberra: Australian Government Publishing, available at: www.hreoc.gov.au/sex_discrimination/publication/strikingbalance/index.html [accessed 6 March 2008].

HREOC (2007) *It's About Time: Women, Men, Work and Family*, Canberra: Australian Government Publishing, available at: www.hreoc.gov.au/sex_discrimination/its_about_time/index.html [accessed 23 January 2008].

Lewis, J. (2001) 'The decline of the male breadwinner model: implications for work and care', *Social Politics*, vol 8, no 2, pp 152-69.

Lewis, J. and Giullari, S. (2005) 'The adult worker model family, gender equality and care: the search for new policy principles and the possibilities and problems of a capabilities approach', *Economy and Society*, vol 34, no 1, pp 76-104.

Lewis, S. and Smithson, J. (2005) 'Sense of entitlement to support for the reconciliation of employment and family life', *Human Relations*, vol 54, no 11, pp 1455-81.

Maher, J. (2008) 'The fertile fields of policy? Examining fertility decision-making and policy settings', *Social Policy and Society*, vol 7, no 2, pp 159-72.

Maher, J. and Dever, M. (2004) 'What matters to women: beyond reproductive stereotypes', *People and Place*, vol 12, no 3, pp 7-12.

Maher, J., Dever, M., Curtin, J. and Singleton, A. (2004) *What Women (and Men) Want: Births, Policies and Choices*, Melbourne: Monash University, available at: www.arts.monash.edu.au/womens-studies/research/projects/what-women-want-report.pdf [accessed 6 March 2008].

Neysmith, S., Reitsma-Street, M., Baker Collins, S. and Porter, E. (2005) '"Provisioning": thinking about all of women's work', *Canadian Women's Studies*, vol 23, nos 3/4, pp 192-8.

NFAW (National Foundation for Australian Women) (2006) *What Women Want: Consultations on Welfare to Work and Work Choices*, Nowra: NFAW.

OECD (Organisation for Economic Co-operation and Development) (2002) *Babies and Bosses: Reconciling Work and Family Life, Vol 1, Australia, Denmark and the Netherlands*, Paris: OECD.

O'Neill, S. (2004a) *Current Issues: Paid Maternity Leave: E-Brief*, Canberra: Australian Parliamentary Services, available at: www.aph.gov.au/library/intguide/ECON/maternity_leave.htm [accessed 23 January 2008].

O'Neill, S. (2004b) *Work and Family Policies as Industrial and Employment Entitlements*, Canberra: Australian Parliamentary Services, www.aph.gov.au [accessed 31 March 2008].

Peetz, D. (2007) *Brave New Work Choices: What is the Story So Far?*, available at: www.qpsu.org.au/data/Your%20rights%20at%20work/0702_brave.pdf [accessed 23 January 2008].

Pocock, B. (2005) *The Impact of the Workplace Relations Amendment Work Choices Bill 2005 on Australian Working Families*, Melbourne: Industrial Relations Victoria.

Probert, B. (2002) 'Clare Burton Memorial Lecture:"grateful slaves" or "self-made women":a matter of choice or policy?', *Australian Feminist Studies*, vol 17, no 37, pp 7-17.

Reynolds, J. and Aletraris, L. (2006) 'Pursuing preferences:The creation and resolution of work hour mismatches', *American Sociological Review*, vol 71, pp 618-38.

Singleton, S. (2005) '"I think we should only have two":men and fertility decision-making', *Just Policy*, no 36, pp 29-34.

Smithson, J. and Stokoe, E.H. (2005) 'Discourses of work–life balance: negotiating "genderblind" terms in organizations', *Gender, Work and Organization*, vol 12, no 2, pp 147-68.

Strazdins, L., Broom, D., Meyerkort, S. and Warren, B. (2006) 'Voting with their feet: friendliness and parent employment in Australian industries, 1981–2001', *Australian Bulletin of Labour*, vol 32, no 1, pp 381-400.

Whitehouse, G. (2005) 'Parenthood and pay in Australia and the UK: evidence from workplace surveys', *Journal of Sociology*, vol 38, no 4, pp 381-97.

Whitehouse, G. and Hosking, A. S. (2005) 'Policy frameworks and parental employment: a comparison of Australia, the United States and the United Kingdom', Paper presented to the conference *Transitions & Risk, New Directions in Social Policy*, University of Melbourne, February, available at: www.public-policy.unimelb.edu.au/Conference2005/Whi1.pdf [accessed 23 January 2008].

FOURTEEN

Working fathers as providers and carers: towards a new conceptualisation of fatherhood

Alison Smith

Introduction

Parental roles surely play a prominent part in determining gender inequalities across the life course, such as the gender pay gap, which still stands at 17% in the UK (ONS, 2007). If we want to understand such mechanisms underpinning gender inequality, then we need to look at both paternal and maternal roles. The importance of considering fathers, as distinct from mothers, when thinking about the division between paid and unpaid work is often given less weight in social policy than it deserves. We may, or we may not, envisage a future of equal parenting roles, where work and care are shared evenly between men and women. Empirically, such a vision of shared parenting remains highly unusual throughout the European Union (EU). And, because the majority of care is still carried out by mothers, the majority of research on families also continues to focus on mothers. Indeed, the wealth of feminist research into mothering, caring and working has perhaps served to mask the issue of the paternal role. It is thus important to also consider fathers, in the context of the realisation that gender does not just equal women.

We need to look not only at how women might manage (or not) to combine employment with care, but also at how men might manage (or not) to combine employment with care. Only with a thorough understanding of the circumstances of the minority of fathers who do spend substantial amounts of time caring for their children can we hope to better support, through social policy or otherwise, those fathers who do want to actively care for their children. And, by supporting those fathers who do want to actively care for their children, we will in turn support mothers. A certain balance between parental employment and parental care has also been shown to be linked to positive child outcomes, particularly for younger children, with evidence that the gender of the parent matters little (Esping-Andersen, 2005).

A common conception of current fatherhood is that there has to be a trade-off between being either a financial provider or an active carer. As a man becomes a father we might expect to see changes in his ability and willingness to do paid work as well as changes to the effort and time he devotes to domestic work. He might be more inclined to work longer hours and be more ambitious as part of an effort to better provide financially for his new family, thus offsetting the increased costs of becoming a parent. Conversely, he might reduce his working hours and place greater emphasis on his domestic life as part of an effort to spend more time caring for his family. Two such competing strategies of co-residential fatherhood are found in the literature, namely that of the 'good provider' and that of the 'active carer' (for example, Kaufman and Uhlenberg, 2000).

However, this chapter argues that the classification of fathers into either good providers or active carers fails to accurately reflect current perceptions of fatherhood. Drawing on recent empirical evidence, the suggestion made here is that factors related to social class are likely to determine a father's ability to be simultaneously a good provider and an active carer.

After an initial discussion of recent conceptions of fatherhood, this chapter suggests that there are two core parental roles, that of provision and that of care. Provision is more easily measured by such indicators as income or expenditure, which are routinely collected by large-scale household surveys. Care is a more difficult concept to operationalise for measurement. Gathering data on the time spent by parents looking after their children is one way that researchers attempt to measure levels of care, in order to compare how much different groups of fathers and mothers 'care' relative to one another. While an imperfect measure, data on parental time enable us to have a more accurate picture of current fatherhood.

An accurate representation of current fatherhood is crucial for the development of effective father-friendly policy. Father-friendly policy is defined here as legislation that affords fathers the opportunity to take leave from employment to spend time caring for their children. Father-friendly policy has been shown to be correlated with increased paternal time (Smith and Williams, 2007), with accompanying benefits for mothers (Oláh, 2003; Cooke, 2006; Hook, 2006) and children

(Cooksey and Fondell, 1996; Büchel and Duncan, 1998). The central aim of this chapter is to challenge the conception that thinking of fathers as either carers or providers is a useful and indeed accurate way to think about current fatherhood. This is done by putting forward the counter-argument that in the absence of statutory father-friendly legislation, it is rather factors related to social class that determine the resources available to men to become both successful providers and successful carers.

Social resident fathers

In most societies and cultures, including in the European and North American context, whether or not a man is established as a child's father carries with it substantial financial, legal and cultural implications. The term 'father' can be used to describe a man who is simply the biological parent (the genitor) of a child. Conversely, father can also be used to describe a man who raises or nurtures a child (its pater), regardless of any biological link. In this sense, it is a term used in acknowledgement of a man accepting responsibility or duty towards a child. To capture this latter description, Hobson and Morgan (2002) coin the term 'social father'. Often, but by no means always, the social father and the biological father of a child will be one and the same. Social fathering practices extend to all aspects pertaining to the maintenance and care of a child, and as such they do not always occur in the presence of the child (Hobson and Morgan, 2002).

Rather than focusing on the state of fatherhood in general, the focus in this chapter is on a particular group of fathers, namely social resident fathers, that is to say men who are living in a household with dependent children for whom they care. As parental roles are often heavily gendered, it is ideal to have information available from both members of a co-resident parenting 'team'. This provides the theoretical rationale for focusing on co-resident fathers. Furthermore, the evidence reviewed here draws on information provided by large-scale household datasets, such as the European Community Household Panel and the Multinational Time Use Study. Such studies rarely collect data beyond an individual's immediate household. It is highly unusual to have large-scale household data available that extends to non-resident parents. This is also a problem for research considering other forms of informal care such as that performed by non-resident grandparents and other friends and relatives.

Resident fathers, in the context of much social policy discourse, are considered to be good fathers, by the merit of simply being present in the household, rather than via any assessment of the nature of their contribution. Furstenberg (1988) coins this the 'good dad–bad dad' dichotomy: a present father is a good dad, and an absent father is a bad dad. However, a non-resident father will normally continue to uphold his role as a social father after he ceases to live with his children, following divorce or separation from the mother, and in the case that she, or another relative, retains custody of the child.

Social resident fathers can also be lone parents. The number of single fathers is very small compared to the number of single mothers and comprises around 10% of single parents (Marsh et al, 2001). There are much greater numbers of non-resident fathers than resident single fathers, as it is still the norm across the EU for mothers to keep custody of children in the event of a relationship breakdown between the couple. More gay men are becoming parents and care for children, either within same-sex couples or as non-resident fathers. Each EU country has opted for a national model of civil partnerships with varied implications for adoption and same-sex parenting (Curry-Sumner, 2005; Dethloff, 2005). However, the numbers remain too small to be picked up in the surveys used to inform the evidence reviewed here.

Whether social or biological, resident or non-resident, fathering practices are very much affected by the dominant culture of fatherhood in a particular time and place. The term 'fatherhood' can be used to refer to the state or condition of being a father, but its most frequent use in the literature is as a collective term to describe the state of being a father in a particular group or society at a particular point in time. Social historians of fatherhood demonstrate that the duties, responsibilities and rights associated with fatherhood have not been static over time, and thus conclude that fatherhood is a social construct (for example, Pollock, 1983; Pleck, 1987; LaRossa, 1997).

There has been an increasing number of studies, beginning in the 1970s, which talk about a 'new fatherhood' ideal (Fein, 1978; Furstenberg, 1988; LaRossa, 1988; Coltrane, 1998). In her chapter entitled 'The good father: reconstructing fatherhood', Segal (1997) cites many adjectives found in the literature that are used to describe the new fathers, such as: good, new, nurturing, modern, full time, older, lone and loving. In short, the new fatherhood refers to the ideal of a nurturing, hands-on father who will perform many of the tasks formerly ascribed to the mother, and who engages in far more intimate emotional relations with his children than previous generations of fathers supposedly have.

Social fathers are frequently conceptualised in terms of being affiliated to one or the other of two roles, for example:

- traditional versus non-traditional (Russell, 1983);
- father-breadwinner versus the new father (Pleck, 1987);
- the economic dimension versus the nurturant dimension (Cohen, 1993);
- breadwinning versus involved (Gerson, 1993);
- financial providing versus nurturance (Hood, 1993);
- good provider versus involved father (Kaufman and Uhlenberg, 2000);
- provider of cash versus provider of care (Hobson and Morgan, 2002; Lewis, 2002).

To take one of these theoretical models of fatherhood, considering only those fathers who are consistently involved with their children, Kaufman and Uhlenberg (2000) suggest two competing models of fatherhood, which will result in opposite effects on the labour market activity of fathers. Their good provider model predicts that fathers will work more than non-fathers, while their involved father model predicts that fatherhood might encourage working fewer hours in the labour market. The good provider is a father who focuses his commitment on the labour market rather than on the family in order to maximise his ability to provide financially. The involved father is a father who tries to combine his commitment to family and work at the expense of a commitment to the labour market. Although the other dichotomies of fatherhood listed above do vary from the Kaufman and Uhlenberg (2000) model, there is a recurrent theme, that fathers are either good providers or more involved with care, but no suggestion that these two states might occur simultaneously. In other words, that fathers might be both good providers and involved carers is not considered.

In summary, there are two polarisations of groups of fathers described above. The first is between groups of fathers who are involved in some consistent way with their children, and those who have abandoned their parental responsibilities (Furstenberg, 1988). The focus in this chapter is on the former group, and even more specifically on social resident fathers. The second takes this group of involved fathers and further polarises them into old and new, modern and traditional, economic and caring fathers. Absent in this literature is a reflection of the empirical reality, that both mothers and fathers are involved, and have historically always been involved, to a greater or lesser degree in both caring and providing for their children.

Parental roles: financial provider and active carer?

The vast majority of social resident fathers are part of a parenting team. In so far as parents can be thought of as members of a team, the roles they perform can be broadly divided into two categories. The first parental role is that of provider or breadwinner. In current European societies, it is parents who are primarily responsible for providing financially for the family and ensuring that the children have sufficient access to nutrition, clothes, education and any other aspect of maintenance involving financial transaction. The state, via social policy or otherwise, can play a greater or lesser part in dictating those elements of child maintenance that must involve financial transaction. The amount of financial substitution enacted by the state will impact on the extent to which parents have to fulfil the role of provider. During the 20th century in Western Europe and beyond, this role has typically been associated with the father, despite numerous occasions where the mother has been the main provider (and/or carer).

The second parental role is that of carer or nurturer. As well as material goods, children require care, which will typically be provided by a family member (mother, father or other relative), but it can be outsourced to either a state-run or a private service provider. The amount of care provision organised and/or paid for by the state will further impacts on the extent to which parents are enabled to combine employment with care. This role has typically been associated with the mother. A body of empirical evidence indicates that mothers are still responsible for the majority of childcare, although the amount of childcare provided by fathers is beginning to catch up (Presser, 1994; Fisher et al, 1999; Bianchi, 2000; OECD, 2001, p 139; Knijn and Selten, 2002, p 178; Gauthier et al, 2004; Smith, 2007).

It is perhaps important at this point to clarify what is meant when referring to fathers providing more care. The suggestion is not that fathers, on average, might become househusbands: that they might undergo a reversal of traditional roles, by which the mother goes out to work full time while the father stays at home and looks after the household and the children as his main activity. Legislation solely designed to increase the supply of informal care as a sole activity would counteract policy goals of increased labour market participation, such as those of the Lisbon Agenda. Rather, the suggestion is that social fathers, on average, would like to be able to play a greater role, not only as an economic provider for the household, but also as a carer. Practically, this would be a similar level of care as provided by a mother who was equally as active in the labour market as the father. As a normative idea, this would be the level of care a parent could reasonably provide within the context of working a reduced or flexible hours working week, with the partner doing the same, while they are having access to affordable, high-quality childcare.

There are a limited number of hours in the day, but the logic to the argument that a father (or indeed a mother) must be either more committed to work or more committed to their family is flawed. Such an argument fails to take many other factors into account, such as the provision and affordability of care services and access to father-friendly leave legislation. Furthermore, such an argument stands counter to government activation policies that encourage welfare recipients, such as lone parents, into work. Fathers do not currently have equal access, as compared with mothers, to legislative arrangements that would make it possible for them to combine participation in the labour market with caring for their children. For example, mothers in the UK will soon have access to 52 weeks' paid maternity leave, while fathers will have access to two weeks' paid paternity leave. They also have little freedom not to engage in paid work (Orloff and Monson, 2002). As such, they are not generally able to spend as much time looking after their children as are mothers. This position stands in contrast to an increasing number of EU member states, where both parents have access to generous leave provision, originally a Nordic model, but now being adopted by other countries. For example, in Germany, legislation introduced in 2002 and extended in January 2007 now offers flexible leave (including the possibility to work part time) to both parents, as well as parenting benefit as compensation for loss of earnings. Since 2007, the measures allow one parent to take up to a year of leave from work after the birth of a child while receiving two thirds of their net pay from the state. Benefits are extended to a maximum of 14 months if both parents take at least two months' leave, thus encouraging fathers to take up some of the leave period.

As Marsiglio (1995) points out, being committed to the provider role does not necessarily preclude a similar commitment to the non-provider aspects of fathering. The couching of this argument in terms of commitment does, however, imply the ability of a father to implement his preferences, which he may not be able to do, and which will typically be a function of social class. Lower-class fathers may not consider balancing time for paid work with time for care as being a viable economic option. Those fathers of a higher social class are more likely to experience better working conditions. They will generally receive higher remuneration allowing them to more easily access high-quality childcare services to help support them to find a balance between employment and care. They are also more likely to be able to afford periods of unpaid or low-paid statutory leave, such as parental leave (currently three months unpaid in the UK) or paternity leave (currently two weeks at a basic rate of approximately £112 per week). They are also more likely to have access to leave arrangements beyond the statutory minimum as well as to flexible working arrangements. Furthermore, they are more likely to have greater autonomy over their working day routine and be subject to less supervision and monitoring. Given this, it becomes likely that there is a positive correlation between a father's success as a financial provider and the time he spends looking after his children. Depending on the level of remuneration, and of levels of state-funded child maintenance (for example Child Benefit), a father may be obliged to work longer hours in the labour market, without father-friendly legislation in place to support his caring activities, and thus spend fewer hours with his children than he would like.

In order to know how much care fathers are able to carry out, as grouped by social class, and therefore to know whether this is indeed taking us towards a new conceptualisation of fatherhood, a measure of care needs to be developed. The next section describes one way of doing this.

A measurement of paternal care: paternal time

Corresponding to the parental roles of caring and providing, resources devoted to children can be similarly understood as financial resources or as care resources. Financial resources are easily measured in monetary terms through the use of family expenditure studies and household data, but care resources are more difficult to take into account. One way to assess a parent's commitment to caring is to consider the quantity of time that they spend looking after their children. Parental time is defined as the amount of time spent by parents looking after their children. It is defined as time actually spent with the children, rather than time spent earning money to provide for the children. Paternal time refers to fathers and maternal time to mothers.

Time spent by parents, both fathers and mothers, with their children, is generally considered to have a positive impact on children's development (Furstenberg et al, 1987; Cooksey and Fondell, 1996; Büchel and Duncan, 1998). Parental time measurement, however, provides sociological insight beyond child outcomes. It is also a starting point for explaining socioeconomic differences between the adults involved. With respect to fathers, paternal time can be used as a measure of a father's contribution to the domestic sphere. It may not say much about the quality or success of the contribution, but it can be taken as an indicator of the increased likelihood of both.

A review of the literature reveals that, despite the media attention around the time pressures with which today's families are confronted, parents are in fact devoting more time to childcare than ever before. The general consensus in the literature is that while mothers still spend more time caring, the gender gap has been reduced, at least within marriage. Paternal time is on the increase at a greater rate than maternal time (Presser, 1994; Fisher et al, 1999; Bianchi, 2000; OECD, 2001, p 139; Knijn and Selten, 2002, p 178; Gauthier et al, 2004; Smith, 2007). About one fifth of European fathers of small children (under six years old) spend substantial paternal time (Smith and Williams, 2007). This is defined as more than 28 hours of childcare per week. However, there are considerable differences between countries in the percentage of fathers who spend substantial paternal time.

But how do these studies mentioned above go about measuring the allocation of time? One of the characteristics of data on the allocation of time is that valid measurements are both difficult and costly to obtain. Most time-use data have to be based, as is the case with most survey work, on self-reported estimates. Self-reported measures are prone to bias. There is always the possibility that a respondent answers with what they consider to be an appropriate answer rather than with a true account. Or as Budig and Folbre (2004, p 52) comment: 'Cultural norms as well as social expectations affect the ways people perceive their own activities'. As shown by Hiller (1984), for example, both husbands and wives see themselves as participating more in domestic work than their spouses report that they do. Husbands were especially likely to see tasks as shared, while wives saw themselves with the major responsibility for housework. Differences in perceptions were larger for childcare than for housework. Men may tend to overstate the amount of time spent caring (Lee, 2005).

The most accurate way to record the activities that parents engage in with children and how much time they spend on each activity would be observation. However, such a method is costly, intrusive and limited in the amount of any particular day that can be covered. Direct observation would also be likely to affect respondents' behaviour. Information on time use is typically collected in one of three ways: by time sampling (also referred to as a random discrete-time log); with continuous time diaries; or with retrospective survey questions. Time sampling can be an efficient way to collect time-use estimates (see, for example, Gershuny, 2004). Respondents typically write down the activity they are engaged in whenever a beeper sounds, or some other sampling device is triggered. However, this methodology is still too costly and intrusive to be used for representative samples. The most extensive and detailed data on time allocation have been obtained using the time-diary method, administered to a sample of individuals in a population and organised in such a way as to provide a probability sample of all types of days and of the different seasons of the year. Time diaries are usually retrospective, asking respondents for a detailed chronology of the previous 24 hours, with responses coded according to a standard list of activities (Juster and Stafford, 1991).

The most simple and widely used method in survey research is to ask parents directly how much time they spend on certain activities. Retrospective survey questions about typical time use (for ordinary household tasks such as childcare, travel, entertainment, socialising, TV viewing, reading and so on) over some past period of time have been criticised for producing biased estimates of actual time use (Juster and Stafford, 1991; Robinson and Godbey, 1997). The major difference in bias when not using time diaries appears to be overestimation as respondents appear to recollect days when the activity asked about was especially prominent, and treat that as an average day. In this respect, validity and reliability of data collected in time-diary form is generally superior. However, there are many strong arguments for using retrospective survey questions. Often, these questions are part of a nationally representative, possibly longitudinal, annual household survey, rich in other socioeconomic information about the respondents. These studies are often well funded, staffed by experienced research teams and well documented.

Childcare is just one type of unpaid work that has to be shared out within the household. Other types of unpaid work include maintenance work (small repairs and gardening), housework (such as grocery shopping and cleaning), food preparation, and other forms of care (such as care for the sick or elderly). This unpaid work contrasts with paid work, voluntary work and with leisure (Sayer, 2005). Sometimes the boundary between what constitutes childcare as distinct from other types of housework is blurred, for example, doing laundry and preparing meals for children. Despite this there are certainly grounds for the stand-alone study of childcare time, set apart from other forms of housework.

Even when the sole activity under scrutiny, childcare can again be classified into various categories of activity. Childcare can be classified as active (also referred to as primary) or passive (also referred to as secondary). Active childcare estimates capture only the time that parents report being solely involved in caring for children. Passive childcare estimates include time that the parent spends with children while engaged simultaneously in other activities. Some measures focus only on childcare in the home environment and others include all activities where children are present, wherever they take place.

Childcare time measures can be either absolute, or relative to the mother. If measures are relative, attention must be paid to the units of comparison. Are full-time employed parents compared, or are full-time employed fathers and non-employed mothers compared? Are single parents being contrasted with cohabiting parents? Are cohabiting parents considered as distinct from married parents? The definition of a parental household can also vary according to the age of the child. Some studies look only at households containing children under a certain age (for example under five), while others consider all children under the age of 16. Finally, estimates are generally reported in terms of hours per week or hours per day. There is rarely a distinction made between weekday and weekend time (Yeung et al, 2001). If estimates are reported in terms of hours per day then it could be that certain days of the week are left without representation in the time sample.

This discussion shows that the measurement of parental time is a complex activity. Despite the difficulties, this activity is nonetheless immensely worthwhile as it allows us to establish how much fathers are involved with care. And, if we are able to answer this question, we can then identify potential determinants for why and how a father may be able to become more active in family life.

Social inequality and the capacity for family life

Drawing on standard measures of income, as well as the time-use information mentioned above, evidence can be gathered to comment on the relationship between social inequality and the capacity for family life, specifically with regard to the amount of financial provision and care that a father is able to provide. Marsiglio (1993) points to two factors frequently associated with the amount of care carried out by fathers – those of race and social class. Griswold (1993) observes that the new father image is very much that of a middle-class man:

The new fatherhood thus becomes part of a middle-class strategy of survival in which men accommodate to the realities of their wives' careers and the decline of their breadwinning capabilities. For these men, pushing a pram becomes less the sign of a wimp than a public symbol for their commitment to a more refined, progressive set of values than those held by working-class men still imprisoned by outdated ideas of masculinity. (Griswold, 1993, p 254)

That working-class men are still imprisoned by outdated ideas, as suggested by the quote above, is contentious. Less contentious perhaps is that they are more likely to be constrained as a result of lower remuneration and less flexible working routines. In a study drawing on time-diary data from 24,546 married mothers and married fathers in Canada, Germany, Italy and Norway to determine whether the effect of education on childcare time varies cross-nationally, findings indicated that, with a couple of exceptions, more educated parents spent more time with children than less educated parents in each country, despite substantial cross-national variation in levels of financial support and services for families (Sayer et al, 2004). The exceptions to this were with respect to fathers. Among fathers, education was found to have no effect on childcare time in Norway, and only weak effects in Germany. The authors suggest that the type of family policies that provide financial support to families, as particular to these countries, may then reduce time constraints on fathers, thus ameliorating educational effects. In other words, fathers with a lower level of education may be finding it harder to combine working the number of hours needed for sufficient remuneration with spending time looking after their children. If there is reduced pressure on the parents for financial provision, the gap in paternal time between fathers with higher and lower levels of education, may be reduced.

As well as there being an education differential predicting levels of paternal time, there also appears to be a link between levels of income and paternal time. We know that married men (assumed to be fathers) earn more than non-married men (for example, Korenman and Neumark, 1991; Schoeni, 1995; Loh, 1996; Chun and Lee, 2001). Furthermore, on average across Europe, childless men earn 5%-6% less and fathers-to-be earn 2%-3% less than fathers, after adjusting for other factors such as age, level of education, marital status, occupational status and sector of employment (Smith, 2007). Fathers-to-be were defined as men in the two years previous to becoming a father. One possible explanation behind these observations is that fathers-to-be are pursuing higher-paid jobs in order to save up in preparation for becoming fathers, as there is some perception that they will need more money when they start a family. Another possible explanation might be that men who command a higher rate of earnings are more likely to attract a partner with whom to have children. In terms of weekly working hours, there seems to be very little difference between fathers, fathers-to-be and childless men.

Fathers who care more also earn more (Smith, 2007). This is not necessarily linked to longer working hours. To the contrary, fathers who report spending the highest level of paternal time work slightly shorter hours than all other men. In other words, fathers who spend more time looking after their children experience better labour market outcomes, in that they earn more per hour, and work fewer hours than fathers who spend less time looking after their children.

Only two indicators related to social class – those of education level and labour market outcomes – have so far been discussed in relation to parental time. The term 'social class' is widely used as a general label to describe structures of inequality in modern societies, both within the discipline of sociology and beyond (Crompton, 1998, p 24). The term is not without controversy within the discipline. I use the term here in the Goldthorpe class schema sense (see Evans, 1992), which, put crudely, allocates people to social classes on the basis of their occupational category and employment relations. An analysis of paternal time by occupational category and employment relations remains important work yet to be done.

Yet taken together, these findings on the positive relationship between level of education, income and paternal time can be used as preliminary evidence that the categorisation of resident fathers as either good providers or active carers fails to properly describe current fatherhood. Rather, it is more appropriate to think about the differences between the super-dad and the ordinary dad. Typically, a super-dad is a father simultaneously successful in the labour market and involved as a carer. An ordinary dad is a father with less success in the labour market and, quite possibly as a consequence of this, is also less involved as a carer. In other words, those fathers who spend the most time with their children also experience the most favourable labour market outcomes, meaning that they earn more money per hour and do not work particularly long hours. One conclusion to be drawn from this is that social inequality is a matter of the capacity for family life and care, not just about material provision.

Conclusion

The importance of considering fathers, as distinct from mothers, when thinking about the division between paid and unpaid work is promoted in this chapter. We need to look at how men might manage (or not) to combine employment with care, as well as at how mothers might manage (or not) to combine employment with care. Care is a challenging concept to operationalise for measurement. One approach is to look at paternal time: the time that fathers report spending looking after their children. We are then able to explore why it is that so few fathers spend a considerable amount of time looking after their children, relative to mothers. Furthermore, by looking at those fathers who do spend relatively high amounts of paternal time, we can begin to understand how to better support fathers' caring activities, via social policy or otherwise.

A common conception of fatherhood in the literature has been that for social resident fathers, there has to be a trade-off between being a financial provider or an active carer. However, a review of the relevant empirical literature – to the extent that it is available, as much more work needs to be done in this area – throws new light on this conceptual framework. Rather, the suggestion is that fathers are more likely to be either *both* a good financial provider and an active carer or *neither* a good financial provider nor, possibly as a consequence, an active carer. In the absence of statutory father-friendly legislation, it will be factors related to social class that determine a father's capacity to fill both parental roles of financial provider and active carer. In other words, social inequality is not just about material provision but also about the capacity for family life and care.

That paternal time, level of education and labour market outcomes are intrinsically linked has significant policy implications. If governments strive to increase fathers' time with their children, including those fathers of a lower socioeconomic class, then they should adopt policies with the following characteristics:

- Fathers should have greater access to leave from employment.
- There should be high wage compensation for such leave.
- Fathers should be able to work flexibly to combine employment with childcare responsibilities.
- Increased child maintenance payments and state-funded childcare provision may reduce the need for fathers to work such long hours, which could rather be spent looking after their children.

Acknowledgements

This project was funded by the Economic and Social Research Council (ESRC) and the European University Institute, and supported by Nuffield College, University of Oxford, and the Social Policy subject area at the University of Edinburgh. For further information please contact alison.j.smith@ed.ac.uk.

References

Bianchi, S. (2000) 'Maternal employment and time with children; dramatic change or surprising continuity', *Demography*, vol 37, no 4, pp 401-14.

Büchel, F. and Duncan, G.J. (1998) 'Do parents' social activities promote children's school attainments? Evidence from the German Socioeconomic Panel', *Journal of Marriage and the Family*, vol 60, no 1, pp 95-108.

Budig, M. and Folbre, N. (2004) 'Activity, proximity or responsibility? Measuring parental childcare time', in N. Folbre and M. Bittman (eds) *Family Time: The Social Organization of Childcare*, London and New York: Routledge, ch 3.

Chun, H. and Lee, I. (2001) 'Why do married men earn more: productivity or marriage selection?', *Economic Inquiry*, vol 39, no 2, pp 307-19.

Cohen, T.F. (1993) 'What do fathers provide? Reconsidering the economic and nurturant dimensions of men as parents', in J. Hood (ed) *Men, Work, and Family*, London: Sage Publications, pp 1-22.

Coltrane, S. (1998) *Gender and Families*, Thousand Oaks, CA: Pine Forge Press.

Cooke, L.P. (2006) '"Doing gender" in context: household bargaining and the risk of divorce in Germany and the United States', *American Journal of Sociology*, vol 112, no 2, pp 442-72.

Cooksey, E.C. and Fondell, M. M. (1996) 'Spending time with his kids: effects of family structure on fathers' and children's lives', *Journal of Marriage and the Family*, vol 58, no 3, pp 693-707.

Crompton, R. (1998) *Class and Stratification: An Introduction to Current Debates* (2nd edition), Cambridge: Polity.

Curry-Sumner, I. (2005) 'Uniform patterns regarding same-sex relationships', *International Law FORUM du Droit International*, vol 7, no 3, pp 186-94.

Dethloff, N. (2005) 'Same-sex parents in a comparative perspective', *International Law FORUM du Droit International*, vol 7, no 3, pp 195-205.

Esping-Andersen, G. (2005) 'Social inheritance and equal opportunity policies', in S. Delorenzi and J. Reed (eds) *Returning Through the Back Door: Social Class and Social Mobility*, London: IPPR, pp 14-30.

Evans, G. (1992) 'Testing the validity of the Goldthorpe class schema' *European Sociological Review*, vol 8, no 3, pp 211-32.

Fein, R. (1978) 'Research on fathering: social policy and an emergent perspective', *Journal of Social Issues*, vol 34, pp 122-35.

Fisher, K., McCulloch, A. and Gershuny, J. (1999) *British Fathers and Children: A Report for Channel 4 'Dispatches'*, Technical Report, Colchester: Institute for Social and Economic Research.

Furstenberg, F. F. (1988) 'Good dads – bad dads: two faces of fatherhood', in A.J. Cherlin (ed) *The Changing American Family and Public Policy*, Washington, DC: Urban Institute Press, pp 193-218.

Furstenberg, F.F., Philip Morgan, S. and Allison, P.D. (1987) 'Paternal participation and children's well-being after marital dissolution', *American Sociological Review*, vol 52, no 5, pp 695-701.

Gauthier, A.H., Smeeding, T. and Furstenberg, F. (2004) 'Are parents investing less time in children? Trends in selected industrialized countries', *Population and Development Review*, vol 30, no 4, pp 647-71.

Gershuny, J. (2004) 'Costs and benefits of time sampling methodologies', *Social Indicators Research*, vol 67, nos 1-2, pp 247-52.

Gerson, K. (1993) *No Man's Land: Men's Changing Commitments to Family and Work*, New York: Basic Books.

Griswold, R. (1993) *Fatherhood in America*, New York: Basic Books.

Hiller, D.V. (1984) 'Power, dependence and division of family work', *Sex Roles*, vol 10, pp 1003-19.

Hobson, B. and Morgan, J. (2002) 'Introduction', in B. Hobson (ed) *Making Men into Fathers: Men, Masculinities and the Social Politics of Fatherhood*, Cambridge: Cambridge University Press, pp 1-21.

Hood, J. (1993) 'Introduction', in J. Hood (ed) *Men, Work, and Family*, London: Sage Publications.

Hook, J. (2006) 'Care in context: men's unpaid work in 20 countries, 1965-2003', *American Sociological Review*, vol 71, no 4, pp 639-60.

Juster, F.T. and Stafford, F.P. (1991) 'The allocation of time: empirical findings, behavioral models and problems of measurement', *Journal of Economic Literature*, vol 29, no 2, pp 471-522.

Kaufman, G. and Uhlenberg, P. (2000) 'The influence of parenthood on the work effort of married men and women', *Social Forces*, vol 78, no 3, pp 931-49.

Knijn, T. and Selten, P. (2002) 'Transformations of fatherhood: the Netherlands', in B. Hobson (ed) *Making Men into Fathers: Men, Masculinities and the Social Politics of Fatherhood*, Cambridge: Cambridge University Press, chapter 6.

Korenman, S. and Neumark, D. (1991) 'Does marriage really make men more productive?', *The Journal of Human Resources*, vol 26, no 2, pp 282-307.

LaRossa, R. (1988) 'Fatherhood and social change', *Family Relations*, vol 37, no 4, pp 451-7.

LaRossa, R. (1997) *The Modernization of Fatherhood: A Social and Political History*, Chicago, IL: University of Chicago Press.

Lee, Y.-S. (2005) 'Measuring the gender gap in household labor: accurately estimating wives' and husbands' contributions', in B. Schneider and L.J. Waite (eds) *Being Together, Working Apart: Dual-Career Families and the Work–Life Balance*, Cambridge: Cambridge University Press, pp 229-47.

Lewis, J. (2002) 'The problem of fathers: policy and behavior in Britain', in B. Hobson (ed) *Making Men into Fathers: Men, Masculinities and the Social Politics of Fatherhood*, Cambridge: Cambridge University Press, ch 4.

Loh, E.S. (1996) 'Productivity differences and the marriage wage premium for white males', *Journal of Human Resources*, vol 31, no 3, pp 566-89.

Marsh, A., McKay, S., Smith, A. and Stephenson, A. (2001) *Low-Income Families in Britain: Work, Welfare and Social Security in 1999*, Technical Report 138, London: DSS Research Report.

Marsiglio, W. (1993) 'Contemporary scholarship on fatherhood: culture, identity, and conduct', *Journal of Family Issues*, vol 14, no 4, pp 484-509.

Marsiglio, W. (1995) *Fatherhood: Contemporary Theory, Research, and Social Policy*, London: Sage Publications.

OECD (Organisation for Economic Co-operation and Development) (2001) 'Balancing work and family life: helping parents into paid employment', in OECD, *Employment Outlook: 2001*, Paris: OECD, ch 4.

Oláh, L. S. (2003) 'Gendering fertility: second births in Sweden and Hungary', *Population Research and Policy Review*, vol 22, no 2, pp 171-200.

ONS (Office for National Statistics) (2007) *Gender Pay Gap*, available at: www.statistics.gov.uk/cci/nugget.asp?id=167 [accessed 28 November 2007].

Orloff, A. and Monson, R. (2002) 'Citizens, workers or fathers? Men in the history of US social policy', in B. Hobson (ed) *Making Men into Fathers: Men, Masculinities and the Social Politics of Fatherhood*, Cambridge: Cambridge University Press, ch 2.

Pleck, J. (1987) 'American fathering in historical perspective', in M. Kimmel (ed) *Changing Men: New Directions in Research on Men and Masculinity*, Newbury Park, CA: Sage Publications, pp 83-97.

Pollock, L. (1983) *Forgotten Children: Parent–Child Relations from 1500 to 1900*, Cambridge: Cambridge University Press.

Presser, H. (1994) 'Employment schedules among dual-earner spouses and the division of household labor by gender', *American Sociological Review*, vol 59, pp 348-64.

Robinson, J.P. and Godbey, G. (1997) *Time for Life: The Surprising Ways Americans Use Their Time*, University Park, PA: Pennsylvania State University Press.

Russell, G. (1983) *The Changing Role of Fathers?*, Brisbane, Australia: University of Queensland Press.

Sayer, L. (2005) 'Gender, time and inequality: trends in women's and men's paid work, unpaid work and free time', *Social Forces*, vol 84, no 1, pp 285-303.

Sayer, L., Gauthier, A.H. and Furstenberg, F.F. (2004) 'Educational differences in parents' time with children: cross-national variations', *Journal of Marriage and Family*, vol 66 (December), pp 1152-69.

Schoeni, R. (1995) 'Marital status and earnings in developed countries', *Journal of Population Economics*, vol 8, no 4, pp 351-9.

Segal, L. (1997) *Slow Motion: Changing Masculinities Changing Men* (4th edition), London: Virago.

Smith, A.J. (2007) 'Who cares? European fathers and the time they spend looking after children', Unpublished doctoral thesis, University of Oxford.

Smith, A.J. and Williams, D. (2007) 'Father friendly legislation and paternal time across Western Europe', *Journal of Comparative Policy Analysis*, vol 9, no 3, pp 175-92.

Yeung, W.J., Sandberg, J.F., Davies-Kean, P.E. and Hofferth, S.L. (2001) 'Children's time with fathers in intact families', *Journal of Marriage and the Family*, vol 63, no 1, pp 136-54.

Index